Fire on the Rim

Pacific Formations: Global Relations in Asian and Pacific Perspectives
Series Editor: Arif Dirlik

Fire on the Rim

The Cultural Dynamics of East/West Power Politics

William H. Thornton

ROWMAN & LITTLEFIELD PUBLISHERS, INC.
Lanham • Boulder • New York • Oxford

ROWMAN & LITTLEFIELD PUBLISHERS, INC.

Published in the United States of America
by Rowman & Littlefield Publishers, Inc.
An Imprint of the Rowman & Littlefield Publishing Group
4720 Boston Way, Lanham, Maryland 20706
www.rowmanlittlefield.com

12 Hid's Copse Road, Cumnor Hill, Oxford OX2 9JJ, England

Material in this book is adapted from the following articles by William H. Thornton, and is used by permission of the journal or copyright holder.

"After the Fall: A Response to Dirlik and Jun," *Development and Society* 29:1 (June 2000).

"Analyzing East/West Power Politics in Comparative Cultural Studies" in *CLCWeb: Comparative Literature and Culture: A WWWeb Journal* 2:3 (2000). Used by permission of Purdue University Press.

"Back to Basics: Human Rights and Power Politics in the New Moral Realism," *International Journal of Politics, Culture and Society* 14:2 (2000).

"Korea and East Asian Exceptionalism," *Theory, Culture and Society* 15:2 (May 1998). Used by permission of *Theory, Culture and Society* and Sage Publications.

"Putting the (Second) Postmodern Question to Japan: *Postmodernism and Japan* Ten Years Later," *Asian Profile* 28:2 (April 2000).

"Reactionary Globalization: Local, Regional, and Global Implications of the 'New Japan Problem,'" *International Politics* 38:4 (December 2001).

"Selling Democratic Teleology: The Case of the Chinese Fortune Tellers," *International Politics* 37:3 (September 2000), 285–300.

British Library Cataloguing in Publication Information Available

Library of Congress Cataloging-in-Publication Data

Thornton, Wm. H. (William H.)
    Fire on the rim : the cultural dynamics of East/West power politics / William H. Thornton.
        p.   cm.—(Pacific formations)
    Includes bibliographical references and index.
    ISBN 0-7425-1706-3 (alk. paper)—ISBN 0-7425-1707-1 (pbk. : alk. paper)
    1. Asia—Politics and government—1945– 2. Asia—Civilization. 3. East and West. I. Title. II. Series.
DS35.2 .T47   2002
950.4′2—dc21   2002017607

Printed in the United States of America

♾ ™ The paper used in this publication meets the minimum requirements of American National Standard for Information Sciences—Permanence of Paper for Printed Library Materials, ANSI/NISO Z39.48-1992.

*For Margery Talbot Thornton, my mother,
and Choi Kum-Im, my mother-in-law.
They meet in us.*

Contents

Foreword

Bryan Turner

For those of us who worry that sociology in particular and the social sciences in general have become merely "decorative" as a result of the cultural turn, William Thornton's analysis of Asian values offers us a way of understanding both the politics of culture through the study of the material basis of society, and the culture of politics through a careful analysis of the religious, legal, and cultural dimensions of state power. While being critical of much post-modern analysis, Thornton extracts some of the useful lessons of postmodernism as a perspective on what he describes as the antipolitics of the authoritarian dimension of Asian political culture. However, the danger that he identifies is a postmodern form of anti-political politics as the defining feature of "Asian values," where citizenship and civil society are collapsed into the goals of the state, and opposition of any kind is seen by definition as subversive of political order and stability.

The debate about social justice in the process of development raises the vexed question of human rights. Can Asian societies afford human rights programs if they want to "catch up" with the West? Alternatively, can they afford not to implement human rights if they want to avoid internal civil conflict? The West has been especially culpable here in promoting an ideology of human rights while in fact giving first priority to economic liberalization. The crunch question is really whether free market economies are the best foundation for democratic liberalization. The mistake, argues Thornton, is the assumption that all rules of law are equal. Thus the legal structures that are necessary for global trade relations may not be wholly or always appropriate to human rights. Singapore is the test case that shows how illiberal legal structures may operate alongside liberal trade relations. Regrettably, the Asian crash gave the neo-liberal arguments of the IMF and WTO an enormous beneficial context to make strategic arguments in favor of unregulated capitalism. Thornton goes on to provide an astute analysis of the dangers of cultural studies as a framework for studying the East. On the political right, Reagan and neo-liberals encouraged the Chinese to follow the pattern of Daoist non-action (let the market decide), and on the political left, cultural relativism silenced Western criticism of Asian authoritarianism. Even Clinton, who promised to support human rights movements in China, gave China Most-Favored-Nation trade status, thereby endorsing the leadership's neglect of human rights provisions after Tiananmen Square. By accepting cultural relativism and defining Western values as reactionary, the cultural left endorsed political authoritarianism and betrayed indigenous reformers, some of whom are in prison precisely because they supported the processes of democratization. Orientalism thus gives way to an equally narrow and pernicious Occidentalism.

The underlying assumption of neo-liberal attempts to quarantine real politics has been that prosperity can be a substitute for social justice. Keeping people fed is a method of keeping them silent. This Western view of China echoes Benjamin Barber's critique of the notion that the world's underdeveloped "others" have one thing in common: basically they want to be like "us"—consuming Western commodities from hamburgers to Ford sport utility vehicles.[1] In this case the "social market economy" is just rhetoric for "the free market." The problem with the post–September 11 coalition is that it justifies all sorts of repression in the name of a general struggle against terrorism. As we all know, yesterday's terrorists may well be tomorrow's legitimate government, and therefore it is always prudent to keep open the lines of communication (with the enemy). The coalition against terrorism provides the perfect excuse for China's leadership to impose its will on dissident forces. These recent events support the reversal of Amartya Sen's[2] argument that democratization ought to be the primary objective of development strategies, and that economic growth follows political modernization rather than vice versa.

Thornton finds that Western views about Japanese development have been equally blind toward or silent about political authoritarianism and lack of democratic openness. The failures of political leadership were identified by Karel van Wolferen in *The Enigma of Japanese Power*,[3] but these lessons were buried by an academic culture that does not want to appear critical of Asian powers. The idea that the Japanese economy could always compensate for the failures of the Japanese polity was shattered by recession and by the inability of Japan to resolve the tensions between bureaucratic and traditional rigidity and economic growth.

In terms of Korea, Thornton argues that again Western assessments are dangerously mistaken. In particular, it is misleading to associate the Korean social system with "bureaucratic-authoritarianism" as if Korea was another Argentina or Brazil. Korea represents a more successful postmodern model that has adapted the local to global pressures. The lesson of Korean politics is that the "authority" can always be challenged by grassroots oppositional groups.

Fire on the Rim is a compelling blend of astute political analysis that is based on a detailed understanding of different political regimes and processes in Asia. Thornton shows how a normative concern for human rights issues can be woven into careful social science description of the economic and political conditions of Asian societies. The importance of the book is that it does not shy away from serious criticism of the authoritarian politics and social failures of many Asian countries, yet it does not fall into the Orientalist trap of accepting an undifferentiated view of Asian values. *Fire on the Rim* should be read by everybody who has a serious concern with democracy and social justice as necessary preconditions of sustainable economic development.

NOTES

1. Benjamin R. Barber, *Jihad vs. McWorld: How Globalism and Tribalism Are Reshaping the World* (New York: Times Books, 1996).
2. Amartya Sen, *Development as Freedom* (New York: Knopf, 1999).
3. Karel van Wolferen, *The Enigma of Japanese Power* (New York: Vintage, 1990).

Acknowledgments

This study was not begun in a research mode, but rather as a very personal reaction to history-in-the-making during my stay in Korea in 1987 and 1988. This was the climactic moment of Korea's democratic takeoff. It struck me that the American press was not reporting events as we saw them unfolding around us. My first appreciation goes to those who were left out of the picture: the Korean working classes. Silent and unseen, they had laid the bricks and mortar of the Korean economic "miracle," and now they were pushing for a political miracle as well. They showed me firsthand that beneath the material accretions of modernization the fire of liberation still burns in some corners of the world—hence the "fire" of my title.

Second I thank the Korea Foundation for helping me, through a 1993 research fellowship, to maintain this Korean connection after my move to Taiwan. Third I thank the Academy of Korean Studies for inviting me, in June of 1996, to talk on East Asian cultural politics. It was here that I ventured the embryonic version of a distinctive Korean development model. Fourth I should thank the Asia Research Foundation for the 1999 grant that helped bring this study to maturity.

Since most of this book had an earlier incarnation in journal articles, I wish not only to acknowledge these journals but to underscore my appreciation of their editors and outside readers for their part in shaping the article series that became *Fire*. These journals include *Theory, Culture, and Society* (with special thanks to Mike Featherstone for his suggestion that I expand my *TCS* article into a book), *Development and Society* (with special thanks to Chang Kyung-Sup, who introduced me to the best researcher in the field, Arif Dirlik), two articles in *International Politics: A Journal of Transnational Issues and Global Problems* (with special thanks to the editor-in-chief Daniel Nelson, of the George C. Marshall European Center for Security Studies in Gar-

xiii

misch, Germany, and to the editor Laura Neack), *CLCWeb* (with special thanks to my old friend Steven Totosy), and the *International Journal of Politics, Culture, and Society* (with special thanks to my frequent adviser Doyle McCarthy), and *Asian Profile*. In addition I owe profuse thanks to Susan McEachern at Rowman & Littlefield for her usually subtle but always vital input, to William Callahan at the University of Durham, U.K., for his invaluable chapter-by-chapter critiques, and to Bryan Turner, chair of sociology at Cambridge, for his always generous encouragement, advice, and (given my rabid anti-globalism) tolerance. My biggest critical thanks, however, are reserved for Arif Dirlik, whose influence on my thought is a patent element of every chapter of this book.

On the personal side, the roots of *Fire*'s methodology run deep in me. My approach to East/West cultural relations traces to my first mentor, Mr. Joseph Ross, who in my teenage years guided me through all the culture-related books of his superb library. Meanwhile he imparted a nonreductionist view of the cultural "other" that exploded liberal platitudes. This sharp-edged but dialogic openness was all the more remarkable because Mr. Ross bore the physical scars of battle on many Pacific islands, the worst being Peleliu, where so many of his Marine Corps comrades were lost. Suffice it to say that he did not need Huntington to inform him about the dangers of civilizational clash.

Nor did my second mentor. I am tragically late in formally expressing my gratitude for my first graduate director, a splendid Crusades scholar and unforgettable friend, the late Elizabeth Hardwicke. Her tough standards were balanced by an unparalleled tolerance (easily extending to my fledgling work on the repressive aspects of late medieval communications advances, and even to my friend's thesis proposal on the sex life of Jesus, which was summarily shot down at higher levels). I would later learn how rare her openness and integrity are in the academic world, but even then I shared with all her students a profound respect for her that never fades. Her utterly nonorientalist approach to non-Western cultures, and to Arab civilization in particular, licensed me to pursue within a history department what today would be called cultural studies.

Finally let me thank my wife and frequent coauthor, Songok Han Thornton, for her rich insights on Asia in general and Korea in particular. A disclaimer may be necessary here: though she is indelibly Korean, she is in no way responsible for the "Korean model" that *Fire* propounds. If a cultural bias crept in here, it was over her objection, and thanks to her screening it is less extreme than it might have been. The same goes for my other polemic excesses. Songok has been, moreover, my best reference on what is politically possible in Asia and what is not—that being the cardinal line dividing realism from utopianism. *Fire* seeks a rapprochement between the two in its contest with conventional readings of Asian development. If any part of this moral realism rings true, much of the credit goes to Songok's critical interventions.

Introduction

The Geopolitics of "Asian Values"

THE DIFFERENCE A DAY MAKES

September 11, 2001, was not just another day of infamy. Even after Pearl Harbor most Americans thought events such as Black Tuesday only happen somewhere "over there." This sense of security was the bedrock of an American exceptionalism that never failed to segregate West from East, "us" from "them." On Black Tuesday that all changed.

Geopolitical modernism has been premised on that same us/them dichotomy. The idea was to make "them" more like us—a project that Americans thought exceedingly generous. While the Cold War intensified this self-reflexive bifurcation of the world, it also skewed the meaning of "us" and "them." Now the line between friend and foe would be drawn on the basis of anti-communism rather than pro-democracy. Thus Pakistan would be in, while nonaligned India would be out. The Shah of Iran and Indonesia's Suharto were very much in, through CIA-assisted coups and mammoth aid packages. Even Osama bin Laden and the future Afghan Taliban were once in, despite the patent fact that their enemy was not so much communism as modernity. That subtle distinction flew over the heads of American policy-makers whose concern was how best to exploit cultural others—such as the pre-Taliban Mujahedeen[1]—not to better understand them. Such modernism was (in the short run, before "blowback" set in) an effective Cold War armament.

It is no accident, then, that postmodern culturalism gained momentum as the Cold War waned. By the 1990s, effusive respect for "difference" was all but obligatory in academic circles. What actually distinguished postmodernism from modernism, however, was not so much its professed pluralism as its far greater sense of security. It could afford to embrace "difference" because modernism's war with the "other" had seemingly been won.

Through the lens of triumphant globalization, difference becomes a game of academic make-believe. The rules of this game prescribe that there is no such thing as even partial truth, much less apodictic truth, for representation is now defined as a mere power play. That spells the end of radical comment, not to mention structural critique. To the extent that postmodernism prevails, the New World Order wins by default. This "anti-paradigm paradigm," as Carl Boggs terms it, is deeply implicated in a conservative politics that operates by dent of anti-politics.[2]

Postmodernists persist in calling this liberation and calling themselves cultural leftists, even as they shun factual reference to real oppression. Seen from a bottom-up angle, there can no longer be any doubt as to the political function of postmodernism. It is to the dark side of globalization what transcendentalism was to the horrors of early industrialization. The only mystery is how this flight from unpleasant reality comes to be liberatory. Jonathan Friedman supplies a plausible answer: The elite "captured" in the class compromise of the old welfare state now feels emancipated by globalization.[3] Notwithstanding its rhetoric of marginality, postmodernism is playing on the winning team. Intellectual honesty would require full disclosure of that fact, but it is precisely the concept of truthful representation that postmodernism proscribes.

September 11 provided a belated wake-up call on the high cost of dodging real issues. In terms of East/West relations, the clock was turned back to the Gulf War, an event that Baudrillard (*The Gulf War Did Not Take Place*, 1995) described as a media-invented fiction. Needless to say, the Islamic world took a different view of the matter. This more than anything turned the Taliban against its former American patrons. Indeed, the "blowback" effect of an all-too-real Gulf War has had a global reach. Apropos of the "fire" of my title, Desert Storm served warning on Chinese strategists that their military must be thoroughly modernized before their larger geopolitical ambitions could be unleashed. That realization pushed China into the waiting arms (pun intended) of Western globalists, who wasted no time in persuading President Clinton to abrogate the human rights agenda he had advertised in his first campaign.

Not even Baudrillard would suggest that Black Tuesday was a media fiction, for this one hit home. It signaled the apodictic fact that cultural difference is no game. Postmodern culturalism has not prepared us for the dark side of difference, nor for the broader networks of commonality that will be necessary to avert such disasters in the future. As the world's "others" are put under increasingly intense pressure to conform, it is a safe bet that some will strike back, and not simply by way of postmodernism's vaunted strategies of "hybridity" or "glocalization." It remains to be seen whether this naive strain of postmodernism can survive the events of September 11. A greater concern is that something even worse could take its place. One can only hope that this day will mark the beginning of a post-postmodern turn in geocultural politics, not a retreat into cultural militarism or its sibling rival, isolationism—the two being equally irresponsible. While seeking an ethical middle path between engagement and disengagement, *Fire on the Rim* searches for a way around the deadly geopolitical schism of the past century: realism versus idealism. *Fire* is, first and foremost, an argument for moral realism.

BALANCING ACT

The two most influential discourses on the Pacific Rim—"miracle" economics and power politics—have had little to say to each other. One thing they share, however, is a deep distrust of cultural analysis. Granted, the "Asian miracle" has commonly been framed in cultural terms, namely "Asian values," but this top-down and highly economized culturalism lost its way after the Asian Crash of 1997. Nor has any other culturalism had much standing within the prevailing realist paradigm of international relations (IR).

Only in the face of mounting ethnic strife and civilizational clash has mainstream IR granted a supporting role to culture.[4] There is a tendency, moreover, for the cure to be worse than the ailment. Too often the cultural corrective takes the form of theoretical imports that are curiously indifferent to the concrete "stuff" of power politics.[5] Nor is there much sustained attention to material structures of oppression. The New Culturalism tends to be worse in these respects than the cultureless realism it displaces.

This study explores the global interface of Rim culture and geopolitics from a very different vantage. Neither IR anti-culturalism nor its anti-realist substitute can cope with the cultural imperatives of the Rim—an area where three times in half a century America has gone to war with enemies it scarcely understood. Sometimes, as in Vietnam, this cultural myopia has led the United States to treat a potential ally as an enemy; whereas recently, in the case of China, it has reversed that error by treating a geopolitical rival as a "strategic partner."

The danger in this case is amplified by the force of demography as well as nuclear warheads: over one billion Chinese are directly involved, and all peoples of East, Southeast, and South Asia live on this volcanic Rim. The United

States can hardly afford a mistake of such magnitude, yet the mental habits that stoke this "fire on the Rim" are seldom questioned. Rather, as Bruce Cumings observes, the American consensus on Asia is naturalized as the one and only objective optic.[6]

Consider the experience of Lucian Pye, who for decades has resisted the American consensus on China. In 1964 he contested the "prudence model" of Chinese political culture, whereby Chinese Communists (China's Great Leap Forward having been somehow forgotten) were credited with having liberated China from its countless layers of cultural inertia. This was in the last days before the outbreak of the Cultural Revolution, which would do much to promote Pye's revisionist study, *The Spirit of Chinese Politics.*[7] *Spirit* would go out of print during the honeymoon years of Nixon's diplomatic reversal, and its message would be all but forgotten during the halcyonic era of Deng Xiaoping's reforms. It would be rediscovered only in the 1980s, when problems started to boil up around the Paramount Leader. By that time its attraction was not due just to the corrective it offered for an almost utopian reading of China's political prospects, but also for the balance it afforded vis-à-vis the more pessimistic accounts of Bo Yang's *The Ugly Chinaman* and the influential television series *River Elegy.*

Pye came across as a moderate insofar as he balanced his dim view of the People's Republic of China (PRC) ruling order with a still hopeful outlook on the Chinese people themselves. A similar dualism tempers my approach to Asian politics in general, and at times puts me at odds with Pye himself.[8] Care is taken throughout this book to distinguish the Asian values of ruling regimes from deeper currents of political culture.

Like Pye I avoid the idealist fallacy that takes a raw cultural potential for a teleological given. Especially I avoid the reverse domino effect of neoliberal globalism: the notion that only poverty stands between the Asian masses and full-fledged democracy. There is no question that poverty is a big part of the problem, and that trade (properly managed) can do much to alleviate poverty. At the end of the Cold War, which some say never ended in the Asia-Pacific,[9] nearly 30 percent of the working population of East Asia and the Pacific brought home less than one dollar per day.[10] To speak of democratization under such circumstances is preposterous. But it is no less absurd to assume that economic development is necessary *and* sufficient for political reform. This book comes down for balanced development and an equitable distribution of the fruits of globalization. This is only fair, since the social and environmental costs of such "growth" will be shared by all.

Though I seek a balance between realist and idealist geopolitical agendas, my first allegiance goes to a qualified realism; for in Asia hard politics is as crucial for humanitarian leverage as for strategic advantage. Moreover, lasting peace and prosperity around the Pacific Rim require a credible balance of power. The "fire" of my title is prompted by the incendiary implications of the region's growing instability. As Zbigniew Brzezinski notes, this area is fast becoming the "world's center of economic gravity," yet at the same time it has all the elements of a political volcano.[11] Similar instability attends globalization in many parts of the world, but in East Asia the dilemma has been camouflaged by record-breaking economic growth. That relative invisibility has made the Rim all the more volatile by delaying badly needed countermeasures. No security issue in today's world is more pressing than this dangerously unexamined "fire on the Rim."

FROM CULTURAL REALISM TO
MORAL REALISM

Again, my working assumptions do not fit neatly into the standard political and cultural categories. While I follow such revisionists as Samuel Huntington and Robert Kaplan in "culturalizing" realism, I depart from them by striking a post–Cold War accord with the pragmatic wing of idealism. Thus I avoid the cultural realist trap of utter pessimism. The (im)balance that concerns me not only involves power politics in the usual sense, but also the mitigating "soft power" of communicable ideals. These include the transcultural or "thin" values that Michael Walzer foregrounds in *The Thick and the Thin* (1994) and Arif Dirlik locates in some forms of Chinese occidentalism.[12]

The catch is that thin values, in defiance of what may be called the Enlightenment fallacy, never exist in pristine isolation. They come interwoven with the "thick" or incommunicable aspects of cultural meaning.[13] It follows that there is nothing so exceptional about cultural exceptionalism. Any culture worthy of the name is "thick" with it. It would be a classic blunder to imagine, as do many globalists, that the mere absence of the thick guarantees the presence of the thin. That is the problem with the current turn toward the "glocal"—the global/local hybrid that in effect puts local culture at the disposal of international capital. By undermining the thick, the glocal also corrodes the cultural politics of the thin. Globalists find advantage in a glocalization that saps the resistance potential of more rooted traditions. "Thick" and "thin" coexist in those traditions, balancing cultural difference against the common (i.e., transcultural) decency that sustained resistance requires.

As Hirst and Thompson argue, it is a myth that corporate globalization cannot be resisted.[14] Globalization faces constant insurgency, if only because the damage it causes (cf. Schumpeter's "creative destruction," which turns out in most cases to be as destructive in terms of social capital as it is "creative" in terms of economic capital) comes back to haunt the corporate order itself. Carl Boggs notes that the new "corporate colonialism," which systematically erodes the public sphere, precludes the kind of public discourse that might address social and ecological crises before they reach critical mass.[15]

There are times when local identity can be reinforced by the threat of globalization, just as the local once drew meaning by contrast with the national.[16] More commonly, however, nationalistic development has rooted out real difference in favor of ersatz localism. Nepalese "generic villages," for example, have been designed by national bureaucrats to rid the country of traditional villages and all they represent.[17] Similar motives were at work in Korea's Saemaul (New Village) Movement, which neutered Korean villages culturally and architecturally, replacing their graceful contours and ample communal spaces with insular block structures that planted urban alienation in the rural heart of the nation, all in the name of modernization.

This movement was the pride of President Park Chung Hee's regime, which not only robbed my future wife of her childhood home, but added insult to injury by requiring her family and their neighbors to provide corvée labor for the building projects that were displacing their community. Contemporary Korean scholars still praise the way this operation mobilized villagers for "popular participation" in the wonders of modernization.[18] What it actually did was disperse communities that had the necessary cohesion for collective resistance.

Today there is an equivalent effort to "save" the local by plugging it into the global, thus "glocalizing" it. No matter how well it is wired, the resulting "glocal village" will be as culturally and politically inert as a Potemkin village. Resistance to such designs will have to come from the impoverished fringes of developed society or from the periphery of the global order. Either way it will erupt from below—from the long-exploited South or the economically bypassed classes of the North, including Japan and the newer Asian "tigers."

Barely noticed by the world press, discontent smolders beneath the Asian "miracle," exacerbated by environmental degradation. China qualifies as the most active yet worst reported "fire on the Rim." While major news media focus on PRC growth rates and investment opportunities, very little attention is given to the worst labor crisis in half a century of communist rule. Workers are being laid off at thousands of factories, while still-employed workers go unpaid and retirees fail to receive their pensions.[19] Meanwhile, a large part of China's rural population is joining a floating urban underclass—roughly 110 million by the mid-1990s[20]—locked in menial and temporary migrant labor. Kaplan sees this as "leading to a crime surge like the one in Africa and to growing regional disparities and conflicts in a land with a strong tradition of warlordism and a weak tradition of central government—again as in Africa."[21] Glocal enclaves only fuel this fire by spreading the gap between haves and have nots.

Unreformed globalization is thus its own worst enemy. Its best friends, in fact, could be the well-wired protesters who have taken to the streets in opposition to its leading institutions, most notably the WTO and the IMF. Few of these activists are from the disfranchised classes whose "coming anarchy" (to borrow Kaplan's title) is more likely to resemble the turmoil in West Africa than the largely symbolic siege of Nike in Seattle, or the subsequent boycott of Nike products at the University of Oregon. In the future these protesters may be looked upon as moderates whose cause reaches so far beyond their immediate self-interest that it is fair to call them "globalists," however distasteful that word would be to them. It is possible, therefore, to see Seattle as a fraternal conflict between globalization's best and worst exponents.

To give force to their point, these reform globalists might have chosen a more potent motto: *après nous le déluge*. Anyone who can contemplate without disgust the McDonaldization of Bhutan, or the continued sinicization of Tibet, is sure to dispute my premises. But there is a growing climate of conviction that some things—ranging from dolphins and sea turtles to Tibetan religion and culture—should be left in peace. A new generation of global radicals holds institutions that systematically break that peace (the IMF, the World Bank, the WTO) accountable for their eco-cultural violence.

A typical case in point was the World Bank's plan to assist in the sinicization of Tibetan lands by loaning $40 million for the relocation of 58,000 ethnic Chinese farmers to an area traditionally used by Tibetan herders. Though strongly endorsed by the Bank's president, James Wolfensohn, the plan was canceled by the Bank's directors under enormous public pressure.[22] China angrily withdrew the project from consideration, vowing to raise the money independently.[23] This was no idle threat. When China's Yangtze River dam project met with similar resistance—eco-cultural criticism that blocked loans from both the World Bank and the U.S. Export-Import Bank—China secured ample funding through bonds underwritten by American financial institutions. Critics of the project faced prison terms in China and could hardly expect sympathy from American investors who had ignored the urgent appeals of forty-five international groups.[24]

Words alone carry no more weight with Western capitalists than with Chinese communists. Idealism must be buttressed with hard politics and, in the case of China, the threat of economic sanctions. These realist methods, however, have their flip side in my case for *moral* realism. The moral qualifier might not have been necessary where classical realism was concerned (e.g.,

Hans Morgenthau's reconciliation of moral principle and national interest),[25] but that balance was lost in the bipolar world of capitalism versus communism that emerged in 1949 with two earthshaking events: the explosion of the first Soviet atomic bomb and the founding of the People's Republic of China.[26] And there is even less moral balance to be found in the globalist New World Order. From the vantage of moral realism, we have moved from Cold War to Cold Peace.

Seen in this light, culture has a moral substance that yields solidarity without being static, hence the cultural *dynamics* of my title. This integrative thrust must be distinguished from both poles of contemporary cultural mythology: the traditionalist myth of place-bound gemeinschaft as well as the postmodern countermyth of unbounded hybridity. The latter, of course, does have its merits. It provides a helpful referent for marketing strategists who want to predict the tides of fashion in First World shopping malls. But it offers no clue as to why Chechens are willing to fight and die for a tragically lost cause, or why Russians are so intent on killing them. Nor can postmodern cultural theory explain, or even address, the volatile issues at stake in Tibet, Taiwan, East Timor, or, indeed, most of the Pacific Rim. To understand the motives of the Southern Mongolian Democracy Alliance—whose leaders have been getting ten- to fifteen-year sentences in China, simply for advocating the cultural preservation of Mongolian culture[27]—culture must be seen as a dynamic political force.

That dynamism is reflected in Huntington's thesis of "civilizational clash" and in Kaplan's focus on cultural migrations.[28] Culture is thus tied to transient politics as well as place-bound traditions. It takes on a resistant function in the face of globalization. But the "force" of a political culture is not altogether negative. It includes a moral dimension that involves two directions of movement. While it draws a line between itself and the "other," it can also supply the cultural confidence to cross that line dialogically.

A NEW CULTURAL CLOSURE

This perspective runs counter to both the universal fiat of modernism and/or globalism and the fatuous, "anything goes" postmodernism that resists universalism by forfeiting critical judgment. It is possible to adopt a *critical* postmodernism—closely akin to what Dirlik calls "critical localism" and what Gearóid Ó Tuathail dubs "critical geopolitics"[29]—while accepting John Gray's admonition, in *Enlightenment's Wake* and *False Dawn*, that the world will no longer submit to the strictures of Enlightenment universalism. Such modernism, Gray contends, has its last true believers in American globalists, if also, paradoxically, in some of their nominal foes, such as the many "multicultural" and "postcolonial" critics who make a show of inverting Western standards while remaining prisoners of the same monological paradigm. This book avoids that trap by adopting more a post-Western than an anti-Western stance. It embraces cultural pluralism without surrendering the precious gains in tolerance and critical judgment that Habermas rightly defends against its postmodern detractors.[30]

During the "miracle" years of East Asian growth, a renegade strain of the "postal" (postmodern and postcolonial) fallacy came to the aid of Asian values: the ritual inversion of Westernism, ironically imported from the West. The region's unprecedented economic record legitimized this anti-Western Westernism on both sides of the Pacific. Writing at the peak of that "miracle," Paul Kennedy (*Preparing for the Twenty-First Century*, 1993) had the prescience to expose the dark side of the area's political and economic prospect. South Korea, for example, lived under perpetual threat from the north. Hong Kong faced repatriation with a politically recidivist China, and Taiwan remained a diplomatic pariah state. Meanwhile, rising oil prices pushed up import bills, higher wages ate away at competitiveness, and inflated stock prices all but guaranteed a regional collapse.[31] Tellingly, Japan was already mired in recession. The remarkable thing is that most putative experts could manage to be surprised by the economic Crash of 1997.

Had this happened in the West, and ten years before, few would have been surprised. The poor showing of Western liberal capitalism relative to the new Asian model seemed to augur a cultural as well as economic eclipse. The pressing question was how the West should prepare for the hard times ahead. Some pundits were suggesting that what was good for Asia—namely the "Japan model"—could also work for flagging Western economies. But this proposal ran aground on the fact that the Japan model (not to mention its even more centralized Asian relatives, such as the Korean "vortex" model) involved intense central direction of the economy, while the emerging Anglo-American model blamed the Western malaise on a plethora of governmental regulation. In Britain and the United States alike, the political pendulum was swinging in the opposite direction: toward a sweeping decentrism that attempted to correct for decades of liberal excess. It was an accident of history that New Right policies in both countries ran counter to the tactical assumptions of their East Asian allies.

Despite those operational differences, the Asian "miracle" made an indelible mark on Western neoconservatism and subsequent neoliberalism—the two having largely converged by the early 1990s, especially after Robert Rubin's neoliberal faction of Clinton's cabinet won out over Robert Reich's humanistic liberalism.[32] If the Asian example undermined faith in *liberal* capitalism, it restored confidence in capitalism per se, expelling the economic insecurities that brought Thatcher and Reagan to power in the first place. By putting welfare liberalism on permanent hold, the stupendous success of the Asian tigers helped legitimize the "lean and mean" neoliberalism that was fast becoming the dominant ideology of the post–Cold War era.

It was enough that, like its East Asian counterpart, the new Anglo-American model subordinated political progressivism to growth-first economism. The flagrant defects of the Asian political system would be conveniently ignored, just as they had been under the sway of Cold War realism. Old-style liberals who had hoped for a more ethical (which is to say a less "realist") geopolitics in the wake of the Cold War would be sorely disillusioned. Already the realist torch was being passed to neoliberal globalism.

Throughout the "miracle" years, economic triumphalism had masked the reactionary aspect of East Asian growth. Even the worst colonial regimes of the early twentieth century—the French in Indochina or the Japanese in Korea and Taiwan—had not been this destructive of local culture and ecology. One can now understand why Graham Greene, in his prophetic novel *The Quiet American* (1955), favored the patent corruption of French colonialism over the postwar alternatives: national movements funded either by foreign capitalism or communism. Whatever its real intentions, the U.S. notion of capitalist development—as inscribed by Greene's fictional York Harding and America's tragically nonfictional W. W. Rostow—would be a recipe for disaster in Vietnam and America alike. Unfortunately, American readers spurned *The Quiet American* in favor of *The Ugly American* (1958), thus missing one of the best warning signs in modern literature. Bad taste never carried a higher price.

Classical realists share Greene's aversion to the American habit of mixing moralism with geopolitics; and structural or neorealism, as R. B. J. Walker notes, is no less pessimistic in this regard.[33] The problem with that idealist/realist mix, however, does not stem from the moral factor per se, but rather from bad moral judgment—bad in the undialogic sense that would apply to any cultural monologue. The crux of the problem is that Americans have never learned to listen to Asian voices.

Frank Baldwin observes, for example, that the U.S. effort to block the Soviets in Korea "overlooked one fact: the Koreans. . . . [The] United States intervened in a local *Korean* revolutionary situation. American power collided not with the Red Army but with the Korean revolution, Korean demands for social justice and rapid political change."[34] The Korean Left had earned its legitimacy through long and perilous resistance to Japanese imperialism. By suppressing this indigenous revolution, the U.S. military government not only rendered itself illegitimate,[35] but set a pattern for invasive foreign policy that constitutes one of the three darkest chapters in American history—the other two being Afro-American slavery and Native American genocide. True to this pattern, America once more turned against a World War II ally, this time in Vietnam, much as the British turned on their former Malayan Communist Party allies.[36] Massive U.S. funding supported the French against the Vietminh resistance that would later give rise to the National Liberation Front (NLF) in the North and the Viet Cong in the South. For years Ho Chi Minh's government tried in vain to communicate its basically nationalistic and nonaligned intentions to the United States. As late as 1963 Ho Chi Minh still expressed hopes for friendship with America.[37] Greene, however, was dead right: They were wasting their ink writing letters to Washington.

Some hoped that the end of the Cold War would remedy America's tunnel vision. But the most distinctive feature of the old realist worldview—its cultural closure—would find a new home in neoliberal globalism. Under the auspices of a new "Washington Consensus," and more particularly the Treasury Department's firm grip on the IMF and the World Bank, the American model of development became the blueprint for late capitalism's most monologic enterprise: the New World Order.

THE MARRIAGE AND DIVORCE OF ASIAN VALUES AND NEOLIBERAL GLOBALISM

At first globalization seemed like another name for Americanization, political as well as economic. The good news was that the United States could conceivably bring its foreign policy "in from the cold," putting it closer to American domestic ideals. No longer was it necessary to support autocratic regimes simply because they promised resistance to communism. Then came the bad news: Much of East and Southeast Asia was seizing the same opportunity in reverse, removing the liberal democratic cloak from development strategies that no longer had to compete with insurgent alternatives.

A cultural cloak was substituted in the guise of Asian values. Modernization, by this standard, would no longer be equated with broad-spectrum Westernization. Dirlik gets to the heart of the matter: "Capitalism at its moment of victory over socialism finds itself wondering about different cultures of capitalism at odds with one another."[38] The assumption has been that "liberal democratic" capitalism would sooner or later insinuate itself on Asia. Increasingly, however, neoliberalism aligned itself with Asian capitalism against the old liberal ethos. The lessons of East Asia seemed all too obvious at a time when neoconservatism was taking hold in economically vibrant

China, and relatively democratic Japan was caught in a protracted recession. Human rights and democracy were cast as luxuries that threatened social order and impeded growth.

Across the Pacific, meanwhile, another kind of retrenchment was in order: the forging of a virulent corporate globalism on the anvil of the fast emerging "Washington consensus." Then it happened: For the newly dominant ideologies of East and West—Asian values and neoliberal globalism—it was love at first sight. The two joined hands in a formidable economic symbiosis, a rearguard alliance on behalf of the New World Order. What made this alliance so "orderly" was that both sides, despite the gap between their respective centrist and decentrist rhetoric, gave full priority to economic over political development. Both tied market forces to traditional institutions such as the family or the nation, as if those were not prime victims of unbridled marketization.[39]

Asia's emerging markets were to this global order what Japan had been to early Cold War America, with one cardinal difference: Here there was no social net of full employment, as Japan had put under its postwar workers. Nor was there any commitment on the part of global investors to long-term development. Post–Cold War globalization was a hit-and-run operation from the first. The IMF was there to bail out investors, should boom give way to bust. No one was looking out for the newly globalized workers of Asia, not to mention the traditional workers outside the corporate gates.

The implantation of "free market" capitalism in Southeast Asia is reminiscent of the first free market in England, which likewise was predemocratic. Gray points out that this puristic capitalism, founded as it was on the ouster of the traditional social market, could not have been spawned if democratic institutions had already been in place. Indeed, "the free market began to wither away with the entry of the broad population into political life."[40] So too, democratic reform movements were still in an infant stage in Southeast Asia when foreign investment crested in the early 1990s. Thus globalization came under the management of unreformed institutions. After the Crash of 1997, the Western press would condemn the region's "crony capitalism," as if *any* capitalism is free of cronyism.[41] Seldom would it be mentioned that this corrupt and authoritarian system had been propped up by the West for decades, first by American Cold War politics and then by neoliberalism's self-proclaimed "apolitics." The dark irony of U.S.-inspired globalization is that it comes exactly as America's most progressive liberal values are in retreat.

So it was that early 1990s globalization led directly to "reactionary modernization."[42] Local reform initiatives that might have offered a balance between economic and political development were overwhelmed. Democratic values, social equity, and ecological sustainability went up in smoke, quite literally in the case of Indonesia's slash and burn assault on its rainforests. The exogenous force of globalization precluded grassroots political development wherever democratization had not achieved a full-fledged "takeoff" prior to the post–Cold War economic boom.

Having reached that point in the late 1980s, Korea and Taiwan escaped the full brunt of reactionary modernization. Indeed, their democratic movements may have been energized by the boom. But similar movements, still in a germinal stage, were retarded if not extinguished in Indonesia, Singapore, and Malaysia, not to mention post-Tiananmen China. Far from being heralds of "growth first" democratization, Korea and Taiwan are the exceptions to Asian exceptionalism. Their democratic takeoffs came just in time, before the full impact of post–Cold War globalization was suffered.

What needs consideration is the role of Asian values, and cultural values in general, "after the fall" (i.e., after the Crash of 1997). There can be no doubt that the cult of Asian values has been greatly buttressed by the East Asian "miracle,"[43] although its basic elements were available by the mid-1940s in the Indonesian concept of the integralist state, modeled in part on ancient Javanese custom, but also on Nazi Germany and wartime Japan.[44] Whereas Weber found in Confucianism a reason for Asia's long economic stagnation, Asian values were conscripted during the "miracle" years to explain the region's unprecedented success. Now those same values, redescribed as crony capitalism, are blamed for the Asian recession. It is seldom mentioned that, prior to the Crash, Asian values were widely used not only to cover the tracks of cronyism but to direct attention away from political repression and ecological holocaust. Singapore school economism officially subordinated politics to commerce, writing human rights off as a Western fetish.

For their part, Western Asianists were all too willing to accept Asian values as an interim station on the road to broader liberalization. Minxin Pei, for example, was there to tell us that "regarding the democratization of neoautocracies, . . . the question is not whether, but when and how."[45] This reform teleology[46] ensured that little pressure would be put on the Singapore school to give its growth-first model of development an expiration date. Nor was its political credo given much scrutiny. Few cared that while Asian values were credited with boosting economic dynamism, it was in fact the economy that legitimated those values and the oppressive policies they sanctioned. Lucian Pye points out the double irony that, first, Asian values only achieved popularity in Asian countries with the least coherent traditional values (e.g., Singapore and Malaysia) or the least certainty about the merits of traditional culture (China); and, second, the collectivity celebrated in the name of those values was nationalism, a Western import.[47]

It would be bad enough if neoliberal globalists simply refrained from applying economic pressure for humanitarian purposes. Many go further, however, by inverting the case for political engagement. Where economic growth is accepted as the main prerequisite for freedom and democracy, doing business with authoritarian regimes becomes a moral imperative, and any action that obstructs "free trade" can logically be considered anti-democratic. It follows that the Seattle protesters against WTO secret agendas and closed door sessions are anti-democratic. Indeed, even pro-democracy dissidents locked away in Chinese prisons can be regarded as paradoxical anti-democrats, while the CEOs of multinational corporations doing business with the PRC can be depicted as heroes of the coming democratic transformation.

Given this logic, it is easy to see how Asian values came to have an almost canonical place in globalist thought "before the fall"—a time when, more than ever, Asian authoritarian regimes were having to defend their domestic legitimacy.[48] Some of these regimes might have been thrown out except for the support they got from the globalist West. A negative symbiosis emerges. Dirlik reminds us that Confucianism had been restored, by no accident, at the moment of capitalism's crisis of the late 1970s and 1980s.[49] Since then global capitalism has become so inextricably tied to Asianism that the Crash of 1997 seemed to implicate both.[50]

CULTURALISM FROM ABOVE AND BELOW

For all its effect on our reading of Asian values, the Crash did little to alter conventional wisdom of the 1990s concerning cultural determinism. Most post-Crash assessments of Asian values still rest, contra Krugman (who along with Alwyn Young denies the Asian miracle) and Bhagwati (who explains it in terms of export policy),[51] on the belief that culture is a prime factor in economic performance. This assumption amounts to a postmodern inversion of the material causality that for decades was as fundamental to modernization theory as to Marxism. Culture is now in the driver's seat, but toward what end? This radical shift in causal theory is anything but radical politically. By eschewing transcultural rights, it unwittingly shuts down a main channel of political reform, while leaving authoritarian traditionalism very much in place. Thus the Asian values/neoliberal alliance has a friend in the New Culturalism.

Prior to this cultural turn, national liberation movements could get past the modernity/tradition or West/past dichotomy by linking themselves to a transnational order of liberation. Now such movements are themselves a thing of the past.[52] The loss of that revolutionary agent is part of the dilemma faced by any local resistance to globalization. The local is thrown into a David and Goliath situation in which globalists join postcolonial postmodernists in denying David his slingshot: the sense of universal justice that seems to have its last world champions, theoretically and administratively, in Jürgen Habermas and Kofi Annan.[53]

Minus that transcultural artillery, local resistance loses much of its staying power—the kind that defeated first the French and then the Americans in Vietnam. Globalists offer the locals a sop in the form of a new glocal identity.[54] They have their reasons: As a stage play for cultural difference, glocalization does a good job of masking the cultural depredations of globalization. Previously the local could count on the national for protection; but increasingly the national itself has been co-opted by the global, leaving "places" to fend for themselves.[55]

Perhaps, as Kaplan suggests in *The Ends of the Earth* (1996) and *The Coming Anarchy* (2000), resistance in the twenty-first century will take the form of pandemic disorder rather than concerted revolution. Huntington takes a different route, that of civilizational clash, to much the same disorderly end; and even when that disorder is downgraded to mere ethnic conflict, as Gray would have it,[56] this is enough to sink any immediate prospect of a *political* New World Order. The question is whether civilizational or cultural resistance can also explode economic globalization. Global capitalism has proven adept at "gulping down any kind of religion or culture in the world."[57] Significantly, however, the global environmental crisis spawned by modernist developmentalism has prompted a neo-Gandhian resistance.[58] It can at least be said for such tradition-based resistance that some cultures or religions are harder for capitalism to swallow.

Islam, for example, has proven a real obstacle to global consumerism.[59] By contrast, Confucian-based Asian values seem highly amenable to some forms of capitalism, though after the Crash, and the subsequent incursions of the IMF, Asian feelings about neoliberal capitalism have understandably cooled. We have already noted how the alliance between Asian values and globalism was strained to the breaking point after the "fall." Confucianism, in any case, was never the perfect springboard for capitalism that globalists imagined it to be, or rather "invented it to be." Much to the embarrassment of theories centered on a unique Confucian/capitalist nexus, non-Confucian success stories (e.g., Thailand, Malaysia, and Indonesia) are now commonplace in Asia.[60] The determining factor in all these cases is not Confucianism or even "Asian values" but the structural relations that empower such values.[61]

The cultural dynamics set in motion by these structures, however, will not always serve the interests of a power elite. Insurgent cultural currents can also be generated, as was the case in Korea and Taiwan during the years leading up to their respective democratic transformations. Here the usual base-to-superstructure causality is problematized, in that the cultural (superstructural) germ of resistance was there prior to its material (infrastructural) activation. Which, then, is the causal "base" of resistance, the emerging economic structure or the grassroots cultural given?

Both, I would argue, are essential for a democratic takeoff. Robert Hefner details how long neglected progressive currents within Indonesian Islam have provided a cultural or "civil" foundation for pluralism and democratization, a process that was systematically thwarted by the regressive politics of Suharto's New Order.[62] Likewise, the politics associated with "Asian values" may have secured the necessary stability for "miracle" economics in Singapore and Malaysia, but these values also froze political development by extirpating the independence and thus the potential opposition of civil society.[63]

Grassroots cultural politics figures heavily in what I call the Korean-oppositional (hereafter simply Korean) as opposed to the Singaporean-hegemonic (hereafter simply Singaporean) model of development. The former was epitomized by Korean president Kim Dae Jung's stance during his oppositional years.[64] This model, which endures despite the apostasy of Kim's IMFism during his presidency, counters the standard image of Korea's political "vortex."[65] It is consistent, therefore, with Dirlik's case for a bottom-up East Asianism that defies "both Orientalist and nationalist mappings of the world."[66]

POLITICAL DEVELOPMENT AND ASIAN GEOPOLITICS

In challenging the normative status of so-called Asian values, *Fire* repositions culture with regard to both development and geopolitics. Its premise is that the place of cultural values in development theory has been suppressed by a specious scientism, while its place in power politics has been obscured by decades of feckless debate between realism and idealism. Globalization perpetuates this dual oversight. Miles Kahler shows how neorealism accommodates many key elements of neoliberalism, such as its stress on global interdependence.[67] Likewise, David Baldwin sees neorealists (such as Joseph Grieco) and neoliberals (such as Robert Keohane) as having converged in important respects. Neither, for example, lays emphasis on the dated question of whether states are the paramount actors in international politics. Baldwin notes, however, that moral issues are hardly mentioned in the current debate,[68] a defect this book seeks to rectify.

Clearly the two dominant factions, neorealism and neoliberalism, are united in their rejection of idealism's moral focus. In that respect realism has won the IR debate of the century. The new line of debate is between the relative priorities given to security issues versus commercial issues, a contest that was graphically played out in 1996 within the Clinton administration with the transfer of jurisdiction over communications satellites and other sensitive aerospace technologies from the State Department to the Commerce Department. The consequent weakening of security provisions for military-related sales to China came under scathing examination in the 700-page Cox report, commissioned by the House of Representatives in June 1998.[69] That dangerous breach of security traced to a presumed affinity between "Asian values" and American interests. *Fire* undertakes to break that mythic linkage by showing both its sides to be truncated representations of a far more complex whole.

It is argued in chapter 1 that Asian values are far more variegated and often more egalitarian than the Singapore model would suggest. Here I expand upon Dirlik's conviction that too much weight has been placed on tendentious readings of Chinese tradition. He was referring specifically to the question of the origins of Chinese anarchism, which Peter Zarrow locates in Daoism and Buddhism.[70] But the causal reductionism that Dirlik rejects has plagued the whole question of Asian values, values that are assumed to be as narrow as they are immutable. On that basis, criticism of Asian authoritarianism becomes not only useless but also "orientalist" in its imposition of Western values on the East. Chapter 1 charges, conversely, that nothing could be more orientalist than the assumption that freedom is a uniquely Western value. Corporate globalists can in good conscience turn a deaf ear to Chinese reformism only so long as the assumption prevails that basic human rights carry a U.S. patent.

To appreciate the broader spectrum of Asian political values, close attention must be given to dissident voices. This book looks to Korean political culture as a window on what has been suppressed in the name of Asian values. Despite Korea's reputation for neo-Confucian centrism, democratic dissent has proven more potent there than in nominally democratic Japan, despite Japan's far more developed economy. Judged by a political yardstick, Korea had emerged by the early 1990s as the most developed country on the Rim.

This alone should dispel the modernist assumption that economic development leads inevitably to political development, and the ancillary notion that democratic activism poses a threat to the democratic process insofar as it

destabilizes the economic environment. Nowhere in the world has rapid economic development been more closely paralleled by political development,
albeit oppositional, than in Korea. My position is that it was precisely the
resistant character of that development that kept it on track. What now threatens to derail this process is its very success. First the door was opened for its
co-optation by Korea's own power structure, and now by the global structure
that rode in with the Asian Crash of 1997.

The issue of oppositional development, as adumbrated in chapter 1, is
developed at length in chapters 4 and 5. Building upon Kim Dae Jung's seminal essay in *Foreign Affairs* (1994), these chapters argue that the popular
resistance that erupted in Korea in the 1980s was not an exogenous import.
Rather it was organically rooted in the "other Korea," outside the "vortex"
of power that has occupied most Korean studies. By contrast to the inherently
rapacious Singapore model, which lends itself to full-scale technical, economic, and military development at the expense of human rights and ecological sustainability, Kim's oppositionalism (or rather the grassroots resistance
that Kim represented) remains dialogically open to the West as well as to
other Asian cultures. Likewise it remains open to voices of dissent within
Korea itself. No thanks to most occupants of Korea's Blue House, the Korean
model has had to fully accommodate the Korean "other."

The double mystery is why this democratic dynamic would surface so dramatically in Korea, of all places, and why its implications would be overlooked by so many for so long. The flip side of that question is why Japanese
democracy has been so overrated for so long. Chapters 2 and 3 take up the
enigma of Japan's political *under*development, which in combination with
the country's economic "miracle" gave rise to the "Japan problem" of recent
decades. If the old "Japan problem" was largely economic, the new one
closely links economics with power politics. The nature of this emerging geopolitics, however, will depend largely on the course of Japan's domestic political development. Here there is cause for hope as well as alarm. The good
news is that without its economic miracle, Japan's Liberal Democratic Party
(LDP) machine finds itself in danger of losing its purchase on legitimacy.
The bad news is that Prime Minister Junichiro Koizumi's refurbished LDP
may find salvation in globalization. In that case Japan could forfeit, along
with its domestic reform dynamic, any chance of a progressive IR role.

Just as Japan's procrustean growth formula helped to suppress noncapital-
ist culture within Japan itself, its export helped to undermine noncapitalistic
values throughout Asia. The Japan model gave unalloyed priority to macro-
managed economic growth. That policy was unfortunately mimicked by most
of East Asia's "flying geese," whose very success killed the idea that the
model owed its effectiveness to the cultural specifics of Japan. This had the

effect of expanding the model to the whole region in the form of East Asian exceptionalism.

That too turns out to have been a transitional exercise in cultural hubris. Neoliberalism's global metastasis is quickly transforming this (or any) exceptionalism into culturally nonspecific globalism, or at best a co-opted glocalism. The resulting ethnocide was softened during the 1990s by the idea that globalization is innately progressive, politically as well as economically. Taiwan and Korea are often cited (their opposition movements being summarily dismissed) as examples of the wisdom of "growth first" development (i.e., economic liberalization without the destabilizing impediment of early political liberalization). The point is simple: Since democracy will follow naturally from economic development, support for democratic activism is unnecessary, unprofitable, and ultimately—in terms of its practical effect—undemocratic.

In fact, activism has been a major factor in the democratization of Korea and Taiwan, the latter case being closely tied to demands for "indigenization."[71] The neoliberal rationale for disengagement (which paradoxically assumes the name of "engagement" where China is concerned) is only compelling where the role of opposition politics, and cultural resistance in general, is surgically removed from consideration. The Korean development model challenges the legitimacy of reactionary modernism. It is true that Korea's power elite *aspired* to authoritarian modernism, or, failing that, to a "pressure release" mode of democracy such as Japan's. But in the post-Park era that cathartic mechanism took on a life of its own. Korea has emerged as the flagship of East Asian democratization.

The core imperative of the Korean model is not that political development should take priority over economic development. The disastrous consequences of such anti-economism were well illustrated in Indonesia of the 1950s, prior to the advent of Sukarno's "guided democracy." Rather this model mandates that economic progress be balanced by political progress at all stages of development. The case for postponing political development is premised on the fiction of a global democratic teleology, as discussed in chapter 6 with regard to China. This myth has had a profound impact on America's China policy in the early post–Cold War years. The original geopolitical motive for the Nixon/Kissinger rapprochement with China, as discussed in chapter 7, was its balance-of-power advantage over the Soviets. That rationale vanished with the collapse of the Soviet power sphere, after which a more "idealistic" reevaluation of America's China policy could be expected, especially in view of the Tiananmen tragedy. But such a sweeping revision of Deng-era China policy would have been anathema to multinational corporations that look to China as their new frontier for massive exports, cheap labor, and miracle-economy investments. To safeguard these prospects, concern over human rights and democracy had to be muted, or at least separated from the *business* of foreign affairs.

This disjunction was premised on a sweeping neoliberal economism: the assumption that economic liberalization contains all the requisites for political liberalization. Early post–Cold War globalists were joined by a host of China experts in support of this teleology as applied to China. Chapter 6 shows how America's China policy, under the spell of globalization, came to be defined by an ideology very close to Fukuyama's liberal-capitalist "end of history." This bipartisan ideology emerged as the foreign policy equivalent of the Cold War's domino theory. Its market-driven vision of the "world as us" became the legitimizing force behind Clinton's "constructive engagement" with China. The same regime that gave us Tiananmen and the Falun Gong crackdown was wishfully perceived as embracing the United States in fair trade and even "strategic partnership," two sides of the same teleological illusion. Meanwhile China's material gains of the past decade were producing a neoconservative "undertow effect" in the form of a well-funded Chinese Communist Party (CCP) and People's Liberation Army (PLA). Teleological confidence has allowed U.S. policymakers to ignore that fact and suspend moral considerations within post–Cold War realism. That is how, with a clean conscience, Washington delinked trade and human rights in the face of CCP retrenchment.

This literal sellout is part of a larger ethical retreat that occurs whenever "U.S. interests" are represented in dollar terms alone. As Perry Link contends:

> [T]he deeper issue is about what is meant by "interests." Are Americans "better off," ultimately, if they have inexpensive shoes yet know very well that the people who make them are deprived of elementary rights? How many toys add up to the equivalent of a feeling about the rightness of there being no double standard among human beings?[72]

A convergence is still possible at this deeper level between American and Chinese interests. Unfortunately, present American "engagement" never dives to that depth.

Chapter 7 critiques current Sino-apologetics from another angle: its violation, in the name of realism, of the most basic tenets of balance-of-power politics. The "realist" merits of the pro-China argument went up in smoke with the Soviet fall, after which geopolitical logic dictated a highly guarded China policy. This strategic reversal was bound to produce tension inside George H. Bush's and Bill Clinton's ranks, for commercial considerations were at that moment tilting the scales sharply in the opposite direction. Rather than argue their case honestly, in terms of cash value rather than security or human rights, corporate interests brought in geopolitical hired guns such as former Secretaries of State Kissinger and Haig to renew the "realist" credentials of pro-China "engagement." This subterfuge was so successful that Clinton was able to sell his largely "incorporated" China policy as a "strategic partnership." Meanwhile he perpetuated the myth—set in stone by Bush before[73]—that market forces alone could transform China into a Taiwan-style capitalist state, ripe for multinational picking.

Oddly, it was from the Right rather than the Left that this market orthodoxy was most forcefully challenged. Huntington's "clash of civilizations" thesis can be classified as a "cultural realism" insofar as it construes culture as a prime mover of geopolitical reality. For Huntington, to be sure, this state of affairs is regretable. To him "civilizational" difference amounts to a geocultural "do not enter" sign, a negatively conceived *cultural realism of the Right*.

This lays the theoretical foundation for George W. Bush's preference—prior to September 11, 2001, at least—for a heavily fortified isolationism. But it also plants a contradiction in the heart of the Bush foreign policy, where unilateralism collides with the globalist tilt of the president's corporate commitments. What emerges is a minimalist policy whereby only moral actions, not commercial policies, are obstructed. The result is an even "leaner and meaner" neoliberalism than Clinton could produce. Nor will the international turn of Bush's antiterrorist campaign rectify this ethical void. The global alliance Bush seeks is one of pure military expedience. Thus September 11 becomes a boon to the very institutions that the World Trade Center symbolized. The attack serves as a catalyst for a far more expansive and militant neoliberalism than was possible at the end of the Cold War, when there was much talk of an international "peace dividend." Far from wounding multinational capitalism, Black Tuesday consummated the militarization of globalization that first surfaced with the Gulf War.

This book is as much at odds with that militant wing of globalism as it is with its rival "cosmopolitan" wing (e.g., the naive global democratism of a David Held).[74] We are thrown back to the very nonutopian devices of realist politics, softened, however, by the recognition that values, social justice, and environmental responsibility are now a vital part of the geopolitical arsenal. While this qualification puts *Fire* within dialogic reach of "bottom-up" cosmopolitans such as Bryan Turner, it also thrusts it into an ideological no-man's-land: out of step with the conventional Left for its balance-of-power realism, and anathema to the realist Right for its social and environmental agenda. *Fire* holds its ground on both fronts.

When Bush announced, just prior to meeting German Chancellor Gerhard Schröder with regard to global warming, that the United States "will not do

anything that harms our economy,"[75] he was throwing away the very principle of moral leadership. After September 11 he learned the hard lesson that
today's geopolitical goals require unprecedented international cooperation.
What he has yet to learn is that lasting cooperation depends upon moral legitimacy. Power politics can no longer be equated with imperialism. For a bona
fide superpower, intervention to prevent genocide is now a moral imperative,
not an expression of nationalistic hubris. Likewise, hard diplomatic pressure
on behalf of human rights must be embraced by any Left that cares about real
results, not just theoretical posturing.

   Fire, accordingly, posits a *cultural realism of the Left.* Call it a moral geopolitics, or simply a moral realism. What this requires is a pragmatic route
around the standard realist/idealist divide. That task is taken up by chapter 8,
which puts cultural complexity to ethical as well as strategic advantage. If
knowledge is power, so too are values. They are the cement of an effective
foreign policy in the post–Cold War era. By crediting the force of ideas and
cultural values, not just warheads and economic growth, moral realism nar-
rows the Cold War gap between realism and idealism.

   Huntington took a paradigm-breaking step in that direction with his insight
that culture is to the post–Cold War era what ideology was to the Cold War.
It is not surprising that more traditional realists have recoiled from this thesis,
since it was on their watch that culture was flatly excluded from foreign policy analysis. In other respects, however, Huntington sticks with the old realist
program. The standard Cold War marginalization of moral considerations is
little changed in the cultural realism of either Huntington or Kaplan. *Fire,* by
contrast, brings realism "in from the cold," offering moral realism as a
counter to the "cold peace" of current globalization. Thus the moral factor is
smuggled in through the back door of power politics.

   This soft-power approach to East/West relations is premised on the cultural
dialogics that was broached in my *Cultural Prosaics: The Second Postmodern Turn* (1998). It is time to resist the undialogic fiat of modernist economism, whose latest incarnation is neoliberal globalism. This book shifts
priority to *political* development, and especially to oppositional politics, with
special reference to indigenous strategies for democratization.

   To the extent that top-down power structures have been globalized, bottom-
up resistance requires and deserves all the outside help it can get. This support would be voided by the insular pluralism that Gray propounds. Neither
does Huntington's cultural retreatism (culminating in his infamous Atlantic-
ism) nor Kaplan's cultural agonistics (including an unabashed apology for
the virtues of war)[76] afford a tenable option in the face of global issues requiring trust and cooperation among nations. What is needed is a realism fit for
the twenty-first century: a culturally informed and morally engaged geopoli-

tics. This is especially crucial in the case of Asia, where the spreading "fire on the Rim," fueled by economic development barren of political development, can no longer be ignored.

Chapter 1 surveys these mounting dangers. If they are not confronted soon, while moral realism is still an available option, the only remaining recourse will be military force. It would be hard to say which of America's recent foreign policies—Clinton's market-idealism or G. W. Bush's market-realism—has done more to make that nightmare vision a reality. The one talks of engagement, the other (prior to September 11) of disengagement, but in moral terms they are equally atavistic. It is time for America to get its Asia Pacific policy out of the twentieth century.

NOTES

1. Ahmed Rashid, *Taliban: Militant Islam, Oil and Fundamentalism in Central Asia* (New Haven, Conn.: Yale University Press, 2000), 13.

2. Carl Boggs, *The End of Politics: Corporate Power and the Decline of the Public Sphere* (New York: Guilford Press, 2000), 209.

3. Jonathan Friedman, "Champagne Liberals and the New 'Dangerous Classes': Reconfigurations of Class, Identity and Cultural Production in the Contemporary Global System," paper given at a conference on New Cultural Formations in an Era of Transnational Globalization, Institute of Ethnology, Academia Sinica, Taipei, Taiwan, October 6–7, 2001.

4. Yoseph Lapid, "Culture's Ship: Returns and Departures in International Relations Theory," in Yoseph Lapid and Friedrich Kratochwil, eds., *The Return of Culture and Identity in IR Theory* (Boulder, Colo.: Lynne Rienner Publishers, 1996), 3–20, 4.

5. For example, James Der Derian, "Post-Theory: The Eternal Return of Ethics in International Relations," in Michael W. Doyle and G. John Ikenberry, eds., *New Thinking in International Relations Theory* (Boulder, Colo.: Westview Press, 1997), 54–76, 65.

6. Bruce Cumings, *Parallax Visions: Making Sense of American-East Asian Relations at the End of the Century* (Durham, N.C.: Duke University Press, 1999), 4.

7. Lucian Pye, *The Spirit of Chinese Politics* (2nd ed.) (Cambridge, Mass.: Harvard University Press, 1992).

8. For example, his dismal treatment of Korean political culture in *Asian Power and Politics: The Cultural Dimensions of Authority* (Cambridge, Mass.: Belknap Press of Harvard University Press, 1985), 215–228.

9. Kimie Hara, "Rethinking the 'Cold War' in the Asia-Pacific," *Pacific Review* 12, no. 4 (1999): 515–536.

10. "The Poor Who Are Always With Us," *The Economist* (July 1–7, 2000), <www.economist.com/editorial/freeforall/current/ ir6164.html>.

11. Zbigniew Brzezinski, *The Grand Chessboard: American Strategy and Its Geopolitical Imperatives* (New York: Basic Books, 1997), 133.

12. Arif Dirlik, *The Postcolonial Aura: Third World Criticism in the Age of Global Capitalism* (Boulder, Colo.: Westview Press, 1997), 117; see also in this regard Xiamei,

Chen, *Occidentalism: A Theory of Counter-Discourse in Post-Mao China* (Oxford: Oxford University Press, 1995).

13. Michael Walzer, *Thick and Thin: Moral Argument at Home and Abroad* (Notre Dame, Ind.: University of Notre Dame Press, 1994), 1.

14. Paul Hirst and Grahame Thompson, *Globalization in Question: The International Economy and the Possibility of Governance* (Cambridge, UK: Polity Press, 1996), 6.

15. Boggs, *The End of Politics*, 20.

16. Arif Dirlik, "Globalism and the Politics of Place," *Development* 41, no. 2 (June 1998), <www.sidint.org/publications/development/vol41/no2/41-2b.html>.

17. Stacey Leigh Pigg, "Inventing Social Categories through Place: Social Representation and Development in Nepal," *Comparative Study of Society and History* 34, no. 3 (1992): 491–513.

18. For example, Dong Hyun Kim, "Decentralization and Implementation of Social Development at the Local Level in Korea," in Gerald E. Caiden and Bun Woong Kim, eds., *A Dragon's Progress: Development Administration in Korea* (West Hartford, Conn.: Kumarian Press, 1991), 181–195, 187.

19. Trish Saywell, "On the Edge," *Far Eastern Economic Review* (February 25, 1999): 46–48, 46.

20. Matt Forney, "Left Behind in the Countryside," *Newsweek* Asia edition (August 21, 1995): 12–13, 12.

21. Robert D. Kaplan, *The Coming Anarchy: Shattering the Dreams of the Post Cold War* (New York: Random House, 2000), 26.

22. "China Resettlement Plan Killed by World Bank's Rich Nations," *New York Times* Late News (July 7, 2000), <www.nytimes.com/yr/mo/day/late/07cnd-world-bank.html>.

23. "World Bank KOs Tibet Resettlement Loan," Associated Press Breaking News, in *New York Times* (July 7, 2000), <www.nytimes.com/online/f/AP-World-Bank-China.html>.

24. "Gigantism on the Yangtze," *New York Times* Editorial (November 15, 1997), <www.nytimes.com/yr/mo/day/editorial/15sat1.html>.

25. Hans J. Morgenthau, *In Defense of the National Interest* (New York: Alfred Knopf, 1951), 33.

26. Bruce Cumings, "China through the Looking Glass," *Bulletin of the Atomic Scientists* 55, no. 5 (November/December 1999): 30–37, <www.bullatomsci.org/issues/1999/so99cumings.html>.

27. Sanj Altan, "Tibetans Aren't Only Victims of China's Wrath," *New York Times* Letters (January 8, 1997), <www.nytimes.com/yr/mo/day/letters/altan.html>.

28. Kaplan, *The Coming Anarchy*, 26–27.

29. Arif Dirlik, *After the Revolution: Waking to Global Capitalism* (Hanover, N.H.: Wesleyan University Press, 1994), 108; Dirlik, *The Postcolonial Aura*, 98; and Gearóid Ó (Gerard Toal) Tuathail, *Critical Geopolitics: The Politics of Writing Global Space* (Minneapolis: University of Minnesota Press, 1996), 228.

30. Jürgen Habermas, *The Philosophical Discourse of Modernity: Twelve Lectures*, trans. Frederick Lawrence (Cambridge, UK: Polity Press, 1987), 336–337.

31. Paul Kennedy, *Preparing for the Twenty-First Century* (Toronto: HarperCollins, 1999), 200–201.

32. For a portrait of the latter see Robert B. Reich, *The Work of Nations: Preparing Ourselves for 21st Century Capitalism* (New York: Alfred A. Knopf, 1991).

33. R. B. J. Walker, *Inside/Outside: International Relations as Political Theory* (Cambridge, UK: Cambridge University Press, 1993), 104–105.

34. Frank Baldwin, "Introduction," in Frank Baldwin, ed., *Without Parallel: The American-Korean Relationship since 1945* (New York: Pantheon Books, 1973), 3–37, 8.

35. Baldwin, "Introduction," 9.

36. Edmund Terence Gomez and K. S. Jomo, *Malaysia's Political Economy: Politics, Patronage and Profits* (2nd ed.) (Cambridge, UK: Cambridge University Press, 1999), 11.

37. Neil Sheehan, *After the War Was Over: Hanoi and Saigon* (New York: Vintage Books, 1991), 58–59.

38. Arif Dirlik, *Postmodernity's Histories: The Past as Legacy and Project* (Lanham, Md.: Rowman & Littlefield, 2000), 63.

39. On this contradictory linkage in neoliberalism see Anthony Giddens, *The Third Way: The Renewal of Social Democracy* (Cambridge, UK: Polity Press, 1998), 12; and David A. Baldwin, "Neoliberalism, Neorealism, and World Politics," in David A. Baldwin, ed., *Neorealism and Neoliberalism: The Contemporary Debate* (New York: Columbia University Press, 1993), 3–25, 9.

40. John Gray, *False Dawn: The Delusions of Global Capitalism* (New York: New Press, 1998), 8.

41. Prabhat Patnaik, "Capitalism in Asia at the End of the Millenium," *Monthly Review* 51, no. 3 (July–August 1999): 53–70, 63.

42. Kanishka Jayasuriya, "Understanding 'Asian Values' as a Form of Reactionary Modernization," *Contemporary Politics* 4, no. 2 (1998): 77–91.

43. Gabriel A. Almond, *A Discipline Divided: Schools and Sects in Political Science* (London: Sage, 1990), 148.

44. Adam Schwarz, *A Nation in Waiting: Indonesia's Search for Stability* (2nd ed.) (Boulder, Colo.: Westview, 2000), 8.

45. Minxin Pei, "The Puzzle of East Asian Exceptionalism," *Journal of Democracy* 5, no. 4 (1994): 90–103, 102.

46. William H. Thornton, "Selling Democratic Teleology: The Case of the Chinese Fortune-Tellers," *International Politics* 37, no. 3 (September 2000): 285–300.

47. Lucian W. Pye, "The Asian Values Ballyhoo: Patten's Common Sense on Hong Kong and Beyond," *Foreign Affairs* 77, no. 6 (1998): 135–141, 140.

48. William H. Thornton, "East Asian Liberalism: The Case of a Politically Incorrect 'Other,'" *Asian Pacific Quarterly* 26, no. 4 (1995): 59–75, 69.

49. William H. Thornton, "After the Fall: A Response to Dirlik and Jun," *Development and Society* 29, no. 1 (June 2000): 111–121, 116.

50. William Greider needed no Asian Crash to reach such a conclusion. For him corruption is a core element of the whole global system (*One World, Ready or Not: The Manic Logic of Global Capitalism* [New York: Touchstone, 1997], 35). To keep such critics at bay, globalists rushed to distinguish Asian "crony capitalism" from their own operations (Ravi Arvind Palat, "Miracles of the Day Before?: The Great Asian Meltdown and the Changing World-Economy," *Development and Society* 28, no. 1 [1999]: 1–47, 3), which stood in danger of being exposed as "crony globalism." As Arif Dirlik puts it, "Asia as the motor force of the world economy has turned once again into an Asia that requires Western guidance to save it from itself, or even an Asia that may be a threat to global order" ("Culture against History: The Politics of East Asian Identity," *Develop-*

ment and Society 28, no. 2 [1999]: 166–189, 175). That threat is compounded by the present "reterritorialization" of Asian capitalism, a trend that has gained momentum after the Crash, but which Dirlik had noticed early in the 1990s (Arif Dirlik, "Introducing the Pacific," in Arif Dirlik, ed., *What Is in a Rim? Critical Perspectives on the Pacific Region Idea* [Boulder, Colo.: Westview Press, 1993], 3–11, 9).

51. Paul Krugman, "The Myth of Asia's Miracle," *Foreign Affairs* 73, no. 6 (November–December 1994): 63–78; Jagdish Bhagwati, "Turnaround Time," *Far Eastern Economic Review* 162, no. 22 (June 3, 1999): 52.

52. Dirlik, "Culture Against History," 169.

53. William H. Thornton, "Back to Basics: Human Rights and Power Politics in the New Moral Realism," *International Journal of Politics, Culture and Society* 14, no. 2 (2000): 315–332; and "Kofi Annan's Millenial Vision," *New York Times* Editorial (April 9, 2000), <www.nytimes.com/yr/mo/day/editorial/09sun2.html>.

54. William H. Thornton, "Mapping the 'Glocal' Village: The Political Limits of 'Glocalization,'" *Continuum* 14, no. 1 (April 2000): 79–89.

55. Dirlik, "Globalism and the Politics of Place."

56. Gray, *False Dawn*, 22–23.

57. Sang-In Jun, "No (Logical) Place for Asian Values in East Asia's Economic Development," *Development and Society* 28, no. 2 (1999): 191–204, 201.

58. Dirlik, *After the Revolution*, 17.

59. Bryan S. Turner, *Orientalism, Postmodernism and Globalism* (London: Routledge, 1994), 91.

60. Yooshik Gong and Wonho Jong, "Culture and Development: Reassessing Cultural Explanations on Asian Economic Development," *Development and Society* 27, no. 1 (1998): 77–97, 92.

61. Jun, "No (Logical) Place," 201.

62. Robert W. Hefner, *Civil Islam: Muslims and Democratization in Indonesia* (Princeton, N.J.: Princeton University Press, 2000), 59.

63. Kanishka Jayasuriya, "The Exception Becomes the Norm: Law and Regimes of Exception in East Asia," *Asian-Pacific Law and Policy Journal* 2, no. 1 (Winter 2001): 108–124, 117–118.

64. William H. Thornton, "Korea and East Asian Exceptionalism," *Theory, Culture and Society: Explorations in Critical Social Science* 15, no. 2 (1998): 137–154; and William H. Thornton, "The Korean Road to Postmodernization and Development," *Asian Pacific Quarterly* 26, no. 1 (1994): 1–11; and Dae Jung Kim, "Is Culture Destiny? The Myth of Asia's Anti-Democratic Values: A Response to Lee Kuan Yew," *Foreign Affairs* 73, no. 6 (1994): 189–194.

65. Gregory Henderson, *Korea: The Politics of the Vortex* (Cambridge, Mass.: Harvard University Press, 1968).

66. Dirlik, "Culture Against History," 187.

67. Miles Kahler, "Inventing International Relations: International Relations Theory after 1945," in Michael W. Doyle and G. John Ikenberry, eds., *New Thinking in International Relations Theory* (Boulder, Colo.: Westview Press, 1997): 20–53, 36.

68. Baldwin, "Neoliberalism, Neorealism, and World Politics," 9.

69. William M. Daley, "Commerce Can Do the Job," *New York Times* Editorial (June 5, 1998), <www.nytimes.com/ yr/mo/day/oped/05dale.html>; and Shawn W. Crispin,

"Technical Problem: Cox Report Is Bad News for U.S. Firms, China and Clinton," *Far Eastern Economic Review* (February 25, 1999): 31–32.

70. Arif Dirlik, "Dimensions of Chinese Anarchism: An Interview with Arif Dirlik," *Perspectives in Anarchist Theory* 1, no. 2 (Fall 1997), <flag.blackened.net/ias/2dimensio.htm.

71. Horng-Luen Wang, "In Want of a Nation: State, Institutions and Globalization in Taiwan" dissertation, University of Chicago, 1999.

72. Perry Link, "The Old Man's New China," *New York Review of Books* 41, no. 11 (June 9, 1994): 31–36, 36.

73. Steven W. Mosher, *Hegemon: China's Plan to Dominate Asia and the World* (San Francisco: Encounter Books, 2000), 121.

74. For example, his *Democracy and the Global Order: From the Modern State to Cosmopolitan Governance* (Stanford, Calif.: Stanford University Press, 1995).

75. "German Leader Questions Bush Plan," the Associated Press, in *New York Times* (March 29, 2001), <www.nytimes.com/aponline/ national.AP-Bush.html>.

76. Kaplan, *The Coming Anarchy*, chap. 9.

Chapter 1

The Postmodernization of Asian Values

AFTER TIANANMEN

For decades culture has been the missing link in the West's comprehension of the modern East. Where it was not willfully ignored, culture simply fell between the cracks of academic compartmentalization. Consider the case of Southeast Asian development. Usually this second Asian "miracle" has been explained in economic terms such as foreign investment or the comparative advantage that accrues from rapidly rising production costs among the established "dragons" of East Asia. Culture has been brought in, if at all, mainly to justify authoritarianism or to discredit the South's leaning toward dependency theory. Rarely has the impact of geopolitics on development been examined, and until recently the impact of culture on geopolitics was categorically denied by IR realists.

A cogent corrective is offered by Benedict Anderson, who situates Asian development within a vast geocultural web. The whole Rim, as he sees it, has been profoundly affected for better or worse by the tides of political culture. Southeast Asia was especially benefited during the Mao era when China removed itself from regional economic competition.[1] However, as Deng's reforms put China back in the running, developing countries found themselves on a collision course with the biggest stock of subsistence labor on earth. Not since the days of postwar communist expansion had the region felt so much at risk, and this time its only viable defense seemed to be surrender to the dictates of globalization.

Geopolitically as well as economically, the resurgent Middle Kingdom China served warning on the Rim, especially after the Asian Crash of 1997. Those who could—Japan, Korea, and Taiwan—sought refuge by investing heavily in the Chinese boom, while those who could not were left in the lurch. It came down to a grim tactical choice between *buying in* or *selling out* (i.e., throwing open one's doors to IMF-directed "free trade"). Few have challenged the globalist logic that promotes these dubious options. One of those few is Amartya Sen, who redefines development in human terms, but with distinctly Asian provenance. Another is Walden Bello, who presents what can fairly be called a "third way" alternative to hermeticism and globalism—not to be confused with the spurious "third way" of Anthony Giddens et al., which amounts to a program for selling out with a clean conscience.

Years before the Crash, Bello recognized the region's impending crisis. He endorsed the slow but sure path of sustainable growth and social equity. Rather than join the "self-defeating race to 'export one's way out of the crisis,'" he advocated a social justice agenda that would augment domestic demand as a dependable engine of development. Nor was this agenda a mere utopian sentiment. Bello witnessed, by the early 1990s, the rise of "organizations and communities throughout both the North and South that . . . were moving toward such a vision, toward communication with one another, and toward alliance."[2]

The question was whether that alliance could "jell fast enough into a critical mass to head off the dark victory of the . . . 'new world order'."[3] If the Crash of 1997 had the effect of extending that Order, it also removed the claim that "core" and "periphery" were obsolete terms in the era of "miracle" economics. After two decades of neglect, dependency theory was back in action. The Crash made it all too clear that Sen and Bello were right: Globalist economism was not in the South's best interest. Others realized too late that the IMF was there to bail out venture capitalists, not developing nations. Unlike past forms of imperialism, the new corporate version was utterly nomadic and unburdened by any sense of political loyalty or human responsibility. In effect, its bags were always packed.

What might have prolonged the "second" Asian miracle was the Tiananmen massacre of June 1989. When China's power elite made their fateful move—the decision to kill political reform in its infancy—they took into account not only the probable domestic consequences of their actions, but also the likely reactions of Western leaders. They bet everything on their belief that after the rhetorical dust had settled, capitalist incentives would triumph over human rights concerns. They judged correctly.

How is it that China's leaders knew the West better than it knew them? Despite countless warning signs, Western analysts were caught off guard by Tiananmen. Bruce Cumings recalls how Deng Xiaopeng's reformism had followed a zigzag course for the past decade, taking back in odd years what it gave in even ones: the Democracy Wall crackdown in 1979; the campaign against "bourgeois liberalism" in 1981; that against "spiritual pollution" in 1983; and in 1987, when Deng pressed for an officially defined "socialism with *Chinese* characteristics,"[4] too few experts registered that what he meant was *authoritarian* characteristics. They could ignore these "odd" signs because they expected political development, the so-called fifth moderniza- tion, to follow naturally in the wake of capitalist transformation. If free mar- ket commerce was indeed the prime mover of democratization, and if international pressure would impede such commerce, then the best way to encourage political reform was obviously to say little and do less about PRC repression.

It was in this vein that President Ronald Reagan, in his 1988 state of the union address, gave market fundamentalism a New Age twist. With a straight face he linked it to Lao-tzu's classic advice on how to govern a great nation: Proceed "as you would cook a small fish; do not overdo it."[5] This is to say that political reform in developing countries should remain epiphenomenal (i.e., strictly subordinate to economic liberalization). It was taken on faith that a full range of reforms would soon be ripe for picking. Had the protesters at Tiananmen not swallowed this notion whole, the tragedy might have been averted. They were simply there, they thought, to do the picking.

The Tiananmen question erupted once more early in 2001 with the publi- cation of *The Tiananmen Papers*,[6] which purports to expose the inner work- ings of the five-member Standing Committee of the Politburo (the highest formal political power in China) in the days leading up to the June 1989 deba- cle. Whatever their broader import, these documents target President Jiang Zemin and his hard-line comrade Li Peng. Li had been instrumental in replac- ing the moderate Zhao Ziyang by the tougher Jiang as the CCP general secre- tary.[7] This action was a veritable coup, since it lacked the legally required vote by the Poliburo and the State Council.[8]

While there is a conservative side to *The Tiananmen Papers*, insofar as it suggests that reform must emanate from within the CCP,[9] its major insight is that China's power elite has been divided on key issues. That could lend sup- port to the case for greater outside pressure on issues such as human rights. This time, however, care should be taken to keep the pace of reform within realistic bounds. The student leadership at Tiananmen, cheered on by Western pundits, lost sight of a crucial piece of local knowledge—the outer bound- aries of the possible.

The Tiananmen Papers reiterates what Mikhail Gorbachev publicly stated after his trip to Beijing just prior to the crackdown: that the buck stopped with Deng. It is clear, moreover, that the People's Liberation Army (PLA) was a sui generis operation answering to no civilian other than Deng.[10] In this respect *The Tiananmen Papers* offers more confirmation than revelation. Orville Schell and Lucian Pye agree that its goal is a resurgent reformism.[11] It could, however, obstruct that very purpose. By tightly focusing responsibility for the crackdown on Deng and his gang of elders, most of whom have passed away,[12] the virus of economic complacency could be passed to a new generation. A balance must be struck, therefore, between two forms of political inertia: that of "futilists" who think nothing will ever alter Chinese despotism and of globalists who think China's economic reform is "driving inexorably toward a fundamental transformation of Chinese politics."[13]

The latter fallacy—let us call it WTOism—follows from the assumption that all "rules of law" are equivalent. Thus the legal structure required by global trade relations is not just conducive to but identical with that required for democratization and human rights. Kanishka Jayasuriya, however, draws a vital distinction between liberal and statist legalisms.[14] The case of Singapore, whose judiciary is formally "autonomous" yet constrained by an executive, statist ideology,[15] removes all doubt that the legal needs of capitalism can be met by a highly illiberal "rule of law." If this fact obtains in little Singapore, it is all the more capable of holding its own in China.

That is not, however, to say that China *must* remain authoritarian. Tiananmen left the West to wonder how China's ill-fated liberalism erupted[16] and where it might lead. Some, such as Peter Lichtenstein, thought it would lead nowhere, that the Chinese democracy movement could not be resuscitated in the present generation.[17] The pall of indifference that fell over this question in both Chinas during the 1990s was not due simply to PRC censorship or ROC fears of disquiet on the mainland. This chapter, and this book as a whole, looks beneath such surface explanations to the cultural logic of repression and reform.

The cultural factor, which was sorely neglected during the Cold War, is crucial to any post–Cold War analysis of Asian politics. But, as Cumings stresses in *Parallax Visions*, this cultural sword must cut two ways. Too often Asia is examined through an unexamined cultural lens. One hopes that the cultural Left is simply unaware of (rather than indifferent to) how its "postmodern" fixations corrode transformational politics. This antipolitics, as Carl Boggs dubs it,[18] comes at the expense of any sustained attention to the material structures of oppression.

One such structure is the IMFism that was foisted on East and Southeast Asian nations in the wake of the Crash. Beneath its development and recovery schemes, IMFism is premised on the antipolitics of spontaneous order. Contradictorily, this neoliberal vision of a New World Order condoned the statist politics of Singapore-style Asian values. After the Crash, however, that fragile alliance dissolved, as a stronger version of IMFism demanded a far less regulated capitalism.

Once again, if only as a sales ploy, an attempt is being made to cast this Newer World Order in terms of Asian tradition. James Dorn of the right-wing

Cato Institute resurrects Reagan's brief flirtation with Taoism, mentioned above, as part of the reinvention of Lao-Tzu as a Chinese Adam Smith or Hayek. China's leaders are exhorted to rediscover "their own ancient culture" in the principle of political *wu wei* (nonaction) and the spontaneous order of market Taoism.[19]

The cultural Left, as Richard Rorty calls it,[20] is also implicated in the capitalist co-optation of Asian culture. While their general turn against Western values has helped to silence criticism of authoritarian Asian values, their vaunted cultural doubt, celebrated under such labels as multiculturalism and postcolonialism, turns its back on the patent occidentalism of Chinese reform, as epitomized by the Goddess of Democracy at Tiananmen. More traditional liberals wonder how far the multicultural embrace of anti-Western dissensus can be taken without betraying the communal ideals of a liberal public. The choice is between an older progressivism, which lacks a viable constituency—its last social base being the striking manufacturing wing of the AFL-CIO[21]—or the politics of corporate accommodation that holds sway in current neoliberalism under the "third way" label.

This was the root of President Clinton's equivocation concerning Chinese political dissent. After criticizing President Bush for coddling Beijing, Clinton promised that human rights would be a top priority in his administration's relations with China.[22] When he later signed an executive order extending China's most-favored-nation (MFN) trade status without restriction, it was contingent upon China's continuing progress on human rights; but the loose wording of those conditions, in combination with the administration's drift toward unconditional "engagement," let both China and Clinton off the hook.[23]

When Clinton chose Winston Lord (a former Kissinger aide and ambassador to China for President Bush) as his assistant secretary of state for East Asia and the Pacific, he was effectively offering Taiwan to China in return for human rights. It was well known that Lord had broken with Kissinger over human rights while endorsing his appeasement policy concerning Taiwan.[24] Those who would write the "other China" off as a nationalistic anachronism in a global age should, as Horng-luen Wang argues, take a closer look at the cultural thrust of globalization.[25] Nationalism no longer carries the moral stigma it once did. If it was the calling card of Serbia's Slobodan Milosevic, it is also the rallying cry of freedom and independence for Tibet and East Timor. Taiwan's opposition politics puts it on the progressive side of the neonationalist spectrum, while its geographic location and economic dynamism make it geopolitically indispensable in balance-of-power terms. This convergence of moral and power-political factors becomes a prime concern of moral realism, as developed in chapter 8.

Clinton's reversal on China not only betrayed his former friends in Taiwan (as governor of Arkansas he visited there several times) but also the democratic hopes of millions in the PRC. Chinese reformists still look to the West and particularly to America as a political beacon if not an actual model. It is paradoxical that such occidentalism would surface at a time when so many American academics seem to equate the word "Western" with "reactionary," unwittingly putting themselves on the side of real reactionaries and at odds with pro-Western reformists, many of whom remain in Chinese prisons.

The plight of these reformists is met with much the same indifference that the Old Left once bestowed on anti-Moscow dissent in Eastern Europe. It is only fair to note, however, that younger Chinese intellectuals have also turned a deaf ear to Tiananmen-style reformism. Politics and ideology are for them associated with statist oppression,[26] which in their view is best contested on a personal rather than social level. Activism has suffered a similar fate wherever global capitalism takes hold. In Thailand, for example, the pro-democracy demonstrations of 1973 seem like ancient history;[27] and the ruling People's Action Party (PAP) of Singapore is having trouble attracting capable young people into government service due to the very success of the party's efforts of years past.[28]

What Chinese reformism and the new Chinese personalism have in common is a generally pro-Western orientation. Where they differ is in their choice of Western values. The former stems from the May Fourth tradition, which combines progressivism with a strong dose of the same occidentalist infatuation that Bertrand Russell once disparaged.[29] In the mid-1980s that tradition was revived at the level of mass culture by Chinese television productions such as the twelve-part series, *New Star*.[30] The immediate cultural antecedent of Tiananmen, however, was the 1988 television series, *River Elegy*. Tellingly, the history department at Beijing University was given the unctuous task of refuting *Elegy* after Tiananmen.[31]

This was probably unnecessary. Chinese occidentalism would soon be absorbed into commercial fashion rather than political critique. Now, even as long sentences are meted out to China Democracy Party leaders, and even longer sentences to organizers of Falun Gong activities, mass culture marches to a different drummer—or rather two different drummers: the Western culture industry and the apolitical tradition of the Chinese merchant class.[32] The new "floating" class of migrant and marginal workers is certainly recalcitrant in the sense of its criminality: theft, prostitution, mendicancy, and so forth.[33] Foucaultian culturalists mimic Maxim Gorky by calling this "resistance," but that is to forget everything Solzhenitsyn taught us in *The Gulag Archipelago* about the chasm dividing criminality from real dissent.[34]

For all its radical posturing, the poststructural phase of Western cultural theory is at a loss when confronted with real reformism. Edward Gunn points out that the identification of *Elegy*'s authors "with modernity as a rational process and their assumption of an autonomous subject acting on the world as an object cannot be shared in part or in whole by scholars of . . . poststructuralist persuasion."[35] Nor can *Elegy*'s patent pro-Westernism be forgiven by cultural theorists who have escaped poststructural textuality only to be engulfed by "postcolonial" sentiments. The liberatory claims of Western cultural studies collide with Xiaomei Chen's observation that "ideas or ideological concepts, whether they stem from a politically dominant or subordinate culture, are never intrinsically oppressive or liberating."[36] Even as "postcolonial" culturalism shrouds itself in a rhetorical defense of "otherness," it universalizes its own political agenda while flatly equating liberalism (in general) with a largely undifferentiated colonial imperialism. Its silence about the ongoing imperialism of globalization borders on complicity.

Given the structural limits set by China's power elite,[37] a big part of Chinese counterdiscourse is understandably devoted to the search for intellectual space. That space, however, requires a material base. Dissidents are prone to link political freedoms with economic concerns such as freedom from inflation. To the limited extent that China's peasantry were even aware of the events at Tiananmen, democracy was less likely to attract their support than concrete material issues such as inflation, corruption, and nepotism.[38] The Tiananmen incident had been preceded by a period of 20 percent inflation. Inflationary pressures contributed, likewise, to the intransigence that Clinton's secretary of state Warren Christopher met in China with his ill-fated human rights diplomacy.[39]

That is not to suggest that diplomacy and other external pressures have no clout with China. The *New York Times* was far off the mark with its assertion that "China needs nothing from America and would never submit to pressure."[40] It is true that China's staunch resistance to human rights reform owes much to the vagaries of domestic politics; but at a time when China needs world trade more than ever, it cannot afford to take trade sanctions lightly. To the degree that Chinese entry into the WTO precludes those sanctions, it augurs hard times for Chinese reformism.

This is Clinton's legacy so far as China is concerned. His administration lost a precious opportunity to make an ethical mark on world affairs in the early days when Tiananmen was still fresh on the public's mind and corporate resistance was not yet fully mobilized. Fortune 500 companies, as James Mann observes, were "noticeable by their absence from this first round of the debate."[41] Now their presence is the paramount force behind America's China policy. For years this corporatism dressed itself in the strained argument that to withdraw MFN status would jeopardize China's reform process.[42]

Beneath such rhetoric, however, the winning argument has always been the cash nexus.

It is a little kept secret that corporate leaders, while pressing Clinton to reverse his China policy, aired their views directly with Chinese leaders. Thus China's economic czar, Zhu Rongji, was well briefed on how to deal with Clinton on MFN.[43] This paradoxical alliance between capitalist "roaders" and CCP hardliners was a main pillar of Deng Xiaiping's reform program, as propounded by younger neoauthoritarians such as Zhang Binjiu and Wu Jiaxiang. All along this strategy has subordinated politics to economic development.[44] As the late Gerald Segal noted, the very legitimacy of Deng's program was tied to its "ability to produce prosperity."[45] The same bottom line would of course apply to any opposing faction. Both liberalism and authoritarianism must ground their legitimacy on economic efficacy.

This explains the acute sensitivity of the Chinese government to any coupling of economic criticism with the broader reform issues of Tiananmen. In 1979 the dissident Wei Jingsheng was arrested and sentenced to fifteen years in solitary confinement for advocating democratic reform in combination with economic reform. Ten years later that combination was still perceived as the regime's worst nightmare. By tying economic relief to issues such as free speech, dissidents such as Wang Juntao and Chen Ziming, in the prelude to Tiananmen, threatened to forge a Polish-style solidarity of intellectuals and workers.[46] The result was unprecedented even by Polish standards: more than a million demonstrators took to the streets in Beijing, with millions more pouring out in towns and cities across the country.[47]

Incredibly, even after Tiananmen, the belief persists in the West that CCP leaders are not inherently averse to liberal democratic reforms. Though Deng's regime insisted it was creating a "socialist market economy," not a free-market economy,[48] Western experts dismissed this as face-saving rhetoric. They believed themselves to have discovered the lodestone of economic and political development (in that order): the democratic teleology that kicks in automatically wherever economic globalization reaches. The important thing is not to disturb its operation with activistic diversions such as the threat of economic sanctions or even sustained rhetorical pressures.

Typical, in this regard, is Suzanne Ogden's notion that the "more secure the Chinese Communist Party leaders feel, the more likely they are to tolerate a pluralistic political system. Economic success . . . will make the CCP leadership feel more secure."[49] The problem in June 1989 was that the regime was not yet "confident enough to consider a further opening up of the society and the political system."[50] Given time and economic success, she avers, the CCP will emulate the multiparty concessions of the Kuomintang in Taiwan.[51]

One is left to wonder how Ogden came to believe that the Kuomintang's concessions were the result of increasing confidence! She seems unaware of the ethnic insecurity of Taiwan's ruling Nationalist Party (KMT), or the long struggle of the Taiwanese opposition for the most rudimentary democratic rights. As the twenty-first century opens, the Democratic Progressive Party (DPP) has finally won a presidential election, the product not of KMT "confidence" but of three decades of political conflict. That struggle put President Chen Shui-bian's wife in a wheelchair for life. Many others were not so lucky. Meanwhile, as Susan Sontag notes, confidence buttresses repression in China: "Persecution is mounting as the Chinese government feels assured that so small an issue as freedom of expression cannot halt the inexorable embrace of China by global business interests."[52] Ogden's reform-through-confidence theory could pass for political humor if it were not taken seriously by so many in high places.

China's foremost dissident Fang Lizhi sees the CCP leadership as dedicated to a permanent separation of economic reform and liberal democracy.[53] Fang independently reached the conclusion of Dreze and Sen (*Hunger and Public Action* [1989]) that developmental priority should go to democratization—an argument that came to full maturity ten years later in Sen's *Development as Freedom*. None of this has a place in globalist development theory. The current "Washington consensus" rests its case for blanket economism on a synergic bond between economic and democratic development, in that order. This growth-first credo, the reverse of Sen's causal sequence, has become as central to post–Cold War foreign policy as the domino theory was to Cold War policy.

Meanwhile East Asia has become globalism's proving ground. Gordon White saw the democratic prospects of East Asia's "four tigers"—South Korea, Taiwan, Hong Kong, and Singapore—as problematic but promising. He expected the PRC to emulate the "Brezhnefication" or predemocratic authoritarianism that these four presumably pioneered.[54] Likewise Thomas Robinson, in crediting the economic success of these repressive systems, underscored the emergence of democracy in at least two of them: South Korea and Taiwan. In the long run, he concluded, political pluralism is tied to economic development through indirect channels such as urbanization, rising education levels, and burgeoning middle classes.[55] Like White he endorsed a gradualism that translates as a no-pressure China policy.

This model assumes that political postponement is just a temporary detour on the road to liberal democracy. The nature of that detour was starkly illustrated by Deng's decree that Chinese prisons must be, in keeping with the new economic liberalism, responsible for their own financial upkeep. No better example of reactionary globalization could be found. China's growing trade in prison exports was a direct result of this nominal "reform."[56] As

Kolakowski argued with regard to Leninist development strategies, there are certain means that in principle are incommensurate with humane ends.[57] It is time to recognize that the authoritarian "detour" is incommensurate with democratic ends. Moreover, there is no certainty that such a strategy would constitute a detour and not a destination.

That question haunted many members of Congress after the Clinton administration agreed in November 1999 to support China's entry into the WTO. Congress would have to ratify this decision indirectly by granting China's application for the permanent normal trading relations (PNTR) that passed the House in May 2000. Meanwhile presidential candidate Al Gore made his position clear by choosing William Daley (Clinton's lobbyist for NAFTA and PNTR) as his campaign manager.[58] Since George W. Bush also favored China's WTO entry, American voters were given little choice on the matter at the presidential level. The rights-first option, as propounded by Sen and Fang, was effectively banished from public consideration.

THE JAPANESE MODEL

The case of Japanese illiberalism may seem less sensational, but its implications for Asian development are far-reaching. The question is why this glaring fact was so long ignored. Now established scholars in the field stand accused of flaccid apologetics: research tainted by years of Japanese funding.[59] Whatever the reason, Western scholarship has been remarkably uncritical of the blatant defects of Japanese democracy. Standard lists of failed democracies in Asia conspicuously omitted Japan during the Cold War. If revisionists now put Japan higher on that list, it is because Japan lacks the usual developmental excuses. It has long since achieved the growth that growth-first strategies mandate as the prerequisite for unfettered democracy.

When it first appeared, Karel van Wolferen's salvo of the late 1980s (*The Enigma of Japanese Power: People and Politics in a Stateless Nation*) infuriated the Japanese with its picture of their government as a headless behemoth that functions in a distinctly illiberal manner. At about that time, however, the uncommonly forceful leadership of Nakasone Yasuhiro (the prime minister from 1982 to 1987, who is best remembered by Americans for his comment that blacks and Hispanics are wrecking American standards of education) was confronting the "headless" issue head-on. Nakasone succeeded in raising military spending, but failed in his larger objective of redefining the job of prime minister.[60] While he overestimated his own power, he clearly underestimated the scope of the larger problem, which was as cultural as it was political. In the recessionary years ahead it would become painfully obvious that Japan suffered from more than a lack of leadership. More fundamentally it suffered from a dearth of effective demand for change.

Foreign revisionists could no longer be accused of Japan-bashing after Ichiro Ozawa's *Blueprint for Building a New Japan* (1994) reproduced many of van Wolferen's charges. Nor could such criticism be written off as the residual effect of a "legitimacy deficit" stemming from Japan's military and colonial legacy.[61] Ozawa internalizes the debate, placing much of the blame for the nation's political stagnation on endemic disrespect for individual autonomy.[62] This lends support to Paul Kennedy's judgment that "it is in the quality of its political leadership that Japan suffers its greatest deficiency."[63] The "1955 system" ensured that becoming the LDP president was tantamount to becoming prime minister; and winning at the LDP level was an exclusively "back room" affair.[64]

Outsiders found it difficult to imagine such bogus politics within a first-rate economic colossus. The economic "miracle" of Japan was taken as prima facie evidence of a sound democratic order; but it was precisely that economic success that legitimized the LDP political monopoly. Though the economic malaise of the 1990s pushed many Japanese intellectuals in Ozawa's direction, a chorus of domestic critics still condemns Ozawa's brand of individualism for eroding the Japanese ideal of *wa* (harmony) and encouraging mutiny inside the 1955 system.

The prospect of real political options is rooted in a political tradition reaching back to 1890, the time of the country's first bicameral legislature. Between 1890 and 1924, Japan's electorate grew sevenfold,[65] inaugurating a period of relative pluralism that the Japanese refer to as their era of "normal constitutional government" or "Taisho democracy."[66] Under Shigeru Yoshida (prime minister from 1946 to 1954), by contrast, the foundation was laid for thirty-eight years of ultraconservative LDP domination. In Ian Buruma's words, "the Yoshida deal turned liberal democracy into a polite ritual of so-called consensus politics, with bureaucrats dictating the terms."[67] This glacial system—condoned (at the very least) by Japan's postwar overlord, the United States—became the unfortunate prototype for "democratic" development throughout Asia.

The Japanese themselves seem to have been remarkably content with this bureaucratic consensualism. Whatever frustrations they felt were usually vented outside politics. When economic recession finally brought down the 1955 system, in July 1993, no viable alternative was found. The nascent reform governments of Morihiro Hosokawa and Tsutomu Hata were soon toppled, leading one observer to wonder if the reform impulse might be a Japanese rock of Sisyphus.[68] Those two reform administrations had lasted only eight months and two months, respectively. Three prime ministers had been jettisoned in less than a year.

The irony was compounded in June 1994 when the obscure socialist Tomiichi Murayama was thrust into the prime ministership, obviously with the blessings of the discredited LDP. Was it really a surprise that he would renounce old socialist policies on defense, foreign relations, the emperor, nuclear power, and so forth?[69] As Edward Desmond observes, Murayama had been "less than enthusiastic" about past struggles for reform.[70] That, from an LDP vantage, was certainly one of his major qualifications for the office, another one being his certain opposition to any efforts on the part of Washington to put Japan at odds with North Korea.

Ozawa complains that Japanese intellectuals have been largely indifferent to the rights of free expression that form the bedrock of liberal democracy in the West. This was never more obvious than when the mayor of Nagasaki, Motoshima Hitoshi, was fatally shot in January 1990. He had audaciously expressed his opinion that the bombing of Hiroshima and Nagasaki, along with the ruinous battle of Okinawa, could have been prevented by imperial intervention. When the Right tried to silence the mayor, few prominent intellectuals supported his right of free speech. Some even charged him with failing to respect the fundamental difference between Western and Japanese values.[71]

That difference is implicit in the cultural continuity that Chalmers Johnson locates in Japanese meritocracy, where dysfunctional traditions such as *Kanryodo* (the "way of the bureaucrat") and *bushido* (the samurai "way of the warrior") are merged. Still, Johnson considers the main force behind Japan's *wa* to be a combination of "situational imperatives," such as population density, a shortage of natural resources, and balance of payments constraints. It was these material factors, he contends, that depluralized Japanese politics in the 1950s and 1960s. This set the stage for "Japan, Inc.," the megainstitution behind Johnson's idea of a developmental state as opposed to a regulatory state such as the United States.[72]

Most interpreters have given more weight than Johnson does to the cultural factor in Japanese political and industrial organization.[73] For that very reason, Johnson's interpretation is more transferable and in that respect more "modernist." Ominously, Johnson endorses the postponement of political development in favor of economic maximization. Not only does he admire the development program orchestrated by the Ministry of International Trade and Industry (MITI), but shows a shockingly high regard for its origins in Japan's prewar and wartime operations: "the experience of the 1930's and 1940's was not by any means totally negative for postwar Japan."[74]

In sum, Johnson accepts the curtailment of Japanese democratic reform as a fair price for progress. This liberal hiatus, a core element of Japanese modernization, attracted many Western admirers until the mid-1990s, when the recession killed its allure. One of its last true believers was David Williams (*Japan: Beyond the End of History* [1994]), who saw in Japan the prototype not only for Asian modernization but also for Western regeneration. Now the question is whether Japanese *post*modernism, as treated in the next chapter, will prove as reactionary as has Japanese modernism.

THE KOREAN ALTERNATIVE

In *MITI and the Japanese Miracle,* Johnson offers an apology for what amounts to reactionary modernization. It follows that he prefers the orderliness of Japanese development over Korea's more fractious approach. Granted, he later softened his judgment on Korea, while toughening his stance on Japan.[75] But the damage was done. His indelible classic would be *MITI*, which lumps Korea in with such bungling "bureaucratic-authoritarian" regimes of the same period as Argentina, Brazil, Chile, and Uruguay.[76] Regretfully this bias has saturated Korean studies, thanks in large part to the classic text on Korean modernization, Norman Jacobs's *The Korean Road to Modernization and Development* (1985). Though Jacobs does not cite *MITI*, he duplicates its treatment of Korea as a model of how *not* to modernize.

Just two years after *Korean Road* came out, the power structure it treated as *the* Korean way was fighting for its life in one of the most dramatic democratic elections of modern history. Although the two opposition parties lost that election, due to their refusal to forge a united front, their combined support amounted to a clear majority. Thus the democratic legitimacy of oppositional politics was the real winner. At that moment, as I argue in chapters 4 and 5, Korea bypassed Japan as the exemplar of Asian values.

It was then, too, that Korean politics can be said to have taken a postmodern turn. Whereas "modernism" denotes transferable modes of development, eventually replacing Japanese exceptionalism with a Japanese *model*, "postmodernism" turns its attention from the general to the particular, from the exogenous to the endogenous, and in this case from the Japanese to the Korean. This view of Korean postmodernization, as taken up in chapter 4, focuses on the populist roots of Korea's opposition politics. A sweeping application of foreign models would uproot these traditions, closing off the distinctly Korean road to democratization.

This is not, however, an argument for developmental autonomy. While imported standards such as "Japanism" or "Americanism" are inappropriate, neither can a developing nation afford the hermeticism of precolonial Korea or contemporary North Korea. A "postmodern" Korea must neither retreat from the world, as did Kim Il Sung, nor uncritically adopt a foreign model of development, as did Park Chung Hee with his fascistic appropriation of an earlier, unreformed Japanese model or Kim Dae Jung with his recent "IMF-ism." What is needed, rather, is a dialogic accord between cultural preservation and openness.

This is the balance that Kim Dae Jung struck in his oppositional years.[77] Even as he screened Western ideas for elements that might be appropriate for Korea, he marshaled an appreciation for what, in a postmodern lexicon, would be termed a "local," "marginal," or "decentered" political agenda. There is no question that the "vortex" of Korean authority, as Gregory Henderson famously terms it,[78] has been the dominant factor in Korean politics for centuries; but the very redundance of Korea's "centered" authority connotes a formidable opposition waiting in the wings. Korean postmodernism, like certain strains of reform Islam in Indonesia,[79] retrieves and foregrounds that marginal undercurrent. Such resistance can surface in surprising places, such as the 1994 protests of Buddhist monks at Seoul's Chogye Temple. This contest precipitated the removal of the Buddhist magnate Suh Eui Hyun and the power elite that had long guarded his hegemony over an order controlling 80 percent of Korea's Buddhists.[80]

The lesson of Korean postmodernism, far from any poststructural/postcolonial apotheosis of the local,[81] is that the ruling "vortex" can be countered by a culturally rooted opposition, so long as it is strategically coordinated. Gradually this countervailing power emerged in the 1970s and 1980s. What hampered the movement was its failure to get beyond regionalism, as in the presidential race of 1987. At that critical moment the local constituencies of the "two Kims" (Kim Dae Jung and Kim Young Sam) pressed their candidates into a no-compromise battle that split the opposition, allowing General Roh Tae Woo to keep the ruling Democratic Justice Party in the Blue House for another seven years.

One must conclude, against those who would all but equate the regional and the progressive in Korean politics,[82] that the opposition had to reach a national and class-based critical mass before it could hope to prevail. To win their respective presidential campaigns in the 1990s, both Kims had to transcend the politics of their regional bases by focusing on common national issues such as corruption and oppression. Nonetheless their success in office, by any postmodern standard, must be measured in large part by their fidelity to the values of their origins. By the standards both helped to install, both failed.

The center still holds in Korean national politics, but unlike the top-down "vortex" outlined by Henderson, this center can be held accountable. That fact was dramatically confirmed when two former Korean presidents became not corpses, like Park, but defendants 1042 and 3124 in an insurrection trial that served warning on Korea's military-political establishment.[83] Still more astonishingly, the son of a sitting president was hauled in on corruption charges.

In its own way, Korea was taking its first feeble steps toward an activist postmodernism, as opposed to Japan's retreatist variety, as discussed in the next chapter. It is too early to say what form a postmodern politics may take in Asia as a whole or Korea in particular. The immediate question is whether Korea will be able to continue its democratic transformation, bringing its political (postmodern) development up to the level of its economic (modern) development. Will it throw off the political incubus of crony capitalism at the national level only to surrender itself to crony globalism?

CONCLUSION

The postmodern dynamic that put two opposition leaders into the Korean Blue House has been an active force in many parts of the Pacific Rim, most notably East Timor and Taiwan. What renders these cases "postmodern" is their move beyond modernist economism, whereby politics is so depluralized as to render democratic processes ornamental. For Jayasuriya this "anti-political politics" is the defining feature of Singaporean Asian values, where citizenship and civil society are collapsed into the goals of the state, and opposition of any kind is seen by definition as subversive of political order and stability.[84]

My appropriation of the term "postmodern" to describe this trend requires some explanation, since this word carries associations I lament. As a postmodern realist, I confess to being a theoretical amphibian, inhabiting two worlds that tend to look on each other with suspicion or outright hostility. On my postmodern side I agree with David Campbell that it is time to write the cultural "other" back into geopolitics, and to contest the universalism that hammers difference into tendentious identity structures. To that extent I share Campbell's skepticism toward the "adequacy to reality" of traditional IR. On my realist side, however, I must reject Campbell's repudiation of the search for "a better fit between thought and the world, language and matter, proposition and fact."[85] It is only by way of that "better fit" that the concrete Other can be retrieved in any meaningful sense. To empty the Other of referential substance in the poststructural manner is not to respect it, but to negate it.

There is much that I find useful and compelling in the broader postmodern critique of power/knowledge impositions. I share the revulsion of Gearóid Ó

Tuathail toward a modernism that codifies and reduces the entire geocultural world to efficient Western categories.[86] That project culminated in the New World Order of corporate sovereignty and unrestricted capital flows. Asian values could be tolerated by that Order so long as they served the interests of corporate globalization. After the Asian Crash, however, tension arose within the Order between Asian values and Western neoliberalism.

Meanwhile, outside the Order, resistance has mounted to both of those ideologies. The West's anti-globalist Other is beginning to discover points of commonality with Asian and/or "Southern" Others, such as the Islamic reformism that took shape in Indonesia in the late 1980s and the 1990s in opposition to Suharto's version of Asian values.[87] Just as power politics is no longer confined to the discrete interests of individual states, so too resistance is no longer confined to the boundaries of domestic opposition.

This syncretist revolt of the margins is no less postmodern than the fractured and ultimately futile resistance that Foucaultian theory endorses. Foucault's cultural agonistics fails to explain the paradoxical global reach of today's anti-globalism. Drawing on Bakhtin, I seek that explanation in a cultural dialogics that contests the naively anti-Western premises of poststructural culturalism. The latter equates order (including any politically effective representation) with repression, and disorder with liberation. That ludic recourse rests on the comforting belief that order, including world order, is in fact unassailable. The game of postmodern "radicalism" can thus be played without danger, and also of course without political impact, except in terms of omission.

This is part of the political entropy that Carl Boggs regards as the leitmotif of postmodernism.[88] Such programmatic impotence in the face of post–Cold War exigencies seemed only natural in the early 1990s, at the high tide of TINAism (the Thatcher-inspired idea that "There Is No Alternative" to global capitalism). Now, however, more strident radicalisms are challenging the view that the New World Order is here to stay. Minus that assumption, the Left credentials of postmodern antipolitics are put in serious doubt. Its whole thrust is exposed as a methodological misfit: a poststructural refusal to recognize, much less contest, the structural reach of today's globalization.

To be sure, the premises of TINAism have been attacked from the Right as well as the Left (e.g., by Huntington's thesis of civilizational clash and Kaplan's thesis of a coming global anarchy). The emerging New World *Dis*order has done much to discredit the notion, rife within cultural and postcolonial studies, that disorder is the best thing to come along since the pill. The postmodern label has also been pinned on the cognate notion that all things Western, being logocentric, are shallow and repressive. What the first post–Cold War decade reveals is that these seemingly antithetical celebrations—

the globalist dream of redemptive world order and the postmodern/ postcolonial vision of redemptive disorder—are sibling rivals. Arif Dirlik notes how postcolonial discourse celebrates a "subaltern" erasure of difference between such incommensurate forms of resistance as criminality and political activism. Even Michael Dutton, who in Dirlik's view is the best poststructural analyst of contemporary Chinese control and resistance, manages to ignore "the democracy movement activists who daily risk their lives . . . or the peasants of Hunan who storm government offices against unfair taxes."[89] Most of today's culturalists likewise manage to evade real politics.[90]

That evasion is abetted by a blanket condemnation of Western metanarratives of resistance. Throughout East and Southeast Asia, postcolonial anti-Westernism (which is itself a distinctly Western product) finds its best ally in the reactionary modernization that Jayasuriya locates in the region's power elites.[91] Now and then these rearguard modernists drop their soft authoritarian pose. Singapore's Lee Kuan Yew, for example, openly defended the actions of China's military against the hapless protesters at Tiananmen.[92]

Another Singaporean, Bilahari Kausikan, accuses human rights advocates of imposing a Western ethos of individualism on the East. In his view the West is "individualistic" or "adversarial," while the East is "communitarian" or "consensus seeking." He sees humanitarianism as masking the material interests of flagging Western economies. Human rights are thus construed as an instrument of economic competition and a tool for remaking the world in the image of the West. Even Kausikan, however, cannot deny that the case for Asian values ultimately rests on a continued economic "miracle."[93] That condition came crashing down in 1997.

Aryeh Neier considers that both East and West have their share of individualistic and communitarian values.[94] This duality, and the politics it stimulates, is not only missed by Singapore school Asianists but by Western academics under the sway of postcolonial discourse. Despite their endless encomiums to "difference" and the special rapport they claim to have with foreign channels of dissent, multicultural and postcolonial critics are at best indifferent to the structural oppression that crushes real difference and activates real resistance. As Dirlik argues, most of what passes for postcolonial discourse amounts to an untimely diversion from real problems of social, cultural, and political domination.[95]

Globalists, meanwhile, regard resistance of any kind as an obstruction to progress. Despite rising post–Cold War dangers,[96] these latter-day modernists imagine the world moving in their direction:[97] toward one big WTO-directed market. Not only has this fostered enormous complacence in the general public, but an equal laxity in liberal standards of judgment among the burgeoning corps of unofficial diplomats who heavily influence Asian-Pacific relations.[98]

Washington's "K-Street" lobbyists, for example, have had astounding success in interweaving their own corporate interests with China's call for trade unrestricted by human rights criteria.[99] In a convoluted sense, this cause can even be defined as "democratic," for just five years after Tiananmen it was obvious that a new generation of educated Chinese were mainly interested in making money, not staging political protests.[100] The new political priorities were suggested in a report of Nanjing youths carrying banners reading "We want democracy, we want freedom . . . , we want Marlboro Long Kent."[101]

Elsewhere a more substantive reformism is taking shape. Paul Kennedy points out that Korea, like Singapore, has assigned its government an active role in preparing its citizens for the future. Both nations prefer this approach to America's laissez-faire inertia;[102] but that is where the similarity ends. Korean oppositional culture has increasingly incorporated populist initiatives into its reform model. It was after the fall of president and would-be dictator Chun Doo Hwan that this grassroots reformism took hold, nipping constantly at the heels of Roh Tae Woo's administration. Presidents Kim Young Sam and Kim Dae Jung have been credited with forging a political reformation. For the most part they were simply riding a populist wave. Korean oppositionalism has been a genuine grassroots phenomenon, close in spirit to Rosa Luxemberg's concept of spontaneous resistance, or the early republican phase of the Spanish Civil War, before its ideological betrayal.[103] The pan-Asian relevance of Korea's bottom-up reformism is suggested by a recent survey of the idea of freedom in East and Southeast Asia (David Kelly and Anthony Reid, eds., *Asian Freedoms: The Idea of Freedom in East and Southeast Asia* [1998]). All contributors to this anthology hold that the presumably Western idea of freedom is in fact common to the whole Pacific Rim, though the form it takes varies widely.[104]

This shatters both versions of the "Asian values" myth: that of Singaporean (soft) and PRC (hard) authoritarianism. Neither represents more than a small sampling of the region's endemic values. Sen suggests that a nonelitist Asianism could herald a more democratic and ecologically sustainable development model. The statism we associate with top-down Asianism has little place in most Asian traditions. Robert Nisbet points out that in

> the traditional Asiatic state prior to the present era, the state's authority rarely if ever touched the individual directly. Between state and individual lay broad strata of authority—family, clan, village, guild, sometimes caste—which were not often penetrated by the power of the king or emperor. Although bureaucracy was very much a reality in the Asiatic state, it did not often seek to supplant but rather to work with and through the deeply rooted social structures.[105]

Anderson adds that the cartographic and juridical sovereignty we associate with the "state" did not even exist in Southeast Asia prior to its colonial advent. Nor did "politics" exist, for active political life requires a social and political cohesion that was wholly lacking.[106]

Paradoxically, when modern statism finally arrived, largely as a Western import, it came with *too much* unity: without the benefit of countervailing Western values and institutions. It was not attended by the concept of an individual's inalienable rights or an effective balance of state powers. While the average East Asian confronts the state more directly than is common in the West, and with far more trepidation, this has less to do with Asian traditions than with a very partial and incomplete process of Westernization. Political "modernization" in Asia has almost always taken the form of a top-down imposition of power, creating a vast chasm between the largely imported or contrived values of a power elite and those of a still rooted social order. This is the gap that Lucian Pye, writing in the fall of 1990, saw as the defining feature of Chinese politics in the aftermath of Tiananmen.[107] It follows that a big step toward democratization and political postmodernization would be a selective retrieval of indigenous patterns of authority. It also follows that real Asian values cannot be held responsible for "crony capitalism" or the Crash of 1997, for these values have never been broadly tested on the modern stage.

Reform in general, not just democratic reform, rests on bottom-up foundations. Gray argues that China's economic reforms, which began in the agrarian sector, have been more effective than Russia's precisely because China's attempt to uproot rural traditions was less successful than Soviet efforts.[108] Insofar as stable political development requires a communal base, a relatively premodern society like China's could provide the bedrock for democratization that Russia lacks.

Unfortunately, the present Chinese regime is doing a fine job of wrecking that foundation. This passes almost unnoticed by media commentators who, ignoring the cogent arguments of "fifth modernization" advocates such as Wei Jingsheng,[109] think the only prerequisite for a successful democratic transition is affluence. They assume that liberal economics leads inevitably to liberal politics, and that the only road to democratization is a Western road. In fact, the growing communitarian branch of Western democratic theory could learn a great deal from Asian traditions, just as Asian reformers could still learn much from the West. It is time for both to face the fact that globalization is coming to the Rim, like it or not, and that a good deal of East/West convergence is bound to follow. It is just a question of what kind of convergence it will be: top-down or bottom-up, proto-fascist or proto-democratic.

So far it would be difficult to answer that question optimistically. Idealists have long dreamed of a democratically ordered world government. But, as Kaplan points out, the world order that has emerged under the rubric of globalization amounts to a "dense ganglia of international corporations and markets that are becoming the unseen arbiters" of a very top-down pattern of global power.[110]

This is bad news for the most notable noncorporate global institution, the United Nations, which has been reduced to a kind of border patrol to keep undesirable elements in line. The organization now deals mainly with the poorest countries,[111] and even that role hangs under a cloud of doubt after the setbacks of the 1990s. William Shawcross describes the days of the great white hope, when Cambodia came under occupation by UNTAC (the UN Transitional Authority in Cambodia) late in 1992. UNTAC consisted of

> about twenty thousand men and women in white cars, white trucks, white airplanes and white helicopters. . . . They were supposed to be giving Cambodia something it never had—democracy—along with something it had not known for twenty-two years—peace. The stakes were high. For Cambodia itself, the UN plan represented the last and best hope to escape the maze. For the UN, the plan was a test case of whether the international organization could adapt to the new realities of the postwar world.[112]

UNTAC was a $2 billion fiasco, taking its place beside the United Nation's similar failures in Bosnia and Somalia, which sped the organization "on its way to becoming a supranational relief agency." Real global power, Kaplan stresses, devolves upon the corporate vanguard that has overtaken the nation-state as the prime mover behind a Darwinian world (dis)order, free of social and environmental constraints. The statistics speak for themselves:

> Of the world's hundred largest economies, fifty-one are not countries but corporations. While the two hundred largest corporations employ less than three-fourths of 1 percent of the world's work force, they account for 28 percent of world economic activity. The five hundred largest corporations account for 70 percent of world trade.[113]

Brian Urquhart notes the irony of today's endless talk about globalization in the face of the virtual collapse of yesterday's dreams of constitutional and enforceable internationalism.[114] Ever the optimist, Kofi Annan pins his millennial vision on the declining leadership function of the nation-state. He would have the United Nations tie its future to the Internet, NGOs and, far more dangerously, in my view, the private sector in general,[115] with the flow of information technology directed against poverty and disease. This "wiring" of poor nations, and the less privileged sectors of affluent ones, could profoundly affect the dynamics of cultural politics. The opportunity it provides for bottom-up counterdiscourse is especially promising in East Asia, given the region's high literacy rates and its relatively wide distribution of educational resources.[116]

Once again Asia is becoming the consummate IR testing ground—this time for the renamed realist/idealist debate between conflict theorists and cooperation theorists. The latter have chosen Europe as their ideal laboratory for cooperation, but that is stacking the deck. Only a non-Western venue can really put humanitarian and democratic values, freighted as they are with Western associations, to the test. This time both bottom-up and top-down authority structures are on trial. If democratic values cannot take root in East Asia, they are unlikely to thrive in any non-Western culture zone.

The question of Asian values, then, is ipso facto a question about global values. That question is problematized, however, by the strikingly diverse patterns of Asian political culture. Consider, for example, the case of Japanese developmentalism, as treated in the next two chapters. Chapter 2 deals with the politics of the Japanese postmodern turn, which in oppositional terms is almost the antithesis of the Korean turn.

NOTES

1. Benedict Anderson, *The Spectre of Comparisons: Nationalism, Southeast Asia, and the World* (London: Verso, 1998), 302.

2. Walden Bello, with Shea Cunningham and Bill Rau, *Dark Victory: The United States and Global Poverty* (new ed.) (London: Pluto Press, 1994), 125, 110.

3. Bello, *Dark Victory*, 110.

4. Bruce Cumings, *Parallax Visions: Making Sense of American-East Asian Relations at the End of the Century* (Durham, N.C.: Duke University Press, 1999), 159; my emphasis.

5. John Clark, "Going With the (Cash) Flow: Taoism and the New Managerial Wisdom," (April 12, 2000), <www. britannica.com/original?article_id = 5406>.

6. These papers were compiled by an alleged CCP insider writing under the pseudonym Zhang Liang, and edited by Andrew Nathan and Perry Link, with assistance on the question of authenticity from Orville Schell. Jiang Zemin was sufficiently disturbed by this book that he staged a special party conference where everyone was made to stand up and swear allegiance to the current regime (see Jasper Becker, "Comrade Jiang Zemin Does Indeed Seem a Proper Choice," *London Review of Books* 23, no. 10 (May 24, 2001), <www.lrb.co.uk/v23/n10/beck2310.htm>.

7. Erik Eckholm, "China Says Protest Papers Are Distorted," *New York Times* International (January 9, 2001), <www.nytimes.com/ 2001/01/09/world/09CHIN.html>.

8. Lucian Pye, "Appealing the Tiananmen Verdict: New Documents from China's Highest Leaders," *Foreign Affairs* (March–April 2001): 148–154, 153.

9. Pye, "Appealing," 149.

10. Andrew J. Nathan and Robert S. Ross, *The Great Wall and the Empty Fortress: China's Search for Security* (New York: W. W. Norton, 1997), 141.

11. Daryl Lindsey, "Vetting the 'Tiananmen Papers'," (February 2, 2001), <www. salon.com/news/feature/2001/02/02/schell/index.html>.

12. Daryl Lindsey, "A Crack in the Wall" (February 2, 2001), <www.salon.com/news/feature/2001/02/02/papers/>.

13. George Gilroy and Eric Heginbotham, "China's Coming Transformation," (500-word preview), *Foreign Affairs* 80, no. 4 (July–August 2001): 26–39, <www.foreignaffairs.org/Search/ document.asp?I = 20010701FAEssay4942.xml>.

14. Kanishka Jayasuriya, "Corporatism and Judicial Independence Within Statist Legal Institutions in East Asia," in Kanishka Jayasuriya, ed., *Law, Capitalism, and Power in Asia* (London: Routledge, 1999), 173–204, 173.

15. Jayasuriya, "Corporatism," 186.

16. On that mystery see Becker, "Comrade Jiang Zemin."

17. Peter M. Lichtenstein, *China at the Brink: The Political Economy of Reform and Retrenchment in the Post-Mao Era* (New York: Praeger, 1991), 146.

18. Carl Boggs, *The End of Politics: Corporate Power and the Decline of the Public Sphere* (New York: Guilford Press, 2000), 230.

19. James A. Dorn, "China's Future: Market Socialism or Market Taoism?" *Cato Journal* 18, no. 1 (Spring–Summer 1998): 131–146, 135.

20. Richard Rorty, *Achieving Our Country: Leftist Thought in Twentieth-Century America* (Cambridge, Mass.: Harvard University Press, 1998), 77.

21. John B. Judis, "Disunion: Gore's Labor Pains," *New Republic* (August 21, 2000), <www.tnr.com/082100/judis082100.html>.

22. James Mann, *About Face: A History of America's Curious Relationship with China, from Nixon to Clinton* (New York: Alfred A. Knopf, 1999), 274.

23. Robert L. Bernstein and Richard Dicker, "Human Rights First," *Foreign Policy*, no. 94 (Spring 1994): 43–47, 43.

24. Mann, *About Face*, 278.

25. Horng-luen Wang, "In Want of a Nation: State, Institutions and Globalization in Taiwan" dissertation, University of Chicago, 1999, 279–280. Wallerstein challenged Wang on this point in the first session of a conference held at Academia Sinica's Institute of Ethnology, Taipei, October 6–7, 2001.

26. Chicago Cultural Studies Group, "Critical Multiculturalism," *Critical Inquiry* 18, no. 3 (Spring 1992): 530–555, 533.

27. Robert Kaplan, *The Ends of the Earth: A Journey into the Frontiers of Anarchy* (New York: Vintage Books, 1996), 375.

28. Trish Saywell, "Singapore: The Young and the Restless," *Far Eastern Economic Review* (December 21, 2000), <www.feer.com/_0012_21/ p024region.html>.

29. Russell cited in Tse-tsung Chow, *The May 4th Movement: Intellectual Revolution in Modern China* (Cambridge, Mass.: Harvard University Press, 1960), 312.

30. James Lull, *China Turned On: Television, Reform, and Resistance* (London: Routledge, 1991), 92.

31. Ruth Hayhoe, "Political Texts in Chinese Universities Before and After Tiananmen," *Pacific Affairs* 66, no. 1 (Spring 1993): 21–43, 37.

32. On the latter see Lucian Pye, "Chinese Democracy and Constitutional Development," in Fumio Itoh, ed., *China in the Twenty-First Century: Politics, Economy and Society* (Tokyo: United Nations University Press, 1997), 205–218, 210.

33. Arif Dirlik, "Reflections on Postmodernity: Streetlife China," *Social Justice* 26, no. 1, issue 75 (Spring 1999): 233–236, 233–234.

34. Aleksandr I. Solzhenitsyn, *The Gulag Archipelago* II, trans. by Thomas P. Whitney (New York: Harper and Row, 1975), 92–93.

35. Edward Gunn, "The Rhetoric of River Elegy: From Cultural Criticism to Social Act," in Roger V. Forges, Luo Ning, and Wu Yen-bo, eds., *Chinese Democracy and the Crisis of 1989: Chinese and American Reflections* (Albany: State University of New York Press, 1993), 247–261, 258.

36. Xiaomei Chen, "Occidentalism as Counterdiscourse: 'He Shang' in Post-Mao China," *Critical Inquiry* 18, no. 4 (Summer 1992): 686–712, 693.

37. Bruce J. Dickson, "What Explains Chinese Political Behavior?" *Comparative Politics* 25, no. 1 (October 1992): 103–118, 104.

38. Bilahari Kausikan, "Asia's Different Standard," *Foreign Policy*, no. 92 (Fall 1993): 24–41, 37.

39. Perry Link, "The Old Man's New China," *New York Review of Books* 41, no. 11 (June 9, 1994): 31–36, 34.

40. "Bottom Line for U.S. and China: No Kowtows on Human Rights," *New York Times* (March 27, 1994), E5.

41. Mann, *About Face*, 232.

42. For example, Bryce Harland, "For a Strong China," *Foreign Policy*, no. 94 (Spring 1994): 48–52, 52.

43. Link, "The Old Man's New China," 34.

44. Yongnian Zheng, "Nationalism, Neo-Authoritarianism, and Political Liberalism: Are They Shaping Political Agendas in China?" *Asian Affairs: An American Review* 19, no. 4 (Winter 1993): 207–227, 207.

45. Gerald Segal, "China's Changing Shape," *Foreign Affairs* 73, no. 3 (May–June 1994): 43–58, 44.

46. Merle Goldman, "Brutality in China," *New York Review of Books* 38, no. 3 (January 31, 1991): 40.

47. Becker, "Comrade Jiang Zemin."

48. Richard Hornik, "Bursting China's Bubble," *Foreign Affairs* 73, no. 3 (May–June 1994): 28–42, 40.

49. Suzanne Ogden, "The Chinese Communist Party: Key to Pluralism and a Market Economy?" *SAIS Review* 13, no. 2 (Summer–Fall 1993): 107–125, 109.

50. Ogden, "The Chinese Communist Party," 109.

51. Ogden, "The Chinese Communist Party," 109.

52. Susan Sontag, "The Crime of Carrying Ideas to China," *New York Times* Op-Ed (August 19, 2000), <www.nytimes.com/yr/mo/day/ oped/19sont.html>.

53. Lizhi Fang, "A Distant View of Tiananmen," interview with Heidi Schulman, *Newsweek* Asian edition (July 18, 1944): 48.

54. Gordan White, *Riding the Tiger: The Politics of Economic Reform in Post-Mao China* (Stanford, Calif.: Stanford University Press, 1993), 249.

55. Thomas W. Robinson, "Democracy and Development in East Asia—Toward the Year 2000," in Thomas W. Robinson, ed., *Democracy and Development in East Asia: Taiwan, South Korea, and the Philippines* (Washington, D.C.: AEI Press, 1991), 279–291, 279, 282.

56. Charles Lane, with Dorinda Elliot et al., "The Last Gulag," *Newsweek* Asian edition (September 23, 1991): 10–12, 11.

57. Iring Fetscher, "Ethics," in Tom Bottomore, ed., *A Dictionary of Marxist Thought* (Cambridge, Mass.: Harvard University Press, 1983), 152–154, 154.

58. Judis, "Disunion."

59. Michael Green, "Who Lost Japanese Studies?" *SAIS Review* 13, no. 21 (Summer–Fall 1993): 87–93, 87–88.

60. James Fallows, "The Real Japan," *New York Review of Books* 31, no. 12 (July 20, 1989): 23–28, 23.

61. Hideo Sato, "Japan's Role in the Post–Cold War World," *Current History* 90, no. 555 (April 1991): 145–81, 146.

62. See his Liberal Party (of Ochiro Ozawa), "A Blueprint for the Renewal of Japan," (May 2, 2001), <www.jiyuto.or.jp/policy_e/gaiyo_e.htm>.

63. Paul Kennedy, *Preparing for the Twenty-First Century* (Toronto: Harper Perennial, 1993), 161.

64. Howard W. French, "Awaiting a Transition, Japan Pushes for Openness," *New York Times* World (March 18, 2001), <www.nytimes.com/2001/03/18/world/JAPA.html>.

65. Ardath W. Burks, *Japan: Profile of a Postindustrial Power* (Boulder, Colo.: Westview Press, 1981), 104.

66. Murray Sayle, "The Party's (Almost) Over," *Far Eastern Economic Review* (August 10, 1989): 19–22, 19.

67. Ian Buruma, "Japan Against Itself," *New York Review of Books* 41, no. 9 (May 12, 1994): 18–22, 19.

68. Frank McNeil, "Rock of Sisyphus or Road to Reform?" *Journal of Democracy* 5, no. 3 (July 1994): 101–106, 102.

69. Charles Smith, "Right Turn," *Far Eastern Economic Review* 157, no. 37 (September 15, 1994): 20; and "Power's Positive Influence," *Far Eastern Economic Review* 157, no. 36 (September 8, 1994): 39.

70. Edward W. Desmond, "The Shock of the Old," *Time* Asian edition (July 11, 1994): 16–17, 16.

71. Ian Buruma, "Against the Japanese Grain," *New York Review of Books* 28, no. 20 (December 9, 1991): 32–36, 32.

72. Chalmers Johnson, *MITI and the Japanese Miracle: The Growth of Industrial Policy, 1925–1975* (Stanford, Calif.: Stanford University Press, 1982), 39–40, 307, 305–306.

73. For example, Naoto Sasaki, *Management and Industrial Structure in Japan* (New York: Pergamon, 1981), 2.

74. Johnson, *MITI*, 308.

75. John Chung Hwan Oh, "The Future of Democracy and Economic Growth in Korea," *Korea Observer* 25, no. 1 (Spring 1994): 47–63, 59; and Chalmers Johnson's much revised position was elaborated in "Democratic Theory and South Korea: Does Economic Development Contribute Toward the Democratization Process?" a paper given at the annual meeting of the Association for Asian Studies, Washington, D.C., March 17–19, 1994.

76. Johnson, *MITI*, 316–317.

77. See for instance Kim's *Mass-Participatory Economy: A Democratic Alternative for Korea* (2nd ed.) (Lanham, Md.: University Press of America, 1996).

78. Gregory Henderson, *Korea: The Politics of the Vortex* (Cambridge, Mass.: Harvard University Press, 1968).

79. Robert W Hefner, *Civil Islam: Muslims and Democratization in Indonesia* (Princeton, N.J.: Princeton University Press, 2000).

80. Jason Booth, "Bad Karma," *Far Eastern Economic Review* 157, no. 17 (April 28, 1994): 22.

81. See Dirlik's critique of both "posts" in *The Postcolonial Aura: Third World Criticism in the Age of Global Capitalism* (Boulder, Colo.: Westview Press, 1997), 9–10; and also my critique of them in Thornton, "Cross-Cultural Prosaics: Renegotiating the Postmodern/Postcolonial Gap in Cultural Studies," *Prose Studies—History, Theory, Criticism* 20, no. 2 (August 1997): 108–124.

82. Sallie W. Yea, "Regionalism and Political-economic Differentiation in Korean Development: Power Maintenance and the State as Hegemonic Power Bloc," *Korea Journal* 34, no. 2 (Summer 1994): 5–29, 26.

83. Don Oberdorfer, *The Two Koreas: A Contemporary History* (Reading, Mass.: Addison-Wesley, 1997), 381.

84. Kanishka Jayasuriya, "The Exception Becomes the Norm: Law and Regimes of Exception in East Asia," *Asian-Pacific Law and Policy Journal* 2, no. 1 (Winter 2001): 108–124, 117.

85. David Campbell, *Writing Security: United States Foreign Policy and the Politics of Identity* (Minneapolis: University of Minnesota Press, 1998), 5.

86. Gearóid Ó Tuathail, *Critical Geopolitics: The Politics of Writing Global Space* (Minneapolis: University of Minnesota Press, 1996), 53.

87. Hefner, *Civil Islam*, 124–125.

88. Boggs, *The End of Politics*, chapter 7.

89. Dirlik, "Reflections on Postmodernity," 236.

90. Arif Dirlik, "Is There History After Eurocentrism? Globalism, Postcolonialism, and the Disavowal of History," *Cultural Critique* 42 (Spring 1999): 1–34, 17.

91. Kanishka Jayasuriya, "Understanding 'Asian Values' as a Form of Reactionary Modernization," *Contemporary Politics* 4, no. 1 (1988): 77–99.

92. Fareed Zakaria, "Culture Is Destiny: A Conversation with Lee Kuan Yew," *Foreign Affairs* 73, no. 2 (March 1994): 109–126, 122–123.

93. Kausikan, "Asia's Different Standard," 27–28, 33, 34.

94. Aryeh Neier, "Asia's Unacceptable Standard," *Foreign Policy*, no. 92 (Fall 1993): 42–51, 42.

95. Arif Dirlik, "The Postcolonial Aura: Third World Criticism in the Age of Global Capitalism," *Critical Inquiry* 20, no. 2 (Winter 1994): 328–356, 331; and *The Postcolonial Aura*, 117, 211.

96. Richard W. Mansbach, "The New Order in Northeast Asia: A Theoretical Overview," *Asian Perspective* 17, no. 1 (Spring–Summer 1993): 5–24, 19.

97. Will Marshall, "The Democratic Concept," *Dialogue* no. 102 (April 1993): 5–9, 5; and John Gray, *False Dawn: The Delusions of Global Capitalism* (New York: New Press, 1998), 234.

98. Lawrence T. Woods, "Diplomacy and Culture: Lessons from the Asian-Pacific Region," *Asian Culture Quarterly* 19, no. 3 (Autumn 1991): 1–11, 6.

99. Susuma Awanohara, "The K-Street Crowd," *Far Eastern Economic Review* 157, no. 22 (June 2, 1994): 25–26, 25.

100. "Healing the Wounds: Why Beijing Should Re-Evaluate the June 4 Incident," *Asiaweek* Editorial (June 15, 1994): 17–18, 17.

101. White, *Riding the Tiger*, 211.

102. Kennedy, *Preparing for the Twenty-First Century*, 336.

103. Ronald Radosh, Mary R. Habeck, and Grigory Sevostianov, eds. *Spain Betrayed: The Soviet Union in the Spanish Civil War* (New Haven, Conn.: Yale University Press, 2001), 106–107.

104. Clark A. Neher, "Freedom in Asia," *International Studies Review* 1, no. 3 (Fall 1999): 174–175, 175.

105. Robert Nisbet, *The Making of Modern Society* (Brighton, Sussex: Wheatsheaf, 1986), 131–132.

106. Anderson, *The Spectre of Comparisons*, 318, 32.

107. Lucian Pye, *The Spirit of Chinese Politics* (new ed.) (Cambridge, Mass.: Harvard University Press, 1998), viii.

108. John Gray, *Enlightenment's Wake: Politics and Culture at the Close of the Modern Age* (London: Routledge, 1995), 50.

109. Jingsheng Wei, "The Missing Modernization," *New York Times* Op-Ed (December 5, 1997), <www.nytimes.com/yr/mo/day/oped/ 05wei.html>.

110. Robert D. Kaplan, *The Coming Anarchy: Shattering the Dreams of the Post Cold War* (New York: Random House, 2000), 80.

111. Kaplan, *The Coming Anarchy*, 80.

112. William Shawcross, *Deliver Us from Evil: Peacekeepers, Warlords and a World of Endless Conflict* (New York: Simon and Schuster, 2000), 73.

113. Kaplan, *The Coming Anarchy*, 80, 81.

114. Brian Urquhart, "In the Name of Humanity," *New York Review of Books* 47, no. 7 (April 27, 2000): 19–22, 22.

115. Broadcasting magnate Ted Turner has already pledged $1 billion toward UN programs, and another $34 million toward America's delinquent UN dues; see Tina Rosenberg, "Building Their Own Private State Departments," *New York Times* Op-Ed (August 12, 2001), <www.nytimes.com/2001/08/12/opinion/12SUN3.html>.

116. Amartya Sen, *Development as Freedom* (New York: Alfred A. Knopf, 1999), 42.

Chapter 2

Japanese Postmodernism and the New "Japan Problem"

GREAT EXPECTATIONS

If the 1964 Summer Games in Tokyo offered the world a window on an Asian "miracle" in the making, the 1998 Winter Olympics in Nagano afforded a very different picture. Steven Weisman points out that when Nagano was selected, seven years before,

> Japan was at the top of its game. Then the economic bubble burst, and the logic of serving as Olympic host turned upside down. To its embarrassment, Japan was forced to scale back its extravagant promises to pay travel and other expenses for athletes. The Japanese are now worried that the billions spent for the Games will leave mountainous debts and useless facilities too costly to keep up.[1]

This reversal invites a more vexing question concerning the "miracle" itself: Was it worth even a fraction of its cultural, political, and ecological cost? A growing number of Japanese believe that the high price of miracles was foisted on them by their supposed benefactor, the United States, which is widely regarded as the postwar Judas. Japan, by contrast, is seen as the uniquely moral missionary of world peace and postimperialist redemption, a cause that America is thought to have subverted in Vietnam, Nicaragua, the Gulf War, and so forth.[2] This may be part of the reason why the Olympic torch at Nagano was lit to the tune of Puccini's "Madame Butterfly," a not-so-subtle reference to American betrayal. But a more immediate reason is suggested by the term "Japan passing," which Japanese journalists and officials have widely used in reference to both America's economic preeminence and her geopolitical circumvention of Japan in favor of alliances with China.[3]

What is being put to the torch is the modernist phase of Japanese/American

55

relations, that curious symbiosis that took shape during the occupation and bore the stamp of America's "victory culture."[4] It is not hard to fathom why few Japanese were inclined to protest this distinctly American pattern of orientalism.[5] Quite simply, they had expected so much worse. Ian Buruma compares Japan's situation to Germany after Versailles, but without the economic repression.[6] Those who favored liberal reforms, in opposition to residual samurai conservatism,[7] looked to their American keepers with great expectations, never doubting that the world's most democratic nation would export, along with Cokes and chewing gum, its own brand of liberal democratic politics. This illusion contributed to the buoyant mood of the "Tokyo spring" of 1946 and 1947, which briefly restored the democratic openness of the 1920s. That previous experiment, which ended with the Great Depression, burst the fragile alliance between the merchant classes and the traditional power structure.[8]

This time the anti-democratic shift—known as the "reverse course"—was spawned by geopolitics rather than economics. It was inaugurated by a national security directive (NSC 13/2) written by none other than George Kennan, author of the *Foreign Affairs* article that first mandated the Cold War policy of containment. The Japanese Left still views this reversal as an American sellout, and American "revisionist" studies of recent years tend to confirm that verdict. At the time, however, most Japanese took the reverse course as a fair trade: material progress purchased at the price of an always dubious liberal prospect. Postwar affluence seemed to vindicate the privileging of economic over political development—an "apolitics" that had deep roots in the imperial system but took on a new life after 1945.[9]

Japan's unprecedented material gains laid the foundation for what appeared to be a new form of capitalism.[10] Chalmers Johnson dubs this model the "developmental state," which in Johnson's recent thought has become a more pejorative label than it once was.[11] Specifically it challenges the halcyonic vision of Japan as a democratic as well as economic model for Asia. Throughout the Cold War, American "Chrysanthemum Club" writers followed Edwin O. Reishauer in downplaying any inkling of a "Japan problem." Meanwhile, despite its averred pacifism, Japan remained America's faithful spear carrier. Not until the 1970s did the economic and military premises of this relationship—in the wake of Vietnam, Nixon's diplomatic shocks, Watergate, and two oil crises—begin to unravel.

By the late 1970s it was abundantly clear that America's economic downturn of those years was more than a simple recession. It was the tip of a global malaise that seemed more likely to worsen than improve. With the fall of the inflated developmental expectations associated with the green revolution, many third world countries seemed destined for fourth world oblivion, while some of the most hallowed assumptions of modernization theory were being questioned. It could no longer be assumed that any undeveloped nation could "take off" into the friendly skies of Westernization if properly directed by the World Bank, the IMF, and at times the CIA.

Just in time, however, modernization theory was offered sanctuary in the Far East, the one part of the world that still enjoyed rising expectations. The "miracle" of Japan's economy had been an acknowledged fact since 1964. There too, of course, the oil crisis of 1973 and 1974 took its toll, as OPEC raised the price of oil from U.S.$1.75 to $11.65 a barrel. Japanese growth slowed while inflation shot up. But the difference between the Japanese and American responses to the crisis was telling:

> In the United States, there were no institutional alternatives to formal legalistic regulation. . . . In Japan, by contrast, MITI continued to manage energy markets through administrative guidance. In the United States, a strong Congress, preoccupied with issues of equity, fairness, and domestic competition, dominated the policy process. The Diet in Japan did not. In the United States . . . many politicians disregarded the interdependence of market forces: supply, demand, and price were often treated as separate policy issues. In Japan, MITI bureaucrats restored market-clearing prices as soon as the crisis passed. . . . With distributive issues easily resolved, the Japanese government could focus on demand management and security of supply. In the United States, distributive issues continued to predominate for years to come.[12]

The crisis, moreover, accelerated Japan's search for high-tech energy economies. Over the next decade these would reduce the nation's dependence on oil by 25 percent. The crisis also stimulated Japan's search for new sources of raw materials—an outward reach that, as Paul Kennedy notes, resembles Britain's nineteenth-century globalism.[13]

By the mid-1970s Japan was economically back on track with a leaner, meaner "Japan, Inc." The myth of Japan's economic superiority was already taking shape, and even the best professional economists were buying into it. The United States as well as Japan did a better job of handling the second oil shock, brought on by the 1979 Iranian Revolution, which prompted OPEC to raise the price of crude oil from U.S.$14 to $32 per barrel. But clearly it was Japan that led the way. In the 1980s, as Bruce Cumings observes, "Japan became for the United States what the United States became for England in the 1920s: the apparent center of world financial and technical prowess."[14]

Writing in the mid-1980s, at the high tide of that myth, Harvard economist Richard Vietor unreservedly measured the defects of the American system against the Japanese standard, stating that "the United States still seems mired in procedural concerns that swamp attempts to set economic objectives. This is a luxury which, by the late 1980s, the United States may no longer be able to afford." He added that "the implementation of economic policy requires at least a minimum of administrative discretion and some institutional channels for meaningful deliberation. Japan has these, the United States has not."[15]

Like geese flocking behind their lead bird, other East Asian nations rushed to reproduce Japan's "miracle." Thus Japan saved modernization theory for East Asia if not for the world. Ezra Vogel's *Japan as Number One: Lessons for America* (1979) marked this changing of the guard with its bold attempt to graft (no pun intended) this new model of capitalism to an America badly in need of redevelopment. What Vogel did not report was the enormous price, in terms of political undevelopment and flagrant corruption, that Japan had paid for its economic success. Nor was there any attention given to the darker side of the miracle, which Vogel himself had acknowledged in some of his earlier works.[16]

JAPAN'S POLITICAL CULTURE

The roots of Japan's developmental trade-off can be traced to the early decades of the century, a time of both liberalization and xenophobic reaction. After World War I, the surface phenomena of progressive innovation and liberalism served to camouflage an underlying drift toward bureaucratic intransigence, flatulent special interests, and reactionary politics.[17] Those who see liberalism as Japan's natural course of development are prone to view the short-lived "Tokyo spring" as a return to that progressive path; whereas they tend to regard the "reverse course" that followed as an aberration imposed on Japan by America.

Others see this reversal as a return to a deeper antiliberal tradition. This would mean that America's deterministic role in the redeployment of Japan's Old Guard has been exaggerated (e.g., by Patrick Smith's *Japan: A Reinterpretation* [1997]). Suffice it to say that the reverse course perfectly complemented America's postwar and then Cold War priorities. What I personally question is not America's willingness to sell democracy out—of that I have full confidence. I simply doubt the effectivity of this U.S. desire.

This interpretation avoids the typical polar split regarding Japan's political teleology: the essentially liberal and the essentially antiliberal. Both poles reduce Japanese political culture to an inert caricature that demonizes either America or Japan itself. America is either blamed for the reverse course or credited for almost inventing Japanese liberalism. Either way, Cold War ideology triumphs over what may be termed cultural realism (to be developed in chapter 7). It is time, John Lie argues, to get back to the inconvenient details of cultural heterogeneity and historical transformation.[18] Such close analysis has been rare in modernist studies that picture Japanese culture as a homogeneous constant.

While the Japanese concept of *wa*, or social harmony, has been accorded the highest place of honor by Japanologists, there is also the dark underside of *wa*. This operates to suppress competition among ideas[19] by exalting the social unit—"anything from a criminal gang to the accounts payable department"[20]—at the expense of the individual. From this countermodernist perspective, *wa* dissolves resistance to the centralizing pressures of technocratization. It thus bridges the bureaucratic ethic of *kanryodo* and the samurai ethos of *bushido*, traditions that are said to lend force to MITI's modernism.[21]

The classic critique of these traditions, which at first sight looks like the antithesis of Vogel's pro-Japanese polemics, is Ruth Benedict's *The Chrysanthemum and the Sword* (1946). While Benedict debunks Japan's conformist militarism, Vogel sees the same consensualism as an engine of economic growth, the perfect remedy for the global malaise of the 1970s. In fact, Benedict and Vogel are both exemplary modernists in terms of what they omit: the many "other" Japans that defy modernist essentialization.

That omission does not, however, justify a full swing to the opposite methodological pole. Nothing could be less helpful at this time than a postmodern condemnation of all social models, all typicality. Satya Mohanty notes that poststructural versions of postmodernism, which until recently were often equated (e.g., in Asada Akira's *Structure and Power* [1983]) with postmodernism as such, make impossible demands on knowledge and objectivity, and then declare all objectivity illusory when those demands are not met.[22]

NIHONJIN IN THE POSTMODERN DEBATE

In the 1980s Japan enthusiastically embraced this obscurantist version of postmodernism, which became not only a methodology (or antimethodology) but a vestment of cultural identity. Japan pictured itself as the definitive postmodern "other" of Western realism and modernism. Traditional Japaneseness (*Nihonjin*) was either retired or recycled in postmodern dress, as the "virtual" quality of a society with no center, no veridical past, and no particular direction. Accordingly, Japanese intellectual life is now marked by a desultory "conversationalism." This lends itself to consensual and increasingly commercialized "talk-think" (*zadankai*, or purchased talk) at the expense of personal expression and engagement,[23] without which modernism quite literally loses its voice.

Distinctly antimodernist voices, however, have also fallen silent. Patrick Smith contends that the dream of rekindling the essence of the Japanese past died with Mishima and Kawabata,[24] both of whom committed suicide in the early 1970s, just as Japan was emerging triumphant on the world stage. But the project of modernization that Mishima so abhorred is typically described as having its prime mover in its ties with tradition. It would be more accurate to say that Mishima wanted to keep tradition in its premodern mold, not as a reconstructed component of the new economism. In his influential essay, "On the Defense of Culture," Mishima lambasted the structured sameness of modern technology, and hence the bureaucratic ethos of the salaryman. Elsewhere he defended cultural anarchy and "aesthetic terrorism,"[25] themes that are more akin to later Japanese postmodernism than to any essentialist vision of tradition.

Thirty years before, with Japan at war throughout Asia, a legendary conference was held in Tokyo on the theme of "overcoming the modern." Such sentiments were swept aside during the occupation and the "miracle" years that followed. Until the 1980s, mainstream Japanese culture lionized the modern as the highway to rapid economic development. Paradoxically, it was the prodigious success of Japan's GNPism—which is also to say its Tokyoism—that revealed the hollow interior of modernism on a broader scale. The project of modernization had left gaping holes, both material and emotional, revealing what Gavan McCormack calls, in his book of that title, "the emptiness of Japanese affluence."[26] At the very peak of the 1980s "miracle," only about a third of Japan's homes were connected with sewers.[27] Nonetheless, the Tokyo version of Japan had become the very archetype of the modern. Here the formlessness of late capitalist modernism was blatantly exposed, much as the corruption and inertia of Japan's bureaucracy would be exposed ten years later in the twisted wreckage of Japan's model city, Kobe, after the Great Hanshin Earthquake of January 1995.[28]

The trick was to turn that public image around, extolling Japanese formlessness as a "postmodern" virtue. (In fact it was more a *hyper*modernism than a *post*modernism, but mainstream usage supports the "post.") Kojin Karatani set the stage for this "postmodern" revaluation in a seminal 1984 discussion with Asada Akira and Jacques Derrida.[29] Against Derrida he argued that there was no structure in Japan to destroy or deconstruct; hence deconstruction would be impossible there. Though Karatani looked upon Japanese capitalism more negatively than Asada and Derrida,[30] he forfeited the resistance potential that a more "centered" or culturally structured view of the past might afford. By imposing a present structural void on the past, he effectively cast Japan, past and present, in the image of present-day Tokyo.

This version of postmodernism is at once the cultural logic of late capitalist modernism and the ideology that places capitalism beyond the reach of serious criticism. Although Japanese postmodernism is hardly a product of traditional values, as Karatani would have it, his error reveals a negative truth: the fact that Tokyo/Japan is so utterly modern, and hence so vacuous, that its ephemeral nature is fully exposed. None of this would much surprise readers of *The Communist Manifesto* or Marshall Berman's *All That Is Solid Melts into Air*, both of which underscore the de(con)structive thrust of capitalism. Tokyo can likewise be read as a text on the meltdown of "all that is solid"— or, structurally speaking, all that is Japan. Karatani's worst error is his belief that this radical deconstruction leaves a structural void where Japan once was. Rather, it threatens to replace one structure with another: that of global capitalism.

As if to fill that cultural void, both Japanese modernism and postmodernism, or rather one of the two major currents of Japanese postmodernism, tend to cloak themselves in selective remnants of tradition. One nominal postmodernist holds that Japan, because "it successfully modernized without losing its soul, . . . is perhaps better positioned than other non-Western cultures . . . to offer guidance to postmodern man."[31] Unlike its Western counterpart, this strain of postmodernism moves beyond the aleatoric or parodic level in its dealings with the past. It finds its paradoxical essence in traditional antiessentialism—most notably the Zen variety. Whereas Japanese modernism draws upon tradition in order to center itself, this mode of postmodernism, which Steven Heine dubs "decentrist,"[32] paradoxically looks to tradition as the vital center of its decentering project.

Heine, meanwhile, notes the rise of a more radically deconstructive postmodernism that vilifies tradition. This ludic variety traces to Roland Barthes's *Empire of the Sun* (1970), which treats Japan as a fluid text where content gives way to a free play of signs (again with the false implication that no structure survives in Japan to constrain freedom). The resulting chaos is lauded as a solution rather than a problem. It is embraced as the "sacred nothing" that raises Japan above the blighted sphere of Western logocentrism.

Heine points out that in the early 1980s this antitraditional postmodernism, inspired by Deleuze and Guattari, captured Japan via Asada Akira's *Structure and Power*. The "AA phenomenon," as it was known, borrowed something from Marx as well as from French poststructuralism (specifically it borrowed one side of Marx—his deconstructive side—while suppressing his structural analysis). But surely this problematizes the liberatory project of Barthes's decentrist nothingness, exemplified as it was by the "empty space" of the imperial palace gardens. Japan's vaunted mediation of the particular and the universal, or atomism and holism (as in the prewar Kyoto School classic by Nishida Kitaro, *The Problems of Japanese Culture*) is more than an aesthetic balancing act. As did the Kyoto School during the war, it has a political mission to keep its sacred silence in the face of domestic oppression and international imperialism.[33]

POSTMODERNISM AND JAPAN— THE TEXT

The contest between these rival postmodernisms had become obvious by the late 1980s, when the standard text on the subject, *Postmodernism and Japan*, was compiled by Masao Miyoshi and H. D. Harootunian. As Tetsuo Najita noted in his contribution to this text, the Barthian "retreat of signs" was not in and of itself deconstructive, for it "still seems to lead to the certitude of cultural knowledge as an ordering reference." Even a "constancy of uncertainty" is an inverted form of certitude and potentially a controlling code. Lyotard's version of postmodernity would abolish all such codes. The danger here, Najita argues, is that such absolute decoding would abolish, along with repressive social codes, any program to prevent "the continuous reconstitution of things as they are."[34] This criticism closely parallels Habermas's critique of Lyotard in their famous debate.[35]

Postmodern Japan, however, tends to amalgamate elements from both Lyotard and Habermas. Consider the political thought of Prime Minister Yasuhiro Nakasone, as discussed by Marilyn Ivy in the same text. Like Lyotard, Nakasone celebrates the eclipse of metanarrative structures that would filter communication ideologically. In his new Japan, the supreme "high-level information society,"[36] information would replace nature as a comprehensive environment. It would become transparent and free of ideological refraction. This bears some similarity to Habermas's ideal speech community, though Habermas would certainly not approve of the ultraconservative tilt of Nakasone's neonationalism, as institutionalized in his International Research Center for Japanese Studies.[37] On this basis Nakasone constructed a postindustrial narrative of legitimization to support his dream of being, in effect, president rather than prime minister. Though he failed in that ambition,[38] Ivy attempts to retrieve the "positive possibilities" of his "new knowledge" model by distinguishing its liberatory and repressive elements. Rather than Habermasian rationalism or any form of dialogics, she rests her case on the energy of consumerism,[39] as if that could be separated from the structures of capitalism she condemns.

The controversy over *Postmodernism and Japan* persists and has even intensified as deconstruction is put on the defensive. This new intensity is indicated by a vitriolic exchange between Miyoshi and one of his harshest critics, Jeff Humphries. No doubt Humphries is right in his charge that while "Miyoshi criticizes the Japanese for being Western-centric, . . . his own perspective is . . . grounded in the West."[40] The argument slides off target, however, when it takes aim at theory in general, even suggesting that the appropriation of "theory" by Japanese studies is inherently neocolonial.[41]

First, the "AA phenomenon" was hardly forced upon Japan under threat of economic sanctions. The Japanese themselves called in these theoretical incursions. Second, it is hard to imagine how any serious study of another culture could be conducted without theoretical grounding. What Humphries means by "theory" is a particular type of theory: that of his nemesis, Miyoshi, and like-minded postmodernists such as Karatani, who is named as the principal proponent of this new colonialism. It is said that in his disagreement with Derrida, Karatoni reveals his considerable ignorance of deconstruction as well as the shallowness of his own mode of postmodernism.[42] What this disagreement actually evinces is the split between two schools of Japanese postmodernism. Karatoni's approach—identified as the decentrist line by Heine, above—upholds the predeconstructive virtues of Japanese tradition. Humphries alludes to this line of tradition when he asserts that

> [A]ll of the academic contributors to *Postmodernism and Japan* seem to share the view that the postmodern in Japan cannot be confined to recent history. The whole volume seems to be inspired by the cliched assumption that everything about Japan, from the karesansui gardens at Ryoonji to the skyscrapers of Tokyo, is somehow "postmodern."[43]

This generalization goes too far. The chapter of *Postmodernism and Japan* that Humphries most disparages includes a badly needed reassessment of contemporary Japan's "relentlessly obsessive 'return to origins.'"[44] This puts in question the cultural exceptionalism that would confirm Japanese identity while banishing the heterogeneous Other.[45] Harootunian's essay dismantles the New Age fetish for advanced communication that Nakasone appropriates, on the Right, and Marilyn Ivy embraces on the Left. More generally it puts the postmodern question to Japan by challenging the place of essentialism in Japanese studies.[46]

Miyoshi has also contributed to that critique, but like so many postmodernists he tends to come full circle, producing an antiessentialist essentialism. His caustic reply to Humphries has all the marks of a losing cause. Returning fire with fire, he accuses his adversary of being "malicious, ignorant, inaccurate, irresponsible, dishonest, fraudulent, lazy, sloppy, unhistorical, and incoherent"—just for starters.[47] Miyoshi and Humphries come together on just one point: their common antipathy toward revisionist intruders such as Ian Buruma and Karel van Wolferen, who have the gall to tackle real issues that

Japanese studies programs have managed to avoid for decades. Though Humphries exhorts his profession to reach out for a wider audience,[48] he shows no patience for those who actually do so.

In its peevish excesses, the Humphries/Miyoshi exchange testifies to what comes from years of disciplinary inbreeding. Japanese culture is too integral to Japanese politics, and the latter is too crucial to the balance of power in Asia, to be left to academic Japanologists alone. What is sorely needed is more, not less, interdisciplinary intrusion.

Though postmodern discourse has pointed us in this direction, too much of it has involved the unilateral export of literary and/or cultural studies obsessions to other disciplines. As van Wolferen argues, it is crucial that we match our cultural understanding of politics with a political understanding of culture.[49] That reciprocity is part of what I call the "second postmodern turn."[50] By putting this "second" postmodern question to Japanese political culture, it is possible to address the problem that arises when a world-class economy takes the *wrong* postmodern turn—a turn toward reactionary globalization.

THE CULTURAL TURN OF THE "JAPAN PROBLEM"

When Junichiro Koizumi in 2001 became Japan's ninth prime minister in ten years, skeptics had reason to doubt his ability to fulfill his campaign pledge to "change the LDP to change Japan." Koizumi is caught in a vicious circle: Only its imminent death can open the Liberal Democratic Party to change, yet to raise party hopes would kill that very incentive. Koizumi's own popularity works against him in that sense. His predecessor, Yoshiro Mori, at least contributed a useful sense of hopelessness. In better times this hope question would not have arisen. The public found political inertia reassuring: More of the same is an alluring prospect for any "miracle" economy. Even now, in the midst of unrelenting recession, moderates have reason to fear fundamental change. Political reform could easily veer to the Right—even the far Right. Many of Koizumi's own supporters (especially within the Buddhist affiliated New Komeito Party, his coalition partner) find it unsettling that he wasted no time in pressing for constitutional reforms to "normalize" military operations.

They are not alone. Inside and outside Japan, the new "Japan problem" is rooted in one irrepressible question: Is there something inherently abnormal about Japanese "normality"? If the old "problem" was primarily economic, the new one ominously ties economics to power politics. There is some irony in the fact that this geopolitical takeoff would occur in the midst of a long economic slump. That timing, however, has as much to do with America's world affairs as with Japan's. Coupled with Japan's "lost decade" and the Asian Crash of 1997, the U.S. economic boom of the 1990s added vast tonnage to America's "unipolar" status. It was at this moment of hubris that corporate America came to see the Pacific Rim as an enormous buying opportunity. That view could be held in good conscience so long as it was believed, with Francis Fukuyama and a broad "Washington consensus," that American corporatism is an engine of democratic as well as economic development. Thus the IMF seized the opportunity to impose its version of the American Dream on the Rim.

Asian reality, however, is seldom the stuff of dreams. Once more Asian regimes are playing hard to get. The Crash put them on guard by raising the question of what it means to be "Asian," politically speaking. So-called Asian values had long treated "Western" democracy as an unaffordable luxury for developing countries. Now that assertion is turned on its head, as Asian values start to look like the luxuries of good times. Without their miracles, political machines ranging from Indonesia's New Order to Japan's LDP find themselves in danger of losing their economic purchase on legitimacy. In the face of sweeping political reform, they look to globalization for salvation. That takes them even further from the broader meaning of Asian values, as treated in the introduction and chapter 1. Again they are abandoning the prospect of a truly democratic Japan, where reforms reach beyond formal institutions such as voting laws.[51] Without such reform Japan will not escape its centrist rut. Nor will it lay the domestic foundation for responsible leadership abroad.

There is no question that Japan will take a prominent role in world affairs in years to come. The question is how. Mayumi Itoh distinguishes two forms of Japanese internationalization, or *kokusaika*: the "inward" and the "outward." The latter is a basically unilateral market strategy inspired by Japan's nationalistic ambitions, whereas the former involves real dialogic encounter with foreign cultures.[52] This "inward" alternative could better be termed "dialogic internationalism," since it has a distinctly Bakhtinian aspect: It is open to foreign cultures without selling out its own values to the latest global fashions.

That qualified openness was harbingered eighty years ago in the thought of Sakuzo Yoshino, who argued for preserving Japanese culture by way of selective inclusion. From this vantage foreign practices such as democracy could be seen as dialogic opportunities rather than threats. The opposite position was taken by Fumimaro Konoe, who would preserve Japanese tradition by way of exclusion.[53] Today a similar dialectic is taking shape between neonationalism and the dialogics of *rinko* or "neighborly relations," where diplomacy is buttressed by cultural interchange.[54] The extremes of this nationalist versus internationalist polarity were represented, respectively, by two works of the early 1990s: the notorious *The Japan that Can Say No* and a small volume by the Japanologist Ronald Dore, recently translated as *Japan, Internationalism and the U.N.* (1997).

In the absence of a dialogics such as Yoshino's or Itoh's, one of two unfortunate scenarios could unfold. First, Japan could resist its present drift toward globalization by way of militant neonationalism. In that case it would forfeit any chance of a progressive IR role. Alternatively, in a desperate bid to revive its economic vitality, Japan could surrender its native progressivism to globalization, much as it surrendered its own liberalism to the "reverse course" of the late 1940s. This would stanch the kind of domestic reform that is necessary for nonhegemonic internationalism around the Rim. Either way, a domestic/foreign nexus is central to the impending "Japan problem."

The crux of the reform issue is how to revitalize the best traditions of Japan; not, as globalists would have it, how to overcome native traditions. Although the "social compact" of Japan's "1955" system has produced a politically inert model of development, this system must be credited with real achievements in other areas. Chief among them is its meliorative effect on some of the social costs of rapid economic growth. The Japan model has afforded more than a blueprint for raw economism. Asian countries have found in Japan's example a way to reconcile the antipodes of development and social solidarity, or liberal internationalism and "Asianism."[55] In their takeoff phase, at least, they have avoided the social deconstruction that the West now suffers in the form of drugs, crime, divorce, and so forth.

It is only fair to note that crime and social disorder are presently a growth industry in Japan.[56] The point, as Bryan Turner argues, is that *all* capitalist societies now face a dearth of solidarity.[57] While Francis Fukuyama (*The Great Disruption* [1999]) attempts to write this off as the growing pains of postindustrial transition, John Gray more convincingly diagnoses it as a process of cultural elimination: not only the surrender of traditional cultures but of alternative modes of capitalism, such as Japan's. For Gray the Japan model is the paradigm case of indigenous modernization. Avoiding the liberal dichotomy of state and society, this model has centered around *wa,* or harmony, achieving modernization with less sacrifice of social structures or cultural traditions than would be expected in such a rapid growth economy.[58] Marx's tenet concerning the destructive dynamics of capitalism—all that is solid melts into air—has been so broadly accepted that Japan seems almost to have defied a natural law.

Prabhat Patnaik argues, moreover, that until recently the Japan model has been instrumental in funneling economic resources toward productive as opposed to speculative investment sites, and in limiting exposure to international financial flows that could be disastrous in times of global recession. Against the common preference of financial interests for tight credit, Japanese policy has consistently maximized growth by keeping credit cheap.[59] Even Richard Katz (*Japan, the System that Soured* [1998]), a harsh critic of the Japanese economic system, must admit that this system worked well in its "catch-up" phase.

Finally, as Amartya Sen observes, Japan has led the way in terms of human development. This example has helped developing countries overcome the reactionary belief that

> [H]uman development is really a kind of luxury that only richer countries can afford. Perhaps the most important impact of the type of success that the East Asian economies have recently had (beginning with Japan—decades earlier) is the total undermining of that implicit prejudice. This economics went comparatively early for massive expansion of education, and later also of health care, and this they did, in many cases, *before* they broke the restraints of general poverty. . . . Human development is first and foremost an ally of the poor, rather than the rich and affluent.[60]

That developmental cushioning is now put in jeopardy by globalization, which undermines the most humane and culturally ingrained components of the Japanese system. As Serge Latouche points out, this system has managed to integrate material production with cultural life. Globalization severs that bond, relegating production to a disenchanted pursuit of profit in the service of passive consumerism.[61] In part this seems to vindicate Japan's postwar literary nativists who turned against the West and even against modernization. But that retreatism also divorced them from their third world counterparts. As Masao Miyoshi observes, third world intellectuals have steadfastly embraced some parts of the Western Enlightenment ethos.[62]

What is lost in both cases—the globalist and the nativist—is the rare balance that the Japan model struck between tradition and modernity, inward and outward development, and ultimately East and West. Either way the result is a dangerously skewed Japanism that exchanges human development and security for reactionary economism. It follows that the current "Japan problem" is not so much the result of the new internationalism being "too Japanese," as so-called "Japan bashers" would contend. Rather, in democratic terms, it is not Japanese enough. The danger is that Japan's internationalization will either collapse into rootless globalization, with policies dictated by market forces, or into a militant nationalism that is as anti-democratic as it is anti-globalist.

The latter impulse is fueled by Japan's geopolitical anxieties. It would be misleading to reduce the reason for this unease to China's rise to the status of a "multipolar" power. Given a state of regional balance, China's military-industrial empowerment could not begin to generate the angst that is being felt around the Rim. That unease can only be explained by the imbalance of power that issues from America's recent "engagement" policy toward China. Nor is that policy the exclusive legacy of Clinton-era economism. President Bush, in extending China's trade privileges on May 29, 2001, spoke of the same strategy for prying open a closed society through commercial engagement.[63]

It is important to recognize that the structural impetus behind this policy is the metamorphosis of Western capitalism—or more specifically capitalism's political agent, liberalism—since the early 1980s. John Judis reminds us that corporate leaders

> used to routinely serve on policy boards and commissions that advocated positions irrelevant, or inimical, to the businesses they represented. In the early twentieth century, businessmen, bankers, and lawyers . . . financed Theodore Roosevelt's Progressive Party, championed child-labor restrictions and workers'-compensation legislation, and encouraged collective bargaining between labor and business. Business leaders lobbied for Lyndon Johnson's War on Poverty and cheered the formation of the Environmental Protection Agency.[64]

Today such public-spirited leadership has all but vanished. In league with a general corporate abandonment of home nations,[65] not to mention local communities, neoliberalism has purged most noncapitalistic elements from American foreign policy. The result is a crisis of trust, as taken up in the conclusion. Allies can no longer count on American commitments unsupported by corporate interest—indeed, very short-term interest. That is one reason why, after half a century of ostracism, Japan is being invited to Asia's geopolitical table. Japan is looked to, however warily, as a balancing agent of last resort.

Many see that prospect as *the* "Japan problem." It is a problem, however, that holds as much promise as peril. This study is not averse to an expansive Japanese role in Asian politics, so long as it is matched by progressive domestic reforms. Japan's electoral reforms of the 1990s fell short of that mark,[66] and in any case more is needed than institutional reform alone. Perhaps the one salubrious effect of Japan's long economic slide could be its negation of the LDP's centrist trade-off: affluence in return for political inertia. Democratic decentralization is definitely in the air. Unfortunately the new incubus of globalization threatens to stunt this reform process at its moment of birth.

CONCLUSION: WARMING TREND

One lesson of the late 1990s is that even a small and seemingly remote economic crisis can have global repercussions. The fall of the Thai baht precipitated the 1997 Asian crisis, but as Paul Krugman notes, Thai purchasing power was no greater than that of the state of Massachusetts. Concern is all the more justified when the economy in question is the world's second largest. It bothers Krugman that Americans who were obsessed by the threat of Japan's success in the 1980s lost interest in its persistent slump in the 1990s.[67]

Most Americans still picture the "Japan problem" as they did in the late 1980s—as a long but emendable list of commercial grievances. It is charged that Japan "still pursues a global trade negotiating strategy more fitting to a small, isolationist developing country."[68] The idea is to get this mega-economy to retire the insularity of "Japan Inc." in favor of neoliberal internationalism. Some, such as Patrick Smith,[69] would stretch this reform mandate to include an expansive role for Japan's Self-Defense Forces (SDF), despite the fact that even present SDF operations may be illegal under Article 9 of Japan's Constitution.[70] In lieu of full militarization, the core proposal set forth by the Clinton administration was "multilateralism," defined by Secretary of State Madeleine Albright as simple "burden sharing."[71]

Many Japanese in turn feel "burdened" by U.S. policies reaching back to "victory culture" days. On the liberal Left they see America as the postwar Judas that betrayed Japan's hopes for substantive oppositional democracy,[72] while on the Right they take umbrage at having to be America's military caddy. Left and Right converge on the issue of American pressure for neoliberalization. In 1993, Kazuo Ogura (a foreign ministry official and later ambassador to South Korea) vented a Japanese counterideology in the form of a "theory of Asian capitalism."[73] After a brief recess following the Asian Crash, this ideology has returned with a vengeance. Perhaps the best representative of such pan-Asianism is Shintaro Ishihara, the best-selling coauthor (with Sony's late boss, Akio Morita) of *The Japan that Can Say No* (1989), and coauthor (with Malaysia's Mahathir Mohamad) of *The Asia that Can Say No* (1992). He blames the United States for the excessive pain of economic reform. Those who think along these lines see Albright's idea of multilateralism as a mere cloak for doing America's post–Cold War bidding.

If this Clinton/Albright agenda was at odds with Japanese perspectives, it was even less mindful of emerging regional attitudes. Its enabling assumption, ironically, was that Japan can be trusted "multilaterally" precisely because it has so few multilateral options. Asia's distrust and antipathy toward Japan since World War II—aggravated by Japan's refusal to come to terms with its own past[74]—can be counted on to keep Japan in check. This dearth of options helps resolve the paradox of Japan's "unrealized power": its failure to "instrumentalize" any but narrow economic goals.[75]

That economism was part of the old "Japan problem." What the Clinton/ Albright plan overlooked was the emergence of a new dilemma in the form of Japan's budding geopolitics—a concern for globalists as well as realists. Witness Japan's efforts to sabotage the neoliberal agenda of the November 1999 WTO meeting in Seattle.[76] This recalcitrance is compounded by the fact that since 1991, due largely to Japan's regional investment strategies, Asia has overtaken the United States as Japan's biggest export market.[77]

The assumption that Japan is "boxed in" internationally lost much of its validity during the Clinton years, when U.S. "constructive engagement" with China sent a strong message to Asian nations that they would be on their own should any conflict arise with America's newfound "strategic partner." That policy was a subset of the administrations' general economism—its own Japan-like subordination of geopolitical strategy to financial or commercial concerns.[78] A security crisis arose when oversight for sensitive missile and computer technology was transferred to the Commerce Department. In one 1995 case, which came under criminal investigation, Hughes Electronics was allowed to tutor Chinese scientists on state-of-the-art rocket launching techniques.[79] By default of both geopolitical realism[80] and "soft power" idealism,[81] the United States has left a power vacuum in Asia that China is gearing up to fill.[82] Asian nations have rightly perceived the United States as being "far less interested in trans-Pacific statecraft than in domestic political gain"[83]—and of course financial gain. Power has once again shifted from the State Department, this time to the Treasury Department.

The definitive mark of that shift was America's weak political response to the 1997 Asian Crash. Major foreign policy decisions were "economized" and effectively relegated to the IMF. Operating with little of the transparency that it demanded from Asian nations, the IMF took a "let them eat cake" attitude toward the common workers of Asia. Its call for a neoliberal restructuration of Asian economies, without social safeguards, punished millions of people who bore no responsibility for the crisis, even as it bailed out those who were directly responsible. Taking its indirect marching orders from Treasury Secretary Robert Rubin, the IMF was more attentive to Wall Street than to Washington's moral or geopolitical imperatives. The message this sent to Asia was one of cold indifference: "While Asia's former 'miracle' economies were reeling in 1998, the White House entourage spent 11 days on a much-heralded African safari."[84] The new "Washington consensus" was so out of touch with Asian perspectives that it believed U.S. influence to have grown in the region after the crisis.[85] That might be true enough in terms of short run economic leverage—the kind of raw economism that dominated modernist development theory after Rostow and was revamped for globalist application by Fukuyama. This worldview, however, obscures the enormous role of moral force in the "winning of the Cold War" and the making of a new geopolitics, as will be treated in chapter 8.

As China rushes to fill the post-Crash power vacuum in Asia,[86] Japan is looked to as a hedge against both China and the United States.[87] Of course, most East Asians long ago took Japan as their developmental mentor, their so-called lead goose. But many now seem ready to go much further in the direction of Japan's own "Miki plan": the idea of a Japan-led Pacific integration that traces to Takeo Miki in the late 1960s.[88] Malaysia's abortive push for a Japan-led East Asian Economic Caucus (EAEC), which Japan backed away from,[89] harbingered the more subtle yet no less potent pan-Asianism of the November 1999 ASEAN (Association of Southeast Asian Nations) summit in Manila.

It was at another Manila ASEAN meeting, in December 1987, that a "warming trend" was first witnessed in Asian attitudes toward Japan, insofar as Japan's Prime Minister Noboru Takeshita, was the only non-ASEAN leader to be invited.[90] Now, in the wake of the Asian crisis, East and Southeast Asian countries have proved more than willing to take Japan as a preferred lender in place of the IMF. Clearly this is not the kind of multilateralism that Albright had in mind. More is involved here than a continued "warming trend," but does it signal a regional paradigm shift?

How, in that case, do these countries deal with the newly official status of the Rising Sun flag and the hymn to the emperor? Can they bring themselves to separate the prospect of Japanese remilitarization from Japan's resurgent nationalism?[91] It would help, of course, if Japan would do more to dispel worries over the link between neonationalism and latent imperialist ambitions. Half a century after Japan's military defeat, much more is needed than expressions of "deep remorse" and "heartfelt apology" for Japan's former imperialism.[92] While Japan is rightly accused of skirting the issue of its past, it is also capable of using the past as a diversion. What should concern Asian workers as well as pro-democracy advocates is the rising tide of Japan's *present* imperialism—the economic rather than military variety.

In years past, along with the usual Cold War imperatives, latent anxieties concerning Japan gave impetus to East Asia's appreciation of Pax Americana. This position was reconfirmed by ASEAN members well into the 1990s.[93] Thus the reversal that took place in Manila has an insurgent aspect: that these countries would opt for Japanese credit over the IMF strikes at least a symbolic blow to America's paramountcy in the region, for it is common knowledge that IMF policies are largely dictated by the United States.[94]

It also strikes a blow against the late modernist assumption that the world is rapidly moving toward a single economic structure, be it (as Fukuyama imagines) a utopian New World Order or (as Wallerstein contends) a dystopian World System. Any "postmodernism" worthy of the name must confront this capitalist omnistructure. In Japan, as in America, most of what passes for postmodernism retreats from that imperative. Incessant talk of difference fails to *make a difference* for the Japanese "other" or the world's oppressed. Rather, mainstream postmodernism and popular culture studies take the course of least resistance: a full retreat into spectatorship,[95] micropolitical fatalism,[96] or the distinctly Japanese "postmodernism" (i.e., hypermodernism) that this chapter has explored.

The next chapter puts the question of political and cultural resistance to Japan as a whole—meaning the country's decentered elements as well as its better known power base. The present weakening of that base affords democratic as well as reactionary opportunities. In short, Japan is at a fateful crossroads. Most of Asia is likely to follow the course Japan takes vis-à-vis globalization. The question is whether that is good or bad news.

NOTES

1. Steven R. Weisman, "Negano Reflects Japan's Glories, and Neuroses," *New York Times* Editorial (February 15, 1998).

2. Ian Buruma, *The Wages of Guilt: Memories of War in Germany and Japan* (New York: Meridian, 1994), 37.

3. John B. Judis, "The Sun Also Rises," *New Republic* (November 3, 1997), <www.tnr.com/archive/11/110397/judis110397.html>.

4. Patrick Smith, *Japan: A Reinterpretation* (New York: Pantheon Books, 1997), 18.

5. Frank Gibney, "The Wilted Chrysanthemum," *New York Times Book Review* (July 13, 1997).

6. Buruma, *The Wages of Guilt*, 296.

7. Ardath W. Burks, *Japan: Profile of a Postindustrial Power* (Boulder, Colo.: Westview Press, 1981), 110.

8. Murray Sayle, "The Party's (Almost) Over," *Far Eastern Economic Review* (August 10, 1989): 19–22, 19.

9. Ian Buruma, "Japan Against Itself," *New York Review of Books* 41, no. 9 (May 12, 1994): 18–22, 21.

10. Haruhiro Fukui and Shigeko N. Fukai, "The End of the Miracle: Japanese Politics in the Post–Cold War Era," in Mark T. Berger and Douglas A. Borer, eds., *The Rise of East Asia: Critical Visions of the Pacific Century* (London: Routledge, 1997), 37–68, 37;

and Michael E. Porter and Hirotaka Takeuchi, "Fixing What Really Ails Japan," *Foreign Affairs* 78, no. 3 (May–June 1999): 66–81, 66.

11. Chalmers Johnson, *Japan: Who Governs?* (New York: W. W. Norton, 1995).

12. Richard H. Vietor, "Energy Markets and Policy," in Thomas K. McCraw, ed., *America Versus Japan: A Comparative Study of Business-Government Relations Conducted at the Harvard Business School* (Boston: Harvard Business School Press, 1986), 193–228, 214.

13. Paul Kennedy, *The Rise and Fall of the Great Powers: Economic Change and Military Conflict from 1500 to 2000* (London: Fontana Press, 1989), 595–596.

14. Bruce Cumings, *Parallax Visions: Making Sense of American East Asian Relations* (Durham, N.C.: Duke University Press, 1999), 32.

15. Vietor, "Energy Markets and Policy," 227–228.

16. Smith, *Japan*, 161.

17. Marius B. Jansen, *Japan and Its World: Two Centuries of Change* (Princeton, N.J.: Princeton University Press, 1980), 75–76.

18. John Lie, "Theorizing Japanese Uniqueness," *Current Sociology* 44, no. 1 (Spring 1996): 5–13, 5.

19. Karel van Wolferen, *The Enigma of Japanese Power: People and Politics in a Stateless Nation* (New York: Vintage Books, 1990), 315.

20. Murray Sayle, "Japan Victorious," *New York Review of Books* 32, no. 5 (March 28, 1985): 33–40, 34.

21. Chalmers Johnson, *MITI and the Japanese Miracle: The Growth of Industrial Policy, 1925–1975* (Stanford, Calif.: Stanford University Press, 1982), 38–40.

22. Satya P. Mohanty, *Literary Theory and the Claims of History: Postmodernism, Objectivity, Multicultural Politics* (Ithaca, N.Y.: Cornell University Press, 1997), 113.

23. Masao Miyoshi, *Off Center: Power and Culture Relations between Japan and the United States* (Cambridge, Mass.: Harvard University Press, 1991), chap. 9.

24. Smith, *Japan*, 252.

25. Tetsuo Najita, "On Culture and Technology in Postmodern Japan," in Masao Miyoshi and H. D. Harootunian, eds., *Postmodernism and Japan* (Durham, N.C.: Duke University Press, 1989), 3–20, 16.

26. Gavan McCormack, *The Emptiness of Japanese Affluence* (New York: M. E. Sharpe, 1996), 7–8.

27. Van Wolferen, *The Enigma of Japanese Power*, 2.

28. Nicholas D. Kristof, "Japan Reluctant to Accept Help from Abroad for Quake Victims," *New York Times* (February 5, 1995): 1, 8.

29. See under Akira Asada, Jacques Derrida, and Karatoni Kojin, "The Ultra-Consumer Society and the Role of the Intellectual" (Choshohi shaki to chishikijin no yakuwari"), *Asahi Journal* (May 25, 1984): 6–14.

30. Marilyn Ivy, "Critical Texts, Mass Artifacts: The Consumption of Knowledge in Postmodern Japan," in Masao Miyoshi and H. D. Harootunian, eds., *Postmodernism and Japan* (Durham, N.C.: Duke University Press, 1989), 21–46, 42.

31. Takeshi Umehara, "Ancient Japan Shows Postmodernism the Way," *New Perspectives Quarterly* 4, no. 2 (Spring 1992): 10–13, 10.

32. Steven Heine, "Ie-Ism (Sacred Familism) and the Discourse of Postmodernism in Relation to Nativism/Nationalism/Nihonism," in Charles Wei-hsun Fu and Steven Heine,

eds., *Japan in Traditional and Postmodern Perspectives* (New York: State University of New York Press, 1995), 25–53, 28.

33. Heine, "Ie-Ism," 45.

34. Najita, "On Culture and Technology in Postmodern Japan," 19.

35. Richard Rorty, "Habermas and Lyotard on Postmodernity," in Richard J. Berstein, ed., *Jürgen Habermas and Modernity* (Cambridge, UK: Polity Press, 1985), 161–175.

36. Quoted in Ivy, "Critical Texts, Mass Artifacts," 23.

37. Miyoshi, *Off Center*, 81.

38. James Fallows, "The Real Japan," *New York Review of Books* 31, no. 12 (July 20, 1989): 23–28, 23.

39. Ivy, "Critical Texts, Mass Artifacts," 44.

40. Jeff Humphries, "Japan in Theory," *New Literary History* 28, no. 3 (Summer 1997): 602–623, 605.

41. Humphries, "Japan in Theory," 602.

42. Humphries, "Japan in Theory," 613.

43. Humphries, "Japan in Theory," 613.

44. H. D. Harootunian, "Visible Discourses/Invisible Ideologies," in Masao Miyoshi and H. D. Harootunian, eds., *Postmodernism and Japan* (Durham, N.C.: Duke University Press, 1989), 63–92, 66.

45. Steve Odin, review of *Postmodernism in Japan*, H. D. Harootunian and Masao Miyoshi, eds., *Philosophy East and West* 40, no. 3 (July 1990): 381–387, 386.

46. Anthony Woodiwiss, "Postodanizumu: Japanese For (and Against) Postmodernism," *Theory, Culture and Society: Explorations in Critical Social Science* 8/4 (November 1991): 111–118, 111–112.

47. Masao Miyoshi, "'Bunburying' in the Japan Field: A Reply to Jeff Humphries," *New Literary History* 28, no. 3 (Summer 1997): 625–638, 625.

48. Humphries, "Japan in Theory," 617.

49. Van Wolferen, *The Enigma of Japanese Power*, 20.

50. William H. Thornton, *Cultural Prosaics: The Second Postmodern Turn* (vol. 10 of the RICL series) (Edmonton: Research Institute for Comparative Literature–University of Alberta, 1998).

51. For a useful but too glowing synopsis of Japan's recent voting reforms see Kazuki Iwanaga, "Dominant Party Democracy and the Politics of Electoral Reform in Japan," in Hans Antlöv and Tak-Wing Ngo, eds., *The Cultural Construction of Politics in Asia* (Surrey, UK: Curzon Press, 2000), 52–85, 70–79; and for a sharply critical assessment see Yoshiaki Kobayashi, "Reading the Election Results," *Japan Echo* 27, no. 5 (October 2000): 29–32.

52. Mayumi Itoh, *Globalization of Japan: Japanese Sakoku Mentality and U.S. Efforts to Open Japan* (Hampshire, UK: Macmillan, 1998), 5.

53. Inoki Takenori, "Japan's Culture and Globalization—Importance of Real Human Contacts," *Global Communications Platform from Japan* (December 14, 2000), <www.glocom.org/opnions/essays/ 200006_inoki_jp_culture/index.html>.

54. Kojima Akira, "Reinventing Japan: Report on the Commission on Japan's Goals in the Twenty-First Century (Outline)," *Japan Echo* 27, no. 2 (April 2000): 17–20.

55. Takashi Shiraishi, "Asia's Regional Order: A Two-Century Perspective," *Japan Echo* 27, no. 3 (June 2000): 9–13, 13.

56. "Sunset for the Men in Suits," *Economist* (July 1, 2000), <www2.gol.com/users/coynerhm/sunset_for_the_men_in_suits.htm>.

57. Bryan S. Turner, *Classical Sociology* (London: Sage, 1999), 262.

58. John Gray, *False Dawn: The Delusions of Global Capitalism* (New York: New Press, 1998), 170–171.

59. Prabhat Patnaik, "Capitalism in Asia at the End of the Millennium," *Monthly Review* 51, no. 3 (July–August 1999): 53–70; also at <www.monthlyreview.org/799pat.htm>.

60. Amartya Sen, *Development as Freedom* (New York: Alfred A. Knopf, 1999), 143–144.

61. Serge Latouche, *The Westernization of the World: The Significance, Scope and Limits of the Drive towards Global Uniformity*, trans. by Rosemary Morris (Cambridge, UK: Polity Press, 1991 [1989]), 40–41.

62. Miyoshi, *Off Center*, 43.

63. Carter Dougherty, "China Wins Renewal of Its Trading Status," *Washington Times* (May 30, 2001), in *Washington Times Online* Archives for 2001, article ID U00573960119.

64. John B. Judis, "Top Down: Whatever Happened to Noblesse Oblige?" *New Republic Online* (March 27, 2000), <www.tnr.com/032700/Judis032700.html>.

65. Robert B. Reich, *The Work of Nations: Preparing Ourselves for 21st Century Capitalism* (New York: Alfred A. Knopf, 1991), 8.

66. Kobayashi, "Reading the Election Results," 32.

67. Paul Krugman, *The Return of Depression Economics* (New York: W. W. Norton, 1999), 83, 60.

68. Greg Mastel, "The Japanese Get Machiavellian," (February 3, 2000), <ic.voxcap.com/issues/issue343/item8096.asp>.

69. Smith, *Japan*, 315.

70. "Japan's Constitution: The Call to Arms," *Economist* 350, no. 8108 (February 27, 1999): 21–25, 21.

71. Quoted in Reinhard Drifte, "An Old Architecture for Peace? Reconfiguring Japan Among Unreconfigured Great Powers," *Pacific Review* 12, no. 3 (1999): 479–489, 481.

72. Buruma, *The Wages of Guilt*, 37; William H. Thornton, "Putting the (Second) Postmodern Question to Japan: Postmodern and Japan Ten Years Later," *Asian Profile* 28, no. 2 (April 2000): 117–124.

73. Christopher B. Johnstone, "Paradigms Lost: Japan's Asia Policy in a Time of Growing Chinese Power," *Contemporary Southeast Asia* 21, no. 3 (December 1999): 365–385, 372.

74. Buruma, *The Wages of Guilt*, 297; Yoichi Funabashi, *Alliance Adrift* (New York: Council on Foreign Relations Press, 1999); Reinhard Drifte, *Japan's Foreign Policy in the 1990s: From Economic Superpower to What Power?* (London: Macmillan, 1996), 156; Frank Ching, "A Tale of Former Allies," *Far Eastern Economic Review* 163, no. 9 (March 2, 2000): 35.

75. Drifte, *Japan's Foreign Policy in the 1990s*, 5.

76. Mastel, "The Japanese Get Machiavellian," 1.

77. Rosemary Foot, "Pacific Asia: The Development of Regional Dialogue," in Louise Fawcett and Andrew Hurrell, eds., *Regionalism in World Politics: Regional Organizations and International Order* (Oxford: Oxford University Press, 1995), 228–49, 245.

78. On Japan's erstwhile economism see Pekka Korhonen, *Japan and the Pacific Free Trade Area* (London: Routledge, 1994), 28–37.

79. Jeff Gerth and David E. Sanger, "Citing Security, U.S. Spurns China in Satellite Deal," *New York Times* International (February 23, 1999), <www.nytimes.com/library/world/asia/022399satellite-sale.html>; Aaron L. Friedberg, "Arming China Against Ourselves," *Commentary* 108, no. 1 (July–August 1999): 22–33, 30.

80. William H. Thornton, "Analyzing East/West Power Politics in Comparative Cultural Studies," *CLCWeb: Comparative Literature and Culture: A WWWeb Journal* (Purdue University Press) 2, no. 3 (September 2000), <www.clcwebjournal.lib.purdue.edu/clcweb00-3/thornton00.html>.

81. Thornton, "Back to Basics: Human Rights and Power Politics in the New Moral Realism," *International Journal of Politics, Culture and Society* 14, no. 2 (2000): 315–332.

82. Julian Weiss, "Asia: America's 'Lost Horizon'?" (January 27, 2000), <ic.voxcap.com/issues/issue341/item8017.asp>, 1.

83. Weiss, "Asia," 3.

84. Weiss, "Asia," 3.

85. Patrick Smith, "A New Asian Cooperation," (November 12, 1998), <ic.voxcap.com/issues/Issue164/item2158.asp>.

86. Robert Taylor, *Greater China and Japan: Prospects for an Economic Partnership in East Asia* (London: Routledge, 1996), 180.

87. "Can Japan Find Its Voice?" *Economist* (May 6, 2000), <www2.gol.com/users/coynerhm/can_japan_find_its_voice.htm>.

88. Korhonen, *Japan and the Pacific Free Trade Area*, 145–146.

89. Drifte, *Japan's Foreign Policy in the 1990s*, 142.

90. Poh Ping Lee, "ASEAN and the Japanese Role in Southeast Asia," in Alison Broinowski, ed., *ASEAN into the 1990s* (London: Macmillan, 1990), 162–183, 162.

91. Raymond Lamont-Brown, "The Closed World of Japan," *Contemporary Review* (October 1998), <www.britannica.com/bcom/magazine/article/0,5744,2656645,00.html>; "Japan Discovers Defense," *New York Times* Editorial (August 26, 1999), <www.nytimes.com/yr/mo/day/editorial/26thu1.html>.

92. Words from a 1995 speech by Murayama Tomiichi; see Todd Crowell and Murakami Mutsuko, "History's Unquiet Ghosts," *Asiaweek* (December 11, 1998), <www.pathfinder.com@@PNrwqwYAGpbbHkjT/asiaweek/98/1211/natl.html>.

93. Graeme Cheeseman, "Asian-Pacific Security Discourse in the Wake of the Asian Economic Crisis," *Pacific Review* 12, no. 3 (1999): 333–356, 334.

94. Krugman, *The Return of Depression Economics*, 114; Joseph Kahn, "I.M.F. Names Official," *New York Times* Business (June 8, 2001), <www.nytimes.com/2001/06/08/business/08FUND.html>.

95. Richard Rorty, *Achieving Our Country: Leftist Thought in Twentieth Century America* (Cambridge, Mass.: Harvard University Press, 1998), 9.

96. Carl Boggs, *The End of Politics: Corporate Power and the Decline of the Public Sphere* (New York: Guilford Press, 2000), 209.

Chapter 3

Reactionary Globalization: Local, Regional, and Global Implications of the New "Japan Problem"

POST–COLD WAR CHOICE

Japan's regional ascendancy, as discussed in the previous chapter, indicates a major shift in Asia's weighing of alternative evils: the distant threat posed by Japanese neonationalism versus the immediate threat of American neoliberalism. It is only the dark shadow of China's rising power that keeps America in the East Asian game and prevents Japan from realizing its earlier tripolar ambition of a rough global parity between three regional "super blocs": the United States, Germany, and Japan.[1]

What was ultimately at issue in Manila, and will be a key question for years to come, is the choice between two capitalist regimes: the Anglo-American or "neoliberal" system of independent, profit-maximizing corporations versus Asian state-administered corporatism.[2] These alternatives are often idealized as the shareholder and stakeholder models of capitalism, respectively. In the former, corporate directors owe their full allegiance to shareholders and bear little or no responsibility for "stakeholders" such as workers, communities, the environment, or even the nation. However, this pure "shareholder" model is hardly an uncontested American tradition. One of its principal advocates, Marina Whitman, admits that it departs from the "good corporation" ideal that prevailed through most of the Cold War. Once America's corporate managers could embrace a wide range of social objectives apart from the bottom line. But as managerial capitalism gave way to what Whitman dubs investor capitalism,[3] those broader objectives were

77

"downsized" along with much of the corporate workforce. It is ironic that a system that so recently subverted the less anomic elements of America's corporate ethos could be exported in the name of "Americanization"; yet this is a core element of the "Washington consensus" that aspires to dominant ideology status the world over. With reference to its softer ideological competitors—Europe's social democratic Second Way and Euro-globalist Third Way—this "lean and mean" corporatism offers a no frills, First Way approach to globalization. It could take the United States by storm because the social contract of American corporations was little more than a private, voluntary appendage.

This was not the case in Europe or Japan, where "stakeholders" have held publicly enforceable rights on a par with shareholders.[4] It is becoming clear, however, that the difference between the Second Way strategies of Europe and Japan is every bit as significant as their similarity. Japan's statist corporatism, part of a distinctly East Asian Second Way, has been strong on social equity but weak on the democratic element that has constrained European corporatism. Both internally and externally the defining feature of Japanese corporatism has been its cooperative centrality: While Japan's workers have constituted a veritable community within each firm, cooperation between firms has been legendary. Likewise, there is a visceral bond between Japan's corporate bureaucracy and the agencies that presumably regulate them.[5]

Prior to the 1990s this model was unquestionably on the rise. Even from 1976 to 1990, when Japanese economic growth fell to 4 percent per annum, after averaging 10 percent in the previous eighteen years, this was still higher than other major industrial countries.[6] Japan and the seven Asian countries that adapted this model in the "miracle years" grew at twice the speed of the rest of Asia, three times faster than Latin America, and twenty-five times faster than sub-Saharan Africa.[7] It is little wonder that developing nations in general have been drawn to a system that so dramatically couples dynamism with stability.[8]

One rarely noted source of this mix has been Japan's relative subordination of both full-fledged democracy and the financial interests that in most Western countries have stood opposed to full employment and hence to unconstrained economic activity. Prabhat Patnaik observes that during the Asian economic boom, countries as different as India and South Korea looked to Japan's example in this respect.[9] Robert Kaplan points out that many third world countries are faced with such massive environmental strain that incipient democratic processes will almost certainly give way to some form of autocracy. The choice is likely to be between what Homer-Dixon calls the "hard regimes" of Muslim extremists and the softer authoritarianism of a Lee

Kuan Yew. Relatively speaking, Lee's Singaporean model could almost pass for progressive,[10] and the Japanese model even more so.

A vital key to East Asian stability, long neglected by Western scholars who accepted Japanese democracy at face value, has been Japan's achievement of relative social equity without the inconvenience of social democracy. Nevertheless, Japan can be justly proud of its equity model, or "Eastern strategy," as Amartya Sen calls this Asian Second Way.[11] In response to the World Bank's 1991 development report, which enshrined neoliberalism as a global imperative, Japan's Overseas Economic Cooperation Fund presented a white paper that politely noted the contrary experience of the "Asian tigers." Their success, it was held, proved the importance of balancing economic efficiency with fairness. The World Bank nominally granted the point in its 1993 book, *The East Asian Miracle*; but of course its actual policies continued on the same neoliberal track that was taken without apology by the IMF.[12] Both institutions applied this policy with a vengeance after the 1997 Crash, thus setting the stage for the ideological rebound of a new East Asian exceptionalism.

Unlike the Islamic resistance that challenges Western globalism from without,[13] the Japanese system threatens it from within. It thus poses the most formidable *capitalist* challenge to the neoliberal world order. While German social democracy has fallen victim to neoliberal globalism under a Third Way cover, Japan has won respect from Asians for refusing to subordinate its own vested interests. It elevated the role of the state at a time when, according to globalization theory, the opposite should have been happening.[14]

Neoliberals were wrong to assume that the Crash of 1997 spelled the end not only of crony capitalism but of East Asian exceptionalism. In both politics and economics, Japan offers an ideological alternative for postrecession Asia. "Revisionists" hold that the Japanese model, far from being the bridge to the West that "Chrysanthemum Club" Japanology imagined, laid the foundation for an exceptionalism that sacrificed political reform on the altar of economic growth. Some Asian reformists, such as Korea's Kim Dae Jung, were never comfortable with that reform hiatus;[15] but most accepted the democratic teleology that allowed for an indefinite developmental "lag" on the side of political reform.[16] Their gradualism was no threat to ruling political factions so long as economic goals remained on the far horizon. It was when those goals began to be met, and even surpassed, that the danger loomed large. The fall of communism compounded the problem and forced "exceptionalists" to raise the banner of "Asian values" against the West.

Western observers have assumed that Japan's long recession, punctuated by the general Asian Crash of 1997, would expunge those "values" and all other serious obstacles to the New World Order of neoliberalism. Instead, the crisis has brought Japan into the heart of a regional counter-Order that not only would entrench Asian values as an oppositional force, but would give them far wider applicability to the third world. Prior to the 1980s the Japanese model of development had been limited by Japan's very success. Even the top "Asian tigers" could not hope to match Japan's performance. But Japan's growth slowed while that of the "tigers" did not. Thus Asian exceptionalism widened its range in the 1980s.[17]

On this larger scale, however, the model was once again all too successful. It came to be viewed as unique to East Asia. The ironic consequence of Japan's economic woes of the 1990s, and the regional Crash of 1997, is that these "exceptions" have been cut down a notch, rendering them more accessible as a universal model of resistance to Washington-based neoliberalism. Now the whole developing world is watching the new Japan model, whose flipside for the West is the "new Japan problem."

JAPAN'S GLOBAL CROSSROADS

The Japanese themselves must confront that problem. In the 1980s the question was how Japan would deal with her immoderate success. Now the salient question is likely to concern stagnation, corruption, waste, and mismanagement (e.g., an antiquated port system that creates a hidden tax on the 98 percent of the country's trade that travels by sea).[18] Lurking behind both questions, that of exceptional growth and protracted recession, is a cultural constant: Japan's uneasy dealings with the outside world. Ian Buruma suggestively asks if Japan's attitude toward trade is not a close cousin of its prewar national myths.[19]

This recidivism works against the dream of a postgrowth cultural renaissance, which was the latest in a long line of utopian, "Japan-at-the-crossroads" visions. Karel van Wolferen reminds us that in the 1960s a cultural revolution was expected once Japan's younger generation gained positions of influence. Labor, likewise, was expected to demand structural change once it gained a political voice. In the 1970s it was again expected that those returning from abroad would relax bureaucratic control over business and the marketplace, thus opening the door for the "internationalization" of Japan's consumer economy and corporate style.[20]

Perhaps the most promising "great expectation" took shape in 1993, when the LDP lost majority control of the lower house of the Diet for the first time in thirty-eight years. The world watched what seemed to be a sweeping generational revolt in the making. *Newsweek* covered the story under the title "No Turning Back," but intimated that the news might be ominous for

Japan's trading partners, since the new generation of leaders might be less amenable to outside pressure.[21] Ichiro Ozawo, the most powerful politician in Prime Minister Morihiro Hosokawa's seven-party coalition, broke with Cold War tradition by avowing (albeit privately) his Japanese nationalism. In that context he called for lifting the military restrictions of Article 9 of the constitution.[22] Ominous as that may sound, many points of Ozawa's *Blueprint for a New Japan* (1994) are commensurate with Mayumi Itoh's concept of "inward" internationalism, as discussed in the previous chapter. Ozawa not only stands for individualism and pluralism, but suggests that corporate Japan never was the faithful representative of traditional values it claimed to be. Rather it produced, under the rubric of a "constitutional state," the largest official corruption in the world.

So too, Japan has promoted environmental rape both domestically and globally, even as it has represented itself to the world as the paragon of harmony with nature.[23] Under the cover of "chequebook diplomacy"—as Helen Clark (New Zealand's Labour prime minister) dubs it—Japan has provided foreign aid in exchange for acceptance of its atavistic whaling industry. The Solomon Islands have already yielded to such aid-for-whaling pressure, and Tonga could be next.[24] By extension, in terms of political purchase, Southeast Asia as a whole could be next. Japan's environmental policies thus provide a window on the darkest side of this nation's domestic/foreign affairs nexus. Here is a country that purports to be a model of sustainable development in Asia, yet does not hesitate to kill minke whales within the Southern Ocean whaling sanctuary, selling the meat as "bacon" and claiming the whole operation is for "scientific" purposes. There is black humor in former Prime Minister Ryutaro Hashimoto's assertion that Japan is taking a leading role in environmental cooperation through strategic research.[25] In July 2000, Japanese whaling ships flagrantly violated an International Whaling Commission ban on the killing of two endangered species—Bryde's and sperm whales—while foreign protesters were charged with "culinary imperialism."[26]

As the need arises, apologists for Japan's environmental record drop their harmony theme and invoke the clash between nature and culture. Conservation is then cast as a uniquely Western value, so any attempt to apply it to Japan becomes an imperialistic act. Clearly this dodge relates to more than environmental matters. Much as Greenpeace members are watching Japanese supermarkets and asking, "What's in the 'bacon'?," the developing world should be asking "What's in the new Japanese internationalism?" Or, apropos of this study, *which* Japan is in it?

On two fronts, the natural and the political, 1993 marked a crossroads for that question. While Ozawa's *Blueprint* mandated environmental leadership on a global scale, the cause of non-Tokyo culture was boosted by the new prime minister, Morihiro Hosokawa, whose 1993–94 cabinet put decentralization into the national agenda.[27] Hosokawa's "revolt from the periphery," based on a fragile coalition of seven small parties, lasted less than a year.[28] Nonetheless his reformism retained great popularity.[29] A Decentralization Law was passed by the Diet in 1995 under the Tomiichi Murayama cabinet, and the Ryutaro Hashimoto cabinet established a very active Committee for the Promotion of Decentralization.

These efforts, however, proved symbolic at best. Indeed, decentralization even got a cool reception from local authorities.[30] The reason is simple: Japan's rural "regions" have been on the take from the LDP system for decades. This is the supreme irony of the ruling party's so-called regionalism: By purchasing support from these districts, and giving itself the appearance of being the quintessential "rural party," the LDP was in fact buying complicity from the "regions" for what remained a centrist politics. Conversely, the victory of urban opposition candidates from centrist Tokyo in the June 2000 elections was a paradoxical victory for *de*centralization. To the extent that the regions are taken off the LDP dole, they are liberated from their own corruption and given, often against their own will, their own voice. The end of the economic "miracle" could similarly free the LDP from its own largesse, through which it has purchased support at the expense of reform.[31]

Needless to say, the LDP does not welcome this liberation and is anxious to forge a new social contract, at least as reactionary as the original, by distributing the spoils of a newly globalized economy. The LDP staged a comeback in the general elections of 1996. In September 1997 Hashimoto drew enough opposition legislators into the LDP to win an outright majority in the lower house;[32] but he was forced to resign when the LDP suffered a smashing defeat in the upper house in July 1998.[33] Although the defeat was widely seen as a repudiation of the LDP's economic policies,[34] Hashimoto was replaced in August 1998 not by a reformist but by an LDP stalwart, the late Keizo Obuchi. Vowing to "adopt a more flexible economy driven by the market,"[35] Obuchi looked to globalization for the party's long-term economic rehabilitation.

In the short term, however, his economic policy amounted to an all-too-familiar "prime the pump" impulse. Abandoning Hashimoto's broad-spectrum reforms, Obuchi focused on "recovery for recovery's sake." In practice this was a dream come true for pork-barrel politicians.[36] It was LDP business as usual, despite the fact that Obuchi had significantly reduced bureaucratic regulations of the economy in favor of political control.[37] Unfortunately that control was not exercised with any programmatic direction in mind, let alone a reformist direction.

It would soon become obvious that "deregulation" can be very much at odds with decentralization. Nor does the center require any identifiable focal point of responsibility. Countries attempting to negotiate with Japan have had to learn repeatedly "that there is no one to deal with on the other side."[38] This is especially true after the retirement of the one individual who could really pull the political strings of the system: Noboru Takeshita, whose last protégé was Obuchi.[39] Ironically, the Clinton administration's effort to prod Japan toward open market regulations had the reverse effect: prompting a retreat toward the MITI-style centrism of the 1960s.[40]

The legitimacy of Japanese centrism is founded on a national myth of homogeneity and hence uniqueness.[41] Peripheral elements are hereby defined out of existence. Centrist purism manifests itself in an amorphous ideology of *nihonjinron* identity, negatively defined as an absence of fundamental disagreement. Japan's governing elite may bicker over paltry matters, but "can be counted on to sustain present power arrangements."[42] This fact is not altered by the existence of ruling coalitions rather than straight LDP rule— the prevailing condition since the Hosokawa administration in 1993. Yoichi Masuzoe observes that the LDP itself functioned as a de facto coalition before 1993, given its many factions. Present coalitions carry on very much as the old LDP did.[43] If anything has changed it is the ruling party's financial capacity to co-opt opposition parties through under-the-table handouts—the major recipient being the old Japanese Socialist Party.[44]

Foreign trade partners are not the only losers in this consensus politics. Another big loser is Japan's own Other. This explains why two major groups—women and the rural population—are less prone than urban males to refer to themselves as "we Japanese."[45] Naturally the Other category includes all of Japan's trading partners. Each of these political nonentities— women, rural communities, and the outside world—stands to benefit from democratic reforms and a political apparatus that is visible and hence subject to revision. As of 1992, however, over 80 percent of Japanese public opinion considered such reform impossible.[46]

That of course was before the full brunt of the 1990s' recession had been felt. Previously the "invisible" nature of the Japanese power structure removed it from dialogic encounter with either its own voiceless minorities or the world community. Such an encounter becomes inevitable as pressure for change builds both within and without. To avert those pressures, Japan reaches out to Asia by exporting, in effect, its own domestic tactics. This did much to spark the Asian Crash, just as the IMF, according to Joseph Stigletz (former chief economist of the World Bank) and Hubert Neiss (former head of the IMF's Pacific Rim operations), did much to worsen the crisis once it began.[47]

A more detailed account of this domestic/foreign bond must start with the fall of Japan's "bubble economy" in the early 1990s. When Tokyo stock and real estate prices plummeted, domestic banks were left with an estimated U.S.$600 billion in loans. Most of this lending had been inspired by rising land values and "paper" returns, rather than real worth. When the decline set in, the government responded by cutting interest rates to further stimulate the economy. This led to more untimely lending, much of which flooded out to Asian neighbors. Currency swings then made repayment impossible.[48] Rather than crack down on derelict banks, in the manner of the U.S. reaction to its savings and loan crisis, the Japanese government undertook a U.S.$238 billion bank bailout, not even asking for full disclosure of the shady operations that had saddled Japanese taxpayers with this burden.

Finding Japan's stagnant economy unpromising, Japanese banks turned aggressively to Southeast Asia, where their lending leapt from U.S.$40 billion in 1994 to $265 billion. Ron Chernow reports how "American and European banks watched aghast as Japanese banks 'dumped' loans in the region. . . . By massively exporting capital to Southeast Asia, the Japanese banks recreated the bubble economy that had been punctured at home and that had sent them abroad in the first place."[49] Japanese banks and corporations fueled the pre-crisis boom via hot money and bad management; and after the Crash struck, they were unwilling to take write-downs on these Asian loans.[50]

This picture of Japan's new Asian strategy will come as no surprise to "revisionists" such as Buruma, van Wolferen, Katz, or Ivan P. Hall. It could, however, serve as a wake-up call for anyone whose idea of Japanese capitalism was set in stone by Chrysanthemum Club apologetics of the postwar era. Undeniably Japan is at a global crossroads—witness Ford Motor's 1996 purchase of Mazda. But the political contours of this globalization are far less clear. Sadaaki Numata, a spokesman for Japan's Ministry of Foreign Affairs, wrote in April 1998 that "the Japanese people are engaged in a democratic debate about how to put the economy back on track to sustained growth."[51] The problem is that there have been so many bad "crossings" in the past. Even if force of circumstance can make Japan alter its course where trade is concerned, that does not guarantee a social democratic outcome. Moreover, the full impact of economic globalization will not be felt so long as the U.S. economy is holding its own. A prolonged U.S. recession (as opposed to a mere stock market correction, as in the summer of 1998) would raise the stakes by removing America's tolerance for Japanese business and banking practices.

Many Japanese heed the warning of Sony's Norio Ohga that the economy is on thin ice. Ohga compares former Prime Minister Hashimoto to Herbert Hoover,[52] though it should be recalled that as late as February 1997 Hashimoto was labeled a free market globalist.[53] In a Japanese context that would make him a dynamic figure, more an F.D.R. than a do-nothing Hoover. The danger, from the perspective of this study, is that centrist voices such as Ohga's will be all too successful in their call for globalization—or, more specifically, in their leaning toward the kind of U.S.-Japan alliance that Zbigniew Brzezinski calls "Amerippon" and C. Fred Bergsten terms "bigemony."[54] This of course would require that part of the "Japan Inc." system be dismantled. The problem, as Kent Harrington notes, is that the people who will have that job are the very ones who assembled the system in the first place: the LDP, the national bureaucracy, and their corporate cronies.

The strength of this Iron Triangle is growing, even as the United States works to make Japan "more like us."[55] The present social foundation of "Japan Inc.," whereby lifelong security was promised (albeit to a much smaller percentage of workers than is popularly believed)[56] in return for corporate loyalty and obedience, is not likely to survive globalization. Foreign experts insist "that deregulation, labor flexibility, individual competition, and so on are the only ways to lift Japan out of its present troubles."[57]

The paradox is that just as Tokyo is extending its cultural aegis over the rest of Japan, its contract with its own salarymen and other corporate "stakeholders" is being nullified. And the situation is even more precarious for the middle and lower classes. They, too, were supposed to inherit a slice of the "Pacific century." Their present plight has brought only cheers from American globalists such as Ron Bevaqua, who is pleased to note that corporate restructuring has now reached "critical mass."[58]

Such neoliberals give scarcely a thought to the human factor in massive layoffs like those at Nissan and NTT, which in October 1999 disposed of 21,000 and 20,000 workers respectively.[59] Protest marches erupted in January 2000 when it was announced that Nissan was planning to lay off another 14 percent of its workers.[60] Older workers, paid more because of seniority, are especially at risk.[61] Even those middle- and lower-level employees who escape layoffs are feeling the onus of regressive tax reform and income stratification.[62] Bill Powell points out that the term "financial crisis" hardly touches the anguish of those who slip through the new economic net. That term is best suited for young investors "who gauge the pain inflicted in terms of lower stock prices, revised earnings expectations and deflated bonuses,"[63] not the possibility of being homeless.[64]

The solution being held out to Asia in general is more and faster globalization. In Japan this translates as a new twist in the old sociopolitical trade-off. Before, political conformity was accepted in return for solid security and upward mobility. Now it is demanded in return for mere solvency. Instead of bright visions of WTO-style enterprise, many Japanese just hope to avoid Sanya—Tokyo's skid row.[65] Many who were pleased to describe themselves as "we Japanese" must revise their mental map of both Tokyo and the world. Their disorientation doubtless contributed to the defeat of the LDP in the July 1998 legislative elections, but could also provide a populist base for rabid neonationalism. At a time when Japan needs 600,000 immigrants a year to maintain its present workforce, 80 percent of the respondents in a recent national poll stood opposed to the entry of any more immigrants; and at a time when internationalization would seem to offer the only ticket out of Japan's chronic decline, foreigners in general are distrusted, and special disdain is reserved for fellow Asians.[66]

THE CENTER HOLDS

Under these straits, the LDP has had to reach out to at least one sector of the Japanese periphery: those small and medium-size enterprises (SMEs) that have survived despite their lack of *keiretsu* (corporate groups) connections. This reform was almost inevitable given the sagging global competitiveness of *keiretsu* business structures. Late in 1999 the Ministry of International Trade provided an unprecedented fiscal package for SMEs—the kind of "post-Fordist" enterprise that is associated with the high tech boom in the United States.[67] Unfortunately this package still requires mediation by banking institutions that strongly favor firms with prior *keiretsu* affiliation. The result is a "two-speed" economy[68] that depresses smaller enterprises while large manufacturers enjoy the best of two worlds: centrist politics combined with global connections. Meanwhile, Japan's banking industry moves toward more monolithic consolidations that offer the perfect apparatus for state capitalism rather than neoliberal globalization.[69]

As if to deflect attention from its real politics, the LDP has shrouded itself in the imagery of "old village" nostalgia.[70] For example, the five residents of a small island off southern Japan, Akashima, are getting a new pier at a cost of $2.5 million. The government also pays for the island's twice-daily ferry and its weekly medical clinic, along with its electric and telephone service via undersea electric cables—*two* cables, just to be sure there is no interruption in the service.[71] Such profligacy, as Ichiro Ozawa complains in *Blueprint*, amounts to virtual reality with a quasi-traditionalist twist. While "culture" is hereby reconstructed out of a centered, rearguard politics, other versions of Japan are ruthlessly deconstructed. Jennifer Robertson traces this process to the concentration of "information capitalism" in the cultural dominant that is Tokyo.[72]

Tokyo itself, however, suffers a similar bifurcation. Already by 1994 the city contained many thousands of unemployed outcasts.[73] By 2000 the official figure for Osaka was 10,000, but such statistics do not account for the armies of day laborers who habitually gather at worksites in the morning with little hope of being used, later to fan out in search of saleable cans and garbage.[74] Buruma draws upon Edward Fowler's recent study of "down and out" life in Tokyo (*San'ya Blues* [1998]) to sketch the symbiotic interplay of Tokyo's conformist mainstream with its derelict subcurrent. The Sanya "Other" serves as a warning as well as a source of cheap labor, prostitution, and social-psychological elastics.[75] It is this dark centrism, not the celebrated decentrism of Japanese postmodernism,[76] that assumes the role of chief architect in Japan's cultural reformation.

As we have seen, Japan's domestic economy has not heretofore conformed very well to its popular, centrist image. It has been comprised of two industrial systems, with only a small fraction of Japanese businesses fitting neatly into the "Japan Inc." category. Smith notes that much manufacturing has taken place through a relatively decentralized satellite system, and 80 percent of retail sales have been through small-scale stores and shops.[77] Presently these businesses are falling into the Tokyo net, victims of a new economic Darwinism.

Unlike South Korea, where industrial and financial *chaebol* were structurally damaged by the Crash, most of Japan's corporate giants went relatively unscathed. Exports and infrastructure projects have flourished despite the financial crisis.[78] This good fortune does not extend to smaller companies, which are being crushed by the influx of cheap imports and the eclipse of old webs of local loyalties. In sum, the central/periphery balance is once more tipping toward Tokyo; and—despite setbacks like the July 1998 elections—it is likely that the political balance will shift in the same direction.[79]

The lasting impact of the recession on Japanese political culture remains to be seen. There is always the hope that it could foment real change; but such hopes have come and gone before. New Age culturalists of the 1980s looked forward to the long-awaited "overcoming of the modern" through a "postgrowth" flowering of culture. Since the "modern" had long meant the West, this "overcoming" was generally seen as a return to what is distinctly Japanese. Its inaugural event, H. D. Harootunian notes, was the 1980 publication by the Masayoshi Ohira government of a plan to move beyond the "age of economy" to one of "spirit."[80] This was to be a "comprehensive Japanese culture,"[81] marking Japan's exceptionalism by "no longer making the modern its goal."[82]

Here modernization was assumed to be the cultural adjunct of GNPism. The modern would be overcome, as materialism is overcome in Maslow's hierarchy, when economic success is sufficient to support a "cultural" or even "spiritual" stage of development. It should be noted that, in functional terms, this "new" ethos bears a suspicious resemblance to the standard Japanese development strategy, whereby consumption is discouraged in favor of maximum savings and investment. Inevitably, as consumption lags behind production, deflationary pressure mounts.[83]

This recessionary tendency was offset in the 1980s by quite a different revolution inside Japan: not toward New Age spirituality, but rather conspicuous consumption.[84] Arthur Koestler once noted that Japanese behavior is divided into extreme social discipline, on the one hand, and unabashed license on the other.[85] Consumerism of the 1980s tipped the scale toward hedonism. It offered, moreover, an easy target for blame when the economic bubble finally burst. Bureaucrats and the media were quick to read the crisis as a moral lesson in support of a managed, high-savings society.[86] When it became obvious that "morality" alone could not get Japan out of its slump, the government turned increasingly to Keynesian policies—deficit spending coupled with income tax reductions—to boost the private sector.[87]

In a literal attempt to "pave the way" for recovery—with new roads, bridges, tunnels, subways, airports, and a few undisguised frills such as concert halls—public assistance was lavished on failing construction companies as opposed to new businesses or assistance for the newly unemployed.[88] This trend was punctuated in June 2000 by the arrest of former Construction Minister Eiichi Nakao on charges of taking U.S.$284,000 in bribes for public works contracts.[89] In compliance with U.S. pressure to stimulate growth at all costs, more than $1 trillion was pumped into the economy between 1992 and 1999, raising public debt to about $5.4 trillion while leaving growth expectations at little more than 1 percent and unemployment at record levels.[90]

Though deficit spending and "roads to nowhere" briefly lifted hopes in the first half of 1999, the economy remained in the grip of recession. Shock set in after a senior official announced, early in 2000, that the economy had been shrinking for the past two quarters.[91] Contrary reports from the Economic Planning Agency (EPA) and the Bank of Japan held that there had been modest improvement over those months, but these claims were belied by falling consumer spending, down 4 percent in December 1999 from the previous year.[92] Even as the Obuchi cabinet approved a budget hike of $165 billion, statistics released in March 2000 indicated a slide back into recession. With a budget approaching a record $8 trillion,[93] the year 2000 closed with jobless rates up and a further decline in consumer spending.[94] This time, moreover, it seemed there would be no safety net. Massive consumer demand had enabled the United States to rescue Asia from its 1997 Crash,[95] but now America itself was on the brink of recession.

Japan's classic "debt trap" is all the more perilous in combination with its aging workforce. With the lowest birthrate of any developed country, and one of the highest rates of longevity,[96] Japan's working population is already dropping at .6 percent per year.[97] This is the demographic foundation for what one economist calls the "dominant gerontocracy," a voting block that for the past decade, in a kind of "inter-generational theft,"[98] has borrowed against future growth to pay for present benefits. Owing largely to renewed regional growth and heavy U.S. demand, spring 1999 saw some long-awaited signs of recovery and a stock market rebound. When these did not last, voters finally registered their discontent.

The most conspicuous result was the election of the unrelenting outsider, Shitaro Ishihara ("Mr. No," as discussed before), in the 1999 Tokyo gubernatorial race.[99] His aim reached far beyond Tokyo and even the nation's boundaries. Domestically he called for tax and environmental reforms, while regionally he targeted the United States in a new book (*Let's Stop America Worship*) and infuriated China by inviting the Dalai Lama to visit his office. His idea of taxing the operating incomes of banks (as opposed to net incomes, which can be reduced through bad-loan write-offs) is catching on with other municipalities and even with the central government; but his most striking influence is seen in the rising popularity of his remilitarization plans,[100] which should be considered in the light of Japan's growing regional status.

EXPORTING THE SYSTEM

In terms of Mayumi Itoh's "inward" and "outward" *kokusaika* (internationalism), Ishihara's foreign policy represents a little of each. If it is "inward" on its pan-Asian side, it is "outward" on the side of its "just say no" reflex. That "no," however, is aimed as much at China as the United States.[101] America's foremost concern must be a Japan that says "no" to the United States while courting a Sino-Japanese pact.[102] As Japan goes, so goes the Asian balance of power, for Japan's military budget is the second largest in the world.[103] Since Japanese public opinion is increasingly wary of China,[104] while the corporate lobby (there as in the United States) is staunchly pro-China, the issue becomes a litmus test for democratic effectivity vis-à-vis the new forces of globalization.

A more immediate concern for America, however, is the prospect of a Japan-led regionalism such as Ishihara's—beginning with the call for base closings throughout Japan and especially in Okinawa.[105] Made-in-the-U.S.A. IMFism paved the way for this reaction throughout East and Southeast Asia in the wake of the Crash. However unjustly, Japan gained prestige relative to the United States.[106] And there is no gainsaying the fact that the "Jurassic

IMF," as Walden Bello calls it, did a fine job of turning West Africa, Mexico, and finally East Asia into economies ripe for fire-sales.[107] As mentioned in the last chapter, this inspired a strident reaction at the November 1999 ASEAN summit, where discussion turned toward an eventual Asian "common market" to rival American and European trade blocs.

A more proximate goal, however, was some form of Asian Monetary Fund (AMF), as proposed by Japan and Malaysia at the peak of the Asian crisis. Here Japan could easily insinuate itself as the natural leader/lender for the region. The plan was to turn Japan's temporary U.S.$30 billion Miyazawa Fund (named after Japanese Finance Minister Kiichi Miyazawa) into a permanent yen-dominated lending institution. Needless to say, development projects supported by this fund would favor Japanese firms and promote the largely unreformed system of Japanese corporatism.[108]

Along with this external threat to the IMF system has come a slightly less subversive internal challenge: the prospect of a Japan-led IMF. Already a Japanese national, Yusuke Horiguchi, has taken over Hubert Neiss's former position as head of the IMF's Asia and Pacific Department; and a leading contender for the director post vacated by Michel Camdessus was Japan's former vice finance minister for international affairs Eisuke Sakakibara.[109] Some idea of Sakakibara's position is suggested by his vocal support for the "Asian values" animus of Malaysia's Mahathir Mohamad. The hidden agenda of this challenge is its defense of Japanese-style political inertia, a domestic and regional Second Way that could offer a global model for political nondevelopment.

From a Third Way perspective, the IMF and AMF systems are equally defective. The Third Way (in theory at least) recognizes the social basis of markets that Western neoliberalism "indifferently casts to the winds."[110] Its conservative components (e.g., its respect for family values that are sorely neglected by liberal social democracy)[111] correspond to some of the less regretful features of East Asian exceptionalism; but its democratic element would put it closer to the values of Amartya Sen or Korea's Kim Dae Jung than to the authoritarian wiles of either Malaysia's Mahathir or Singapore's Lee Kuan Yew.[112] In place of social democracy's Second Way (i.e., welfare statism), the Third Way seeks a more flexible "positive welfare."[113] As applied to Japan, this would offer an alternative to the bad choice between guaranteed employment-for-life and its zero-security antithesis, Sanya. So too, by promoting a broader distribution of economic goods and political rights, the Third Way can mediate between two Japans: a stentorian Tokyo and a voiceless Japanese Other. The former, Peter Hartcher notes (*The Ministry* [1998]), is centered in the Ministry of Finance, which in turn is a virtual appendage of the University of Tokyo.

Rather than relieving domestic pressures by exporting its current system, Japan needs to come to terms with its own internal crisis. It led the way toward the "Asian miracle" by matching economic dynamism with social equity. It failed, however, by not matching socioeconomic achievement with political development. The first test of its present leadership will be the political voice it offers or denies its own peripheral elements.

One such voice is that of Yasuo Tanaka, the author-turned-governor of Nagano Prefecture. Here and in other prefectures such as Kochi and Tochigi, independent governors are rejecting the public works proffered by the central government, which always come with hidden costs and political strings attached. Nagano City, for example, was supposed to have enormously benefited from the U.S.$1 billion spent there in support of the 1998 Winter Olympics. Instead, the upkeep on redundant facilities costs the local government many millions per year, while a high-speed train line not only operates at a loss, but cuts into the business of local hotels and restaurants by enabling visitors to hop in and out without staying overnight. When Tanaka's grassroots supporters tried to investigate Nagano's $14 billion debt, they found the records had been mysteriously burned. Tanaka's response is not a blanket denunciation of all public works, but rather a redefinition of public works to include public-spirited projects: schools and facilities for the handicapped rather than bridges and dams that better serve construction interests than the community or the environment.[114]

That same public spirit could carry the new Japan model past the politics of East Asian exceptionalism. To offer an alternative to the ways and means of Camdessus-style modernization, Japan must acknowledge the democratic rights and privileges of the Other within itself. In addition to its intrinsic value, this could have a catalytic effect on Japan's economy, since social insecurity contributes to a chronic deflationary malaise. Substantive democracy could foster the kind of security that promotes consumer demand.

Like Sen's democratically empowered development model, this new Japan model stands opposed to First Way globalization. Both would temper market forces with varying degrees of social equity. Sen's model, however, is arguably "more Asian" in that it synthesizes the best of two Asian systems: the inveterate democratic ideals of Sen's native India and the distributive virtues that helped launch East Asia's "miracle" economies. To this amalgam Sen would add the crucial ingredient of economic security.[115] It may seem that he borrows this concern from European welfare capitalism, but in fact the most dramatic working example of this principle is found not in Europe but in the Indian state of Kerala. Here progressive politics has secured a decent standard of living, a rare ethnic accord, and an impressive degree of participatory democracy. It has done all this despite the fact that Kerala is poor even by Indian standards.[116]

Sen is not endorsing Gandhian economics or the Second Way inertia of European labor politics. Rather he suggests a way of avoiding the worst defects of both Western and East Asian capitalism. By emphasizing human development, he adumbrates a distinctly Asian Third Way, close to what Stephan Haggard sees as Asia's post-Crash "middle way": a growth model "that builds on the strengths of East Asia's past growth strategy while addressing the new requirements of those vulnerable to external shocks."[117]

It is unfortunate that this model, so good in theory, is unlikely to have much impact on developmental policy in the near future. Once East and Southeast Asia are out of their economic doldrums, they will probably revert to old habits. That is the bad news. The good news is that they will surely mount resistance to the Anglo-American package of "reforms" they have been forced to swallow as a condition of IMF assistance. This drift was already apparent in Kim Dae Jung's October 1998 visit to Tokyo. As Patrick Smith observes:

> Kim listened attentively to the ritual apologies for Japan's wartime behavior—as visiting Koreans must. . . . But . . . Kim was ready with a startling agenda. He began by calling for a new epoch in relations between Korea and Japan and ended by proposing a seven-nation security dialogue. The latter proposition is especially striking, given that Koreans have long mistrusted any notion of Japan in a regional security role.[118]

Not surprisingly the region is looking toward Tokyo rather than Kerala for a post-Americana agenda. The fate of all Asian Others rests in some measure on the politics of Japan's own Others. Just as Krugman warned against ignoring the economic plight of Japan in the 1990s, close attention needs to be given to the regional and global implications of Japan's domestic politics. At all three levels Japan is at a crossroads. The ruling coalition (the LDP plus the New Komeito and New Conservative Parties) barely held its own in the June 2000 election for the crucial lower house of the Diet,[119] as even rural areas turned against the LDP.[120] Every statement of the gaffe-prone Yoshiro Mori seemed to reduce LDP support,[121] with the prime minister's personal approval rating dropping to 16 percent.[122] What saved the coalition, Paul Krugman conjectures, was the fact that the opposition seemed to have an even weaker grasp of what to do if elected.[123] By opting for the devil it knew, Japan once again voted for business as usual.[124] In December Mori defeated a no-confidence vote when the reform faction of his party, lead by Koichi Kato, itself split. To many Japanese this signaled the last hope for structural reform from within the LDP system. Old-style politics had weathered the storm.[125]

The present question is where Junichiro Koizumi stands on reform. Clearly his economic views are neoliberal, yet his ties to the Japanese Right are no secret. Among other things, he wants to make the emperor the actual head of state (*genshu*), as opposed to a mere symbol (*shocho*), as has been the case since 1946. He supports new textbooks celebrating Japan's imperial past. And, to the horror of Asian neighbors, he paid an official visit to a shrine honoring Japan's World War II dead, including fourteen Class A war criminals who were executed during the occupation. Twenty demonstrators in Seoul chopped off the tips of their little fingers in protest.[126]

This is all in the spirit of Koizumi's notion of "reform." Heretofore the LDP has been politically static, but that very inertia has applied a brake to reactionary agendas of the domestic and globalist Right. The two have so far been at odds, but the possibility of a rapprochement via a "reformed" LDP darkens the domestic and geopolitical horizon. If that is what Koizumi's reform comes to, Mori could begin to look good in retrospect.

CONCLUSION:
A REGIONAL IMPERATIVE

Early in the Cold War the LDP forged a social contract with the Japanese public whereby the radical thrust of democracy was forfeited in return for economic development and security. Japan's phenomenal growth legitimized that trade-off and the centrist politics it supported. After the Cold War, when this arrangement finally faltered, the LDP lost much of its political base and decentralization emerged as the defining issue of the 1990s.

It would be hard to dispute Roger Buckley's conclusion that "the experiences of the 1990s are a warning to Japan that economism has its high price and that complementary values need to be considered."[127] That is simply to say that the Japanese Other needs more consideration. Unfortunately the LDP establishment is turning in quite the opposite direction: toward the new economic prop of globalization, the bargaining chip for a new social contract. Globalists equate deregulation with decentralization, but the center more than holds in this new globalist politics. Globalization provides the financial underpinning for an unfortunate trade-off: a strong dose of globalist "reform" in return for a renewed LDP power base (i.e., neoliberalism in return for neocentrism).

Since this globalized politics is being instituted at the same time Japan is establishing itself geopolitically, the connection between the two developments requires examination. Such a question hardly arises in the orthodox discourse of globalization, where it is assumed "that as the integration of the world economy advances, national governments are becoming less relevant."[128] Just as globalism holds itself aloof from issues of distributive justice (on the utopian ground that the free market will amply distribute benefits for all), so too it ignores the volatile subcurrents of Asian power politics (on the historically dubious ground—famously propounded by Thomas Friedman's "golden arches" fable—that globalist "free trade" precludes war). This well-funded flight from reality, by discouraging the kind of geopolitical thought that would foster a stable balance of powers, increases the likelihood of war and forces Japan to reconsider its security needs.

Two events reported on January 14, 2001, in the *New York Times* confirm that the Cold War alliance between Japan and the United States is anything but obsolete. Just as China and Russia were announcing their new "strategic partnership," the leader of China's Parliament Li Peng was in New Delhi urging India to take its recently warmed relationship with China to "new heights."[129] Only a few months before, Prime Minister Mori was himself in India seeking closer security relations, while India for its part was extending its reach in the South China Sea through joint naval exercises with Japan and Vietnam—developments the Chinese were watching closely.[130]

The celebrated summit between the two Koreas in June 2000 activated Japan's latent anxiety concerning China. North Korea had long provided Japan with diplomatic cover for its security arrangement with the United States, which now includes a possible missile-defense system. Real peace on the Korean peninsula would remove that cover at a time when China is exercising its regional clout as never before. On seventeen occasions in the first half of 2000 Chinese ships defied Japan's 200-mile exclusion zone. In September Japan's foreign minister Yohei Kono personally delivered a complaint to Beijing. Meanwhile the LDP threatened to delay a U.S.$161 million soft loan to China,[131] and in December the Japanese government approved a $223 billion weapons buildup over the next five years, including $90 billion for refueling aircraft that will greatly enhance Japan's offensive striking capabilities. China immediately protested, to no avail.

While the opposition Democratic Party was calling for the removal of constitutional restraints on Japan's regional peacekeeping service, Mori was joined by the Buddhist-backed New Komeito Party, his coalition partner, in a push for better regional security. Although most New Komeito members resist Koizumi's call for constitutional remilitarization, the tide is clearly running against the geopolitical apathy of previous decades. As a representative of Japan's defense academy explained it, China's nuclear missile program had never really gripped the imagination of the Japanese public until "one real missile" fired from North Korea woke them from their slumber.[132]

Obviously Japanese globalization will not follow the "golden arches" formula. Koizumi offers a bridge between globalism and realism—a union that the Japanese may be better prepared to grasp than most Americans. The Japanese have long tied their national security to economic policy, thus avoiding the American "traders versus warriors" syndrome.[133] So far, on the American side, globalism and realism have not been on such good speaking terms. Japan is ahead in that regard, but faces an equally serious geopolitical impediment: the stigma of its past aggressions, military and otherwise. The development model of prewar Japan was as politically defective as it was economically and technologically robust. That imbalance helped take Japan into war,[134] and was not rectified under U.S. auspices after the war. It has lived on under the cover of pure economism and must be redressed if the new Japan model is to serve the cause of Asian democratization. Emphatically, WTO-style globalization is not a solution to this problem.

If Japan is to globalize *and* achieve security, it must radically revise the standard discourse of globalization. A whiff of revisionist dissent could be detected at a June 2000 New York symposium on Japanese globalization. Although its program was billed as a debate between "two contrasting evaluations of globalization," that was false advertising. One glance at the panel choices reveals how the deck was solidly stacked in favor of business-as-usual globalism: Roland Robertson and Emmanuel Todd headed the list of invited apologists for unreformed globalization. Nonetheless, a trace of resistance crept in from the Japanese side, starting with the keynote address by Hayao Kawai, director general of the International Research Center for Japanese Studies in Kyoto. Stressing the need for "empathetic understanding" between cultures, Kawai added a caveat (as radical as this globalist venue would permit) concerning the fact that money is becoming the global arbiter of human values. He closed, moreover, with a call for the preservation of nature, of all things.[135]

Clearly Kawai doubts that "free market" globalization is in Japan's best interest. This chapter has argued, furthermore, that a "globalized" Japan would be highly injurious to the whole Pacific Rim. This would not be the case with Mayumi Itoh's "inward" internationalization, as previously discussed. Indeed, in balance-of-power terms, that alternative is becoming a regional imperative. The question is whether Japan can finally liberate the progressive wing of its own political culture. Otherwise the reactionary modernization[136] of the old Japan model will give way to an even more virulent reactionary globalization.

NOTES

1. On that ambition see Christopher B. Johnstone, "Paradigms Lost: Japan's Asia Policy in a Time of Growing Chinese Power," *Contemporary Southeast Asia* 21, no. 3 (December 1999): 365–385, 366.

2. William Greider, *One World, Ready or Not: The Manic Logic of Global Capitalism* (New York: Touchstone, 1997), 187.

3. Marina V. N. Whitman, *The World, New Rules: The Changing Role of the American Corporation* (Cambridge, Mass.: Harvard Business School Press, 1999), chap. 1.

4. Charles Derber, *Corporation Nation: How Corporations Are Taking Over Our Lives and What We Can Do About It* (New York: St. Martin's Press, 1998), 250–51; David C. Korten, *The Post-Corporate World: Life After Capitalism* (West Hartford, Conn.: Kumarian Press, 1999), 170.

5. Aurelia George Mulgan, "Japan: A Setting Sun?" *Foreign Affairs* 79, no. 4 (July–August 2000): 40–52, 49.

6. Yoshio Suzuki, "The Japanese Economy at a Historical Crossroads," in Craig Freedman, ed., *Japanese Economic Policy Reconsidered* (Cheltenham, UK: Edward Elgar, 1998), 17–27, 17.

7. Greider, *One World, Ready or Not*, 276–277.

8. Greider, *One World, Ready or Not*, 278.

9. Prabhat Patnaik, "Capitalism in Asia at the End of the Millennium," *Monthly Review* 51, no. 3 (July–August 1999): 53–70, 55; also at <www.monthlyreview.org/799pat.htm>.

10. Robert D. Kaplan, *The Ends of the Earth: A Journey to the Frontiers of Anarchy* (New York: Vintage Books, 1996), 126.

11. Amartya Sen, *Development as Freedom* (New York: Alfred A. Knopf, 1999), 82.

12. Greider, *One World, Ready or Not*, 278; Johnstone, "Paradigms Lost," 371.

13. Bryan S. Turner, *Orientalism, Postmodernism and Globalism* (London: Routledge, 1994), 12.

14. George Friedman, "Japan Moves Closer to State Capitalism," *Asian Wall Street Journal* Editorial (September 9, 1999): 10.

15. William H. Thornton, "Korea and East Asian Exceptionalism," *Theory, Culture and Society: Explorations in Critical Social Science* 15, no. 2 (May 1998): 137–154; and for other salient examples see David Kelly and Anthony Reid, eds., *Asian Freedoms: The Idea of Freedom in East and Southeast Asia* (Cambridge, UK: Cambridge University Press, 1998).

16. William H. Thornton, "Selling Democratic Teleology: The Case of the Chinese Fortune-Tellers," *International Politics* 37, no. 3 (September 2000): 285–300.

17. Takatoshi Ito, "Japanese Economic Development: Idiosyncratic or Universal?" in Justin Yifu Lin, ed., *Contemporary Economic Issues: Proceedings of the Eleventh World Congress of the International Economic Association, Tunis* (London: Macmillan; New York: St. Martin's Press, 1998), 18–37, 18.

18. Gavan McCormack, *The Emptiness of Japanese Affluence* (New York: M. E. Sharpe, 1996), 11; Alan Larson and Clyde J. Hart, "Japan's Ports Keelhaul the Economy," *Asian Wall Street Journal* (October 18, 1999): 10.

19. Ian Buruma, "What Keeps the Japanese Going?" *New York Review of Books* 35 (March 17, 1988): 39–43, 39.

20. Karel van Wolferen, *The Enigma of Japanese Power: People and Politics in a Stateless Nation* (New York: Vintage Books, 1990), 151.

21. Bill Powell, "No Turning Back," *Newsweek* Asian edition (August 2, 1993): 10–14, 13.

22. Peter McKillop, "A Nation Tired of Bowing," *Newsweek* Asian edition (November 15, 1993): 20–23, 20.

23. Patrick Smith, *Japan: A Reinterpretation* (New York: Pantheon Books, 1997), 183.

24. Colin James, "Green Queen," *Far Eastern Economic Review* 163, no. 5 (February 3, 2000): 24.

25. Kazuo Matsushita, "Environment and Development in Asia," *Japan Echo* 27, no. 3 (June 2000): 14–18, 18.

26. Calvin Sims, "Japan, Feasting on Whale, Sniffs at 'Culinary Imperialism' of U.S." *New York Times* International (August 10, 2000), <www.nytimes.com/library/national/science/081000sci-animal-whale.html>.

27. Gilbert Rozman, "Backdoor Japan: The Search for a Way Out via Regionalism and Decentralization," *Journal of Japanese Studies* 25, no. 1 (Winter 1999): 3–31, 5.

28. Smith, *Japan: A Reinterpretation*, 185–186, 321.

29. James Fallows, "Hosokawa's Prophecy," National Public Radio broadcast of April 8, 1996, published in *Atlantic Unbound* (January 20, 2001), <www.theatlantic.com//unbound/jf-npr/jr604-08.htm>.

30. Rozman, "Backdoor Japan," 5.

31. Ikuo Kabashima, "The LDP's 'Kingdom of the Regions' and the Revolt of the Cities," *Japan Echo* 27, no. 5 (October 2000): 22–28.

32. Yoichi Masuzoe, "The Obuchi Administration," *Japan Echo* 27, no. 2 (April 2000): 24–28.

33. Takeshi Sasaki, "Assessing the Obuchi Administration," *Japan Echo* 27, no. 4 (August 2000): 21–25, 21.

34. Fumitoshi Takahashi, "Manipulations Behind the Consumption Tax Increase? The Ministry of Finance Prolongs Japan's Recession," *Journal of Japanese Studies* 25, no. 1 (Winter 1999): 91–106, 96.

35. Keizo Obuchi, "Japan's Quiet Reforms," *New York Times* Op-Ed (April 29, 1999), <www.nytimes.com/yr/mo/day/oped/29obuc.html>.

36. Sasaki, "Assessing the Obuchi Administration," 24.

37. Sasaki, "Assessing the Obuchi Administration," 25.

38. Van Wolferen, *The Enigma of Japanese Power*, 413.

39. "Japan's New Politics," *Economist* (May 6, 2000), <www.britannica.com/bcom/magazine/article/0,5744,359194,00.html?query=japa n>.

40. Michael Green, "Who Lost Japan Studies?" *SAIS Review* 13, no. 2 (Summer–Fall 1993): 87–93, 91.

41. Van Wolferen, *The Enigma of Japanese Power*, 267.

42. Van Wolferen, *The Enigma of Japanese Power*, 269.

43. Masuzoe, "The Obuchi Administration," 28.

44. "Japan's New Politics."

45. Van Wolferen, *The Enigma of Japanese Power*, 270.

46. François Godement, *The New Asian Renaissance: From Colonialism to Post-Cold War*, trans. by Elisabeth J. Parcel (London: Routledge, 1997), 175.

47. On Stigletz see Michael Hirsch, "Stigletz Resigns," (November 24, 1999), <newsweek.com/nw-srv/tnw/today/ps/pslps01we_1.htm>; and on Neiss see Teofilo C. Daquila, "Japan-Asia Economic Relations: Trade, Investment, and the Economic Crisis," *East Asia* 17, no. 3 (Autumn 1999): 88–115, 105.

48. "Dangerous Inertia in Japan," *New York Times* Editorial (March 29, 1998).

49. Ron Chernow, "Grim Reckoning in Japan—and Beyond," *New York Times* Op-Ed editorial (November 17, 1997).

50. G. Pierre Goad, "Post-Crash and Burn—What's Next?" *Far Eastern Economic Review* 163, no. 4 (January 27, 2000): 64–65, 65.

51. Sadaaki Numata, "Japan Can Solve Its Economic Crisis," *New York Times* Letters-to-the-editor section (April 24, 1998).

52. Michael Elliot, "A Delicate Imbalance," *Newsweek* Asian edition (April 13, 1998): 4.

53. Paul A. Gigot, "The Great Japan Debate Is Over. Guess Who Won?" *Asian Wall Street Journal* (February 4, 1997): 10.

54. Zbigniew Brzezinski, *Out of Control: Global Turmoil on the Eve of the Twenty-First Century* (New York: Touchstone, 1993), 129; on Bergsten see Richard Cronin, *Japan, the United States, and Pacific Prospects for the Asia-Pacific Century: Three Scenarios for the Future* (New York: St. Martin's Press, 1992), 107.

55. Kent Harrington, "Japan Has Lots of Woes—and Lots of Money to Solve Them," *Washington Post* (Sunday, November 30, 1997): C01.

56. Chalmers Johnson, *MITI and the Japanese Miracle: The Growth of Industrial Policy, 1925–75* (Stanford, Calif.: Stanford University Press, 1982), 12.

57. Ian Buruma, "Down and Out in East Tokyo," *New York Review of Books* 45, no. 11 (June 25, 1998): 9–12, 10.

58. Ron Bevaqua, "The Lingering Death of Japan, Inc." *Asian Wall Street Journal* (October 22–23, 1999): 10.

59. Bevaqua, "Lingering Death of Japan, Inc.," 10.

60. CNN "Biz Asia" report, aired in Taiwan at 7:15 P.M., January 25, 2000.

61. "Sunset for the Men in Suits," *Economist* (July 1, 2000), <www2.gol.com/users/coynerhm/sunset_for_the_men_in_suits.htm>.

62. Stephanie Strom, "Japan Slowly Embraces Greater Income Inequality over Social Harmony," *New York Times* International (January 4, 2000), <www.nytimes.com/library/world/asia/010400japan-econ.html>.

63. Bill Powell, "The Great Betrayal," *Newsweek* Asian edition (August 3, 1998): 11–12, 11.

64. Stephanie Strom, "Tradition of Equality Is Fading in New Japan," *New York Times* International (January 4, 2000), <www.nytimes.com/library/world/asia/010400japan-econ.html>.

65. Buruma, "Down and Out in East Tokyo," 10.

66. Howard W. French, "Still Wary of Outsiders, Japan Expects Immigration Boom," *New York Times* International (March 14, 1999), <www.nytimes.com/library/world/asia/031400japan-immigration.html>.

67. John Tomaney, "A New Paradigm of Work Organization and Technology," in Ash Amin, ed., *Post-Fordism: A Reader* (Oxford, UK: Blackwell, 1994), 157–194.

68. "Japan's Newly Re-Elected Prime Minister Appoints New Cabinet," Reuters report in *New York Times* Late News (July 4, 2000), <www.nytimes.com/yr/mo/day/late/04japan-politics.html>.

69. Friedman, "Japan Moves Closer to State Capitalism," 10.

70. Jennifer Robertson, "Empire of Nostalgia: Rethinking 'Internationalization' in Japan Today," *Theory, Culture and Society* 14, no. 4 (November 1997): 97–122, 103.

71. Nicholas D. Kristof, "Empty Isles Are Signs Japan's Sun Might Dim," *New York Times* International (August 1, 1999), <www.nytimes.com/library/world/asia/080199japan-decline.html>.

72. Robertson, "Empire of Nostalgia," 99.

73. Edward W. Desmond, "Down-and-out in Tokyo," *Time* Asian edition (September 5, 1994), 41.

74. Howard W. French, "Japan's Struggles in Dealing with Its Homeless," *New York Times* World (February 2, 2001), <www.nytimes.com/2001/02/02/world/02JAPA.html>.

75. Buruma, "Down and Out in East Tokyo," 10.

76. Masao Miyoshi and H. D. Harootunian, eds., *Postmodernism and Japan* (Durham, N.C.: Duke University Press, 1989); William H. Thornton, "Putting the (Second) Postmodern Question to Japan: Postmodern and Japan Ten Years Later," *Asian Profile* 28, no. 2 (April, 2000): 117–124.

77. Smith, *Japan: A Reinterpretation*, 119.

78. Harrington, "Japan Has Lots of Woes," C01.

79. Nicholas D. Kristof, "Shops Closing, Japan Still Asks 'What Crisis?'" *New York Times* Editorial (April 21, 1998).

80. H. D. Harootunian, "Visible Discourses/Invisible Ideologies," in Masao Miyoshi and H. D. Harootunian, eds., *Postmodernism and Japan* (Durham, N.C.: Duke University Press, 1989), 63–92, 78–79.

81. Harootunian, "Visible Discourses/Invisible Ideologies," 80.

82. Harootunian, "Visible Discourses/Invisible Ideologies," 81.

83. Clyde Prestowitz, "Retooling Japan Is the Only Way to Rescue Asia Now," *Washington Post* (December 14, 1997): C01.

84. Sheldon Garon, *Molding Japanese Minds: The State in Everyday Life* (Princeton, N.J.: Princeton University Press, 1997): 231.

85. Ian Buruma, "Japan: In the Spirit World," *New York Review of Books* 43, no. 10 (June 6, 1996): 31–33, 31.

86. Garon, *Molding Japanese Minds*, 232.

87. Bevaqua, "The Lingering Death of Japan, Inc.," 10.

88. Stephanie Strom, "Economic Stimulus in Japan: Priming a Gold-Plated Pump," *New York Times* International (November 25, 1999), <www.nytimes.com/library/world/asia/112599japan-econ.html>.

89. "Japan's Newly Re-Elected Prime Minister Appoints New Cabinet."

90. Sheryl WuDunn and Nicholas D. Kristof, "Japan as No.1? In Debt, Maybe, at the Rate Things Have Been Going," *New York Times* International (September 1, 1999), <www.nytimes.com/library/world/asia/090100japan-debt.html>; "Building the New Japan," *Asian Wall Street Journal* (November 9, 1999): 14.

91. Paul Krugman, "The Japan Syndrome," *New York Times* Op-Ed (February 9, 2000), <www.nytimes.com/library/opinion/Krugman/020900krug.html>.

92. "Japan Says Economy Improves," from AP Breaking News, *New York Times* (February 14, 2000), <www.nytimes.com/aponline/f/AP-Japan-Economy.html>.

93. Stephanie Strom, "Japan Is Back in Recession, Statistics Show," *New York Times* Business Section (March 14, 2000), <www.nytimes.com/yr/mo/day/news/financial/japan-econ.html>.

94. Miki Tanikawa, "A Year to Forget for the Japanese Stock Market," *New York*

Times Business (December 27, 2000), <www.nytimes.com/2000/12/27business/
27NIKK.html>.

95. David E. Sanger, "Slowdown at Home Spells Risks Abroad for Bush," *New
York Times* Business (January 7, 2000), <www.nytimes.com/2001/01/07/business/
07CONT.html>.

96. Tanikawa, "A Year to Forget for the Japanese Stock Market."

97. David Asher, "Japan's Debt Trap," *Asian Wall Street Journal* (September 7,
1999): 8.

98. Simon Ogus, "Consuming Interest," *Far Eastern Economic Review* 162, no. 48
(December 2, 1999): 49.

99. "Tokyo Says Yes to 'Mr. No.'" *Asian Wall Street Journal* Editorial (April 13,
1999): 12.

100. Ayako Doi, "Japan's Right Stuff," [Book review of *Ishihara Shintaro no Tokyo
Dai-kaikaku (Shintaro Ishihara's Overhaul of Tokyo)*, 2000, by Akio Sakurai and the
Tokyo Shimbun "Ishihara Watch" Team] *Foreign Policy* (January–February 2001),
<www.foreignpolicy.com/issue_janfeb_2001/IOWjanfeb2001.html>.

101. "Japan's New Politics."

102. Steven W. Mosher, *Hegemon: China's Plan to Dominate Asia and the World* (San
Francisco: Encounter Books, 2000), 115.

103. Andrew J. Nathan and Robert S. Ross, *The Great Wall and the Empty Fortress:
China's Search for Security* (New York: W. W. Norton, 1997), 82.

104. Nathan and Ross, *The Great Wall and the Empty Fortress*, 227.

105. "Tokyo Governor Criticizes U.S. Military Base," AP Breaking News, *New York
Times* (February 4, 2001), <www.nytimes.com/aponline/world/AP-Japan-Near-Miss
.html>; Masaaki Gabe, "Futenma Air Station: The Okinawa Problem in Japan-U.S. Relations," *Japan Echo* 27, no. 3 (June 2000): 19–24.

106. M. Diana Helweg, "Japan: A Rising Sun?" *Foreign Affairs* 79, no. 4 (July–August
2000): 26–39, 39.

107. Walden Bello, "Reform the Jurassic IMF," *Far Eastern Economic Review* 162,
no. 49 (December 9, 1999): 44; Robert L. Pollock, "An IMF Prelude to the Asian Meltdown," *Asian Wall Street Journal* Editorial (November 29, 1999): 10.

108. Yusuke Horiguchi, "Finish the Job" [A February 16, 2000 interview by Murray
Hiebert] *Far Eastern Economic Review* 163, no. 9 (March 2, 2000): 29; "ASEAN's Initiatives," *Asian Wall Street Journal* Editorial (December 1, 1999): 10.

109. "ASEAN's Initiatives," 10.

110. Anthony Giddens, *The Third Way: The Renewal of Social Democracy* (Cambridge, UK: Polity Press, 1998), 15.

111. Giddens, *The Third Way*, 90.

112. On Kim and Lee see Thornton, "Korea and East Asian Exceptionalism," 138.

113. Giddens, *The Third Way*, 117.

114. Stephanie Strom, "Governor's Taking a New Broom to Japan's Politics," *New
York Times* World (January 10, 2001), <www.nytimes.com/2001/01/10/world/
10JAPA.html>.

115. Amartya Sen, "Human Development" [An interview with Amartya Sen] *Atlantic Unbound* (December 15, 1999), <www.theatlantic.com/unbound/interviews/
ba991215.htm>.

116. Akash Kapur, "Poor but Prosperous," *Atlantic Monthly* (September 1998), <www.theatlantic.com/issues/98sep/kerala.htm>.

117. Stephan Haggard, *The Political Economy of the Asian Financial Crisis* (Washington, D.C.: Institute for International Economics, 2000), 231.

118. Patrick Smith, "A New Asian Cooperation," (November 12, 1998), <ic.voxcap.com/issues/Issue164/item2158.asp>.

119. "Mori's B Team," *Economist* (July 8, 2000), <www.economist.com/editorial/freeforallf/current/as4980.html>; Yoshiaki Kobayashi, "Reading the Election Results," *Japan Echo* 27, no. 5 (October 2000): 29–32, 29.

120. Howard W. French, "Japan's Governing Party Suffers Severe Election Setback," *New York Times* World (June 26, 2000), <www.nytimes.com/library/world/asia/062600japan-election.html>.

121. "Mori Is More Than a Bad Joke for Fiscal Reform," *Financial Times* (December 11, 2000), <http://globalarchive.ft.com/globalarchive/articles.html?print = true&id = 0 01211000102>.

122. Kobayashi, "Reading the Election Results," 30.

123. Paul Krugman, "Japan's Memento Mori," *New York Times* Op-Ed (June 28, 2000), <www.nytimes.com/library/opinion/krugman/062800krug.html>.

124. Jonathan Watts, "Japan's Damaged PM Scrapes Home," *Guardian Unlimited* (June 26, 2000), <www.guardian.co.uk/international/story10,3604,336545,00.html>.

125. "Ally of Japanese Prime Minister Resigns," Breaking News from Reuters, *New York Times* (December 1, 2000), <www.nytimes.com/reuters/world/japan-politics-nonaka.html>.

126. Herbert P. Bix, "Japan's New Nationalism," *New York Times* Editorial/Op-Ed, <www.nytimes.com/2001/05/29/opinion/29BIX.html>; Edward J. Lincoln, "The Sounds of Silence," *New Republic* (August 15, 2001), <www.thenewrepublic.com/express/Lincoln081501.html>.

127. Roger Buckley, *Japan Today* (3rd ed.) (Cambridge, UK: Cambridge University Press, 1998), 199.

128. Linda Weiss, "Globalization and State Power," *Development and Society* 29, no. 1 (June 2000): 1–15, 1.

129. On the former, see Erik Eckholm, "Power of U.S. Draws China and Russia to Amity Pact," *New York Times* World (January 14, 2001), <www.nytimes.com/2001/01/14/world/14CHIN.html>; on the latter, see Agence France-Presse, "Chinese Guest Woos India," *New York Times* International (January 14, 2001), <www.nytimes.com/2001/01/14/world/14INDI.html>.

130. As reported in the Hong Kong communist newspaper *Wen Wei Po*; see Frank Ching, "Japan and India Forge New Links," *Far Eastern Economic Review* (September 7, 2000), <www.feer.com/000907/p32eoa.html>.

131. "Japan and China Eye Each Other Warily—As Usual," *Economist* 356, no. 8186 (September 2, 2000): 27.

132. Charles Bickers, "Extending Tokyo's Reach," *Far Eastern Economic Review* (January 18, 2001), <www.feer.com/_0101_18/p026region.html>.

133. Colin H. Williams, "Towards a New World Order: European and American Perspectives," in Colin H. Williams, ed., *The Political Geography of the New World Order* (London: Belhaven Press, 1993), 1–19, 17.

134. Kojima Akira, "Reinventing Japan: Report on the Commission on Japan's Goals in the Twenty-First Century (Outline)," *Japan Echo* 27, no. 2 (April 2000): 17–20, 19.

135. "International Symposium—Perspectives of the 21st Century: Culture and Globalization," Global Communications Platform from Japan (June 19, 2000), <www. glocom.org/debates/200006_miyazaki_sympo>.

136. Kanishka Jayasuriya, "Understanding 'Asian Values' as a Form of Reactionary Modernization," *Contemporary Politics* 4, no. 1 (1998): 77–91.

Chapter 4

The "Other" Korea:
An Oppositional Postmodernism

POSTMODERNISM'S RADICAL
INDIFFERENCE

It is no accident that postmodernism and development theory have traveled separate roads.[1] For all its "decentered" posturing, the bulk of what passes for postmodernism has little application in the "developing" world. It lumps that world into a suspiciously global category where "difference" is collapsed into the "labyrinth of textuality," as Edward Said dubs it.[2] Even more than modernism, which simply bypasses the Other, postmodernism silences its Others epistemologically,[3] blacking out the margins it purports to cherish. It ends up supporting the very ethnocentrism it is pledged to resist.[4]

If postmodernism and its allied discourses—postcolonialism, muliticulturalism, and cultural studies—are to have meaning outside the privileged sectors of the New World Order, they must be held accountable for their indifference to the extant colonialism of corporate globalization. So too they must be purged of the simplistic polarities that turn historical analysis into moralistic hype.[5] The work of Bruce Cumings amply proves that there is no inherent incompatibility between moral vision and empirical investigation. Cumings faces up to the sometimes inconvenient particulars of the colonial past (e.g., the chasm dividing Taiwanese memories of Japanese colonialism from that of Koreans or Manchurians). Many Taiwanese have good reason to remember their Japanese overlords (relative to their Chinese overlords, before and after) with a degree of nostalgia.[6] The standard postcolonial critique, by contrast, homogenizes the colonial experience while placing it conveniently in the past, far removed from the cutting edge of neocolonial corporatism.

The real target of this "critique"—in line with postmodernism's micropolitical animus against the activist Left[7]—is the very concept of oppositional politics, or what Richard Rorty dubs the reformist as opposed to the cultural Left. The latter not only refuses to engage in national politics, but, in the name of "theory," fails to confront the inroads of corporate globalization.[8] By repudiating all "master narratives" of resistance, postmodernism and its cognates substitute parody for radical critique. The result is an eclipse of public responsibility, as "parody turns without notice into complicity in the ideological consolidation of social, political, and cultural relationships produced by Global Capital."[9]

As a corrective, this chapter puts postmodernism and development onto the same track, with Korea posited as a case study of real and compelling difference. Today's Korea exhibits a uniquely postmodern blend of tradition and transformation in its turn toward a people-centered model of development. This shift, as Gerald Caiden observes, is increasingly based upon "the uniqueness of a culture rather than . . . a pale imitation of the West."[10] From this vector Korean postmodernism points toward a possible reconciliation between development and difference, for Korea (prior, at least, to its recent colonization by the IMF) has managed to have it both ways.

KOREA'S POSTMODERN POLITICS

A large part of Korea's difference stems from the unusual scope of its political discourse, making the line between political and nonpolitical culture extremely hard to draw. Visitors to Korea are often struck by the political sophistication of taxi drivers, by the political climate of ordinary coffee houses, and by bookstores that cater to a growing body of politically literate readers. While this political consciousness certainly reflects the diffusion of higher education, the roots of political awareness run deep in Korean culture. Survey data from the lean years of the early 1970s reveal that the conversations of workers living scarcely above a subsistence level were as likely to revolve around politics as issues of daily livelihood.[11] Long before its full democratic impact would be felt, the germ of Korea's political postmodernization was already planted in this extended social discourse. Political "postmodernization" as such began when that discourse could no longer be suppressed by those in power.

While it is hard to assign a precise point of origin to this event, as good a date as any might be Roh Tae Woo's presidential inauguration on February 25, 1988. Roh himself was a militarist whose best political asset was his predecessor's inability to smile for cameras or otherwise avoid the appearance of an aspiring military dictator. Roh was much better at not looking the part.

And for a military man he was remarkably adept at bending with the wind—the postmodern wind of bottom-up political reform. Early on his inauguration day, Ian Buruma reports, the former general seized a photo opportunity with cleaning ladies at his party headquarters. His was to be the "Great Era for Ordinary People," and the new atmosphere was epitomized by nothing so much as the president's photogenic smile. That winning smile signaled a departure not only from the stern visages and administrative styles of Roh's predecessors, Park Chung Hee and Chun Doo Hwan, but also from an era dominated by the Japanese model of development.

Buruma was quick to relate Roh's new populist image to the substantive shift of Korean political culture:

> When the ordinary people open their newspapers in the morning they see evidence of change: editorials and cartoons are sometimes mildly critical of the Government. And new papers and journals are being published. Books by authors who had been banned because of their political sympathies are now on sale.[12]

Indeed, the joke was on me. When I moved to Korea in 1987, the bookstores were stocked with many of the same books I had discarded after being warned not to bring them into Korea, due to intense censorship. Just a year before that warning would have been well taken.

It was only with the inauguration of President Kim Young Sam, however, that political postmodernization would storm the palace, or rather the Blue House. The line between modern and postmodern was drawn decisively with the censure, dismissal, or arrest of more than a thousand high-level officials in government and business.[13] Populist values pulsed through an expanded political discourse that made the Blue House seem less remote.

In America a similar populist movement had taken shape early in the twentieth century, as one feature of modernization. But in the Asian NICs the modernizing phase of development came and went without such indulgences. Here modernism was a distinctly "top-down" affair. It is appropriate, therefore, to apply the term "postmodern" to the "bottom-up" issues raised by Asian oppositional politics since the late 1980s. Japan, as we have seen, has been commonly looked to as the main locus of Asian postmodernism. But where political development is concerned, Korea offers a more fertile field of postmodern investigation. First, it has been recognized that Japanese postmodernism is extremely weak in terms of critical resistance.[14] Korea's less conformist political climate yields a more "resistant" strain of postmodernism, one as concerned with substantive criticism as with style. Second, insofar as Korea is still less developed than Japan, it provides better insight into postmodernism as an element of the development process. Finally, Korea may be a better choice for an exploration of non-Western postmodernism, for

Korea has been more guarded in its appropriation of Western values. In that sense it is simply more Other than Japan. That otherness has too often been put in a purely negative light. Writing during the administration of Chun Doo Hwan, Lucian Pye dismissed public dissent against Chun as just so much theater. Pye misread both sides of the conflict, the state and the society, by taking them to be equally static and nondialogic. The dance of contention that Pye read as stylized "theatre" was indeed performative, but it also constituted, from both sides, a highly developed rhetoric of commendably nonviolent intent (as compared, say, to the far less theatrical patterns of dissent and control in many Latin American countries). As a rhetorical exchange, moreover, this performance was seldom monological. Both sides had their choreography and their lines to recite, but between the lines they imparted messages that were comprehensible enough to Koreans, if often inscrutable to outsiders. Behind the stage effects, the gains and losses were real. Pye was wrong, furthermore, in his conclusion that it made little difference who might replace President Chun, since one Korean leader is basically like another.[15] Pye could hardly have imagined that in the next decade both Kims, icons of the Korean opposition, would occupy the Blue House.

THE OTHER KOREAN ROAD

Nor did these postmodern reversals issue from a cultural backwater. There was cultural dynamism in the Other Korea during the course of the country's modernization, though most of this has gone unnoticed by scholars such as Morris Janowitz and Samuel Huntington,[16] who associate Korea's developmental potency with Blue House authoritarianism. Cumings reminds us that a more traditional Korea would have disdained Park Chung Hee's militaristic style.[17] His reactionary modernism was more in keeping with Japanese values than Korean ones. Norman Jacobs cogently argues that Parkian modernization has in fact been an obstacle to development.[18] Unfortunately Jacobs's *The Korean Road to Modernization and Development*, which applies Max Weber's theories of domination to Korea,[19] remains mired in its own methodological modernism—measuring Korean development against an ideal of pure objectivism.[20] From a postmodern perspective, no such objective grounds exist outside discursive practice. Jacobs operates out of a positivist tradition,[21] which is prone to focus on overt authority at the expense of more amorphous cultural resistance. As had Gregory Henderson,[22] Jacobs lays stress on the centralizing "vortex" of power. The image one gets is of a two-tiered society: the vortexers and the vortexed. While both authors are concerned over the plight of the vortexed, they continue to read the social and political contribution of this Other Korea in negative terms, scarcely noticing the very real oppositional force mounting on the political periphery.

The main body of scholarship on Korean development has followed Henderson and Jacobs on this negative track, looking toward the "vortex" rather than the margins for solutions. The Right has applied this approach with unmitigated venom, as in a coauthored study by Bun Woong Kim and David S. Bell extolling the virtues of Korea's "elitist heritage." This study concluded that the opposition movement could not have developed domestically, since Koreans by their very nature respect authoritarianism. In short, so far as politics is concerned, there is no Other Korea. Korea's oppositionalism could only have been implanted from the outside.[23]

A more tempered expression of this same approach is found in a study of popular protest by Aie-Rie Lee. Lee attributes postwar oppositionalism almost entirely to the culture shift that resulted from government-sponsored and largely Westernized higher education. Again, the possibility that resistance could have originated in the political margins of Korea itself is dismissed. Like Kim and Bell, Lee reduces Korea's past to one "long tradition of subservience to authority."[24] This neglects the plausible hypothesis, taken up in the next chapter, that the severity of Korean authority was partly motivated by the existence of real resistance potential outside the "vortex."

Henderson himself does not deny this, but views such resistance as a losing cause. He frames his entire thesis around his lament over the eclipse of localized political and economic initiative, such that "even what passed for local power was central power extended."[25] He traces the early modern phase of this "vortexization" to the Taewongun period, when high social mobility contributed to social atomization. In his view this made individuals all the more vulnerable to central control.

James Palais counters that the lives of ordinary Koreans of the Taewongun era were still very much circumscribed by "traditional ties to family, lineage, and village."[26] Palais, however, roughly equates tradition and local initiative with the continued hegemony of the *yangban* class, which he does not consider to have been under serious threat from either the royalty or the peasantry during the late Yi period. Though Palais does grant that the threat of peasant insurrection induced limited reforms, he dismisses the widespread suspicion among *yangban* intellectuals that the Taewongun intended to court the masses and usurp *yangban* privileges.[27] For Palais popular unrest was a sideshow that lacked the infrastructure for systemic change. But it should be stressed that his position—that grassroots resistance lacked the means to seriously challenge the *yangban* ruling class—in no way supports Aie-Rie Lee's depiction of ordinary Koreans as naturally subservient. Rather, the image that Palais projects is of a social powder keg waiting for the right conditions to explode. In the absence of those conditions, Henderson and Palais can agree that the political challenge from Korea's social margins was negligible. The fact remains that the politically charged populism of recent decades did not drop out of thin air. It was shaped and intensified by several decades of brutal Japanese occupation. A social base for ludic insurrection was laid in the last years of Japan's rule, when the pace of Korea's forced industrialization was twice or three times that of Japan's Taiwan colony.[28] An incipient working class was torn from the land yet given no secure place in the emerging order. Japanese oppression germinated a counterauthoritarian spirit that never fully developed in Taiwan. This was the germ of the Other Korea that won my admiration when I met it in clouds of tear gas in 1987. I came to feel, as Cumings somewhere wrote, that no people on earth more deserves democracy than the Koreans.

HARD TRUTHS FOR
SAMUELSON ET AL.

Like Jacobs's *Korean Road*, Kim Dae Jung's *Mass-Participatory Economy* (1985) distinguishes modernization and development, but defines development more in terms of the needs of the Korean people. Koreans have never been so quiescent as the postwar Japanese when it comes to the machinations of the nation's industrial giants. The name *chaebol*, as Carter Eckert observes, carries roughly the same negative connotations that Japan's *zaibatsu* had in prewar days;[29] but while the Japanese absorbed corporatism into their new cultural identity, postwar Koreans refused such accommodation.

Socioeconomic modernization, therefore, has taken very different courses in Japan and Korea, and consequently their postmodernization is also bound to be different. This is to say that postmodernism is not constitutionally co-opted—as Fredric Jameson implies in *Postmodernism, or, The Cultural Logic of Late Capitalism* (1991)—but neither is it inherently "radical." We are left with a cacophony of new questions, but with few answers. In years past it could be asked if Korean postmodernism would in the long run better serve the government or the opposition. This question became all the more pressing when the erstwhile opposition *became* the government, and all the more convoluted when that government became, after the 1997 Crash, indentured to the IMF.

A similar ambiguity arises where individualism is concerned. Surely some manner of individualism is essential for any nonconventional political critique, but it is also obvious that concerted resistance will be the loser as hyperindividualism and other "decentered" values gain ground. This is happening, moreover, at a time when the opposition, facing in globalization its most formidable adversary, needs solidarity more than ever. Is this just bad luck, or does globalism actively foster hyperindividualism as a divide-and-conquer tactic? The opposition, after all, has depended for its organization and fortitude upon a degree of solidarity that is utterly inconsistent with the narcissism being imported from the West under globalist auspices.

Some, of course, are more concerned about the destructive impact of bottom-up solidarity. In *Hard Truths for Korea*, Paul Samuelson targets "populist reform" as one of the most serious threats to Korea's economic prospect. He cites Uruguay as a classic case of how a developing country can be ruined through overzealous egalitarianism.[30] This unfortunate comparison ignores the crucial role of populist elements in the making of the economic "miracle" that Samuelson wants to preserve. It was not bottom-up reformism, but top-down corruption that pushed Korea to the brink of insolvency by the late 1990s.

Son-Ung Kim considers the innate productivity of workers to have been more important than entrepreneurship in sustaining the economic growth of Asian NICs in general.[31] But in Korea, especially, the engine behind the "miracle" has been the Korean work ethic. A Korean mother I know worked such hours as a factory day laborer that she could not see her children for days on end, throughout their childhood. A close relative of mine, "retired" from the coal mines with no health benefits, just died of black lung disease. These are the "populists" that Samuelson blames for obstructing Korea's growth. They are the pages ripped out of the history of Korea's development.

Many confuse the legitimate claims of populism on a fair share of the nation's GNP with the narcissism and mindless consumerism that President Kim Young Sam justifiably condemned, in keeping with the austerity policy launched by President Roh in September 1991. At that time Korea's average per capita income was around U.S.$6,000. The typical Korean hardly needed a lecture from either president on why he or she should not shop at Seoul department stores where a set of golf clubs could cost U.S.$6,000 and a pair of underwear $600.[32] Samuelson should have taken a closer look at the "hard truths" of working-class lives. Populism posed a danger only to Korea's power elite, not to its efficiency or solvency. Indeed, populist values might offer the best hope for securing sustainable economic growth.

The prime targets of populist criticism have always been the corruption and shady operations that the IMF would identify as *the* major threat to Korea's continued prosperity. In cheering the IMF on, Western commentators arrogantly assumed that "crony capitalism" is natural to Asia in general and to

Korea in particular. Their strident call for transparency presupposed that this demand had never been heard from inside Korea. Notwithstanding this anticrony rhetoric, the IMF quickly bailed out the cronies who brought on the Crash, leaving the working classes to fend for themselves.

Too often economists fail to realize that injury to the working classes will kill the goose that laid the economic miracle. Most studies parallel Henderson, Jacobs, and Samuelson in foregrounding the developmental contribution of Korea's power elite. Such studies tend to denigrate tradition, treating it as little more than an obstacle to modernization. By contrast, postwar Japanese scholarship has not only recognized the importance of Japanese tradition for modernization, but has welded it into a virtual ideology of Japanese uniqueness.

Meanwhile, a small school of revisionists, originally out of the Japanese studies department of the University of Chicago,[33] has challenged Japan's vaunted exceptionalism, or *nihonjinron*, from a structuralist and now poststructuralist vantage. This critique questions the ideological wedding of modern technologism with traditional Japanese values such as *bushido*. It likewise casts suspicion on outside observers such as Ezra Vogel,[34] who have been fatuous enough to take the self-representation of *nihonjinron* at face value.

While Vogel converts Japanism into a blueprint for America's reconstruction, Jacobs castigates Korean patrimonialism on much the same basis. This judgment falls short on both sides: first, Japanese development was not the sterling democratic model it claimed to be, and second, patrimonialism was not the last word on Korean political culture. Larry Burmeister points out that

[P]rewar Japan appears to have been on the same trajectory as "modernizing, nondeveloping" Korea—that is, modernization (industrialization, urbanization, militarization) *without political development*. Were internal social forces promoting "development" temporarily sidetracked? Is the prewar rise of Japan to world power status (based often on the conscious appropriation of centralized, autocratic Prussian models of . . . organization) a stage in the "development" process? If so, is Korea, too, not passing through an equivalent stage, rather than being mired in patrimonial "nondevelopment"?[35]

That corrective leaves Korea on a Japanese developmental track where success is defined as getting closer to the lead goose. As early as 1988 I argued that a better corrective would be to put a country's development on its own cultural track.[36] Ex-Thatcherite John Gray (*False Dawn: The Delusions of Global Capitalism* [1998]) comes to a similar conclusion. Whereas Takeshi Umehara contends that postmodern development "will need to be drawn primarily from the experience of non-Western cultures, especially Japanese civilization,"[37] Gray's pluralism prevents him from privileging any one culture or civilization. That is certainly a big improvement over his former Thatcherism, but it leads to an antidialogic retreatism not unlike Huntington's. The Other is thereby saved from globalist usurpation only by being taken out of circulation. Once again the voice of the Other is muted.

In Korea and most Asian NICs the cultural Other has been dealt a similar kiss of death. It has been effectively set in stone through lavish funding for the preservation of traditional dance, music, and crafts. "Culture" thus becomes a museum artifact, as inert as it is politically impotent, which is the whole point. Likewise the Saemaul movement, mentioned in the introduction, undertook to "save" rural communities while razing their aesthetic traditions and treating their residents with contempt. The timing of the movement suggests that its real target was the political Other. Jacobs points out that what drove Park in this direction was his awareness, after the sordid 1971 election returns, that support for his regime was declining rapidly in the rural sector.[38] This was understandable, given his attitude toward the Other Korea. Burmeister has shown (in *Research, Realpolitik, and Development in Korea: The State and the Green Revolution* [1988]) that the rural sector had been consistently treated as a hindrance rather than a contributor to Korea's industrial transformation.

A classic case of "vortexization" is seen in the government's Tongil ("unification") rice campaign, which coerced farmers into planting a strain of rice that not only proved unpalatable to most Koreans but was far less resistant to cold and disease than traditional japonica rice.[39] A belated appreciation of the old strain is emblematic of a new, postmodern attitude toward traditional values. In postwar years, the social sciences had forfeited responsibility in such matters to developmental economics,[40] where the salutary role of tradition was sure to be missed. The same antithetical view of tradition and modernization has guided Korea's public funding of cultural projects such as film, literature, and especially architecture. Fortunately a small but dynamic coterie of artists, architects, composers, and writers have sought to integrate traditional values and motifs with functional modernization. It is time to do the same for development theory.

NEW PRIORITIES

A precedent-setting example of this cultural regeneration was provided by an amateur film director from Taegu, Professor Bae Young-Kyun. Bae's internationally acclaimed film of 1989, *Dal-Ma ga Dong Jok uhro gan gah dohl un* (Why Dal-Ma Went to the East), represents the ambiguities of Buddhism's place in modern Korea. *Dal-Ma* is not only "postmodern" in terms of the deep silences of its narrative form, but in its frankly marginal content as well. Its focus is on the survival of the same Buddhist values that Henderson identifies as a mainspring of decentered values in traditional Korea. Moreover, the marginality of *Dal-Ma* is matched by the terms of its financial production. Taking seven years to produce, and drawing on the acting talents of students and other amateurs, Bae circumvented the industry's usual financial apparatus and thus safeguarded his own regional authenticity.

In *Dal-Ma*'s closing scene, a young monk cremates his dead spiritual teacher and departs for the "East," leaving the viewer to wonder where he is going and what he will do. One plausible interpretation is that he is carrying the living faith of his teacher back to the spiritually defunct world of the modern city. Spiritual replenishment, then, is not to be found in the isolation of old and new, but in their postmodern fusion. This not only contravenes the modernist exile of tradition, but also the bogus retrieval of culture in the frozen and depoliticized manner of a cultural museum such as the Han Hahk Village, outside Taejon.[41]

Bae's bridging of traditional and contemporary culture has its corollary in the postmodern integration of popular and "high" cultures. In popular music, for example, a blend of new and old was achieved as early as the 1970s by Lee Mi-Ja and is manifest in all of Song Chang-Sik's performances. Another milestone toward that end was achieved symbolically when Patty Kim, long one of Korea's most popular singers, was belatedly invited to perform at the Saejon Culture Hall, previously reserved for "high" or "classical" (meaning *Western* classical) performances.

Efforts to popularize Korean musical traditions have taken two distinct paths. On the one side there is the unrestrained eclecticism of Im Dong-Chang, who bridges elite and popular forms with a rare existential intensity. More commonly, however, postmodernism takes the form of camp (to borrow Susan Sontag's term)[42]: an arbitrary mix of traditional elements with the latest musical refuse. This relativistic stew, in Park Yong-ku's opinion, is indicative of Korea's current culture crisis.[43] Indeed, it is part of the general postmodern dilemma that Jameson identifies with the cultural "logic" of global capitalism and Dirlik locates at the level of assumption in academic disciplines that would be expected to challenge this logic. My only point of difference with these dark visions lies in my conviction that it need not be so. Postmodernism can offer, like Bae's melding of past and present cultural forms, an indeterminate vision of meaningful possibilities—the Korean equivalent of Richard Rorty's postmodern vision of America in *Achieving Our Country*.

One must wonder, however, if Korea's rising tide of individualism will remedy or worsen the critical malaise that Park Yong-ku identifies. It is worth noting that the great age of individualism in the West was also the great age of industrial development, corporatism, the welfare state, and the cultural exaltation of an antipopulist elite. The word modernism is shrouded in these associations. By way of reaction, "postmodernism" should invite their inversion: the rise of a resistant popular culture (as opposed to a Frankfurt School mass culture), the return to localism (as opposed to hegemonic nationalism), or communitarianism (as opposed to liberal atomism). Obviously postmodernism must assume a different meaning in Asian countries where modernism was not allied to liberal individualism in the first place.

Recognizing that the East Asian experience undermines the standard association of modernity with capitalist individualism, Peter Berger argues that Western-centered models of development are no longer adequate.[44] Marion Levy explains the Asian dissociation of modernization and individualism by distinguishing the function of individualism in "first-comer" and "late-comer" modernizations. In the former, individualism helps to forge the necessary work ethic and savings habits for sustained growth economies, whereas in the latter this is unnecessary and perhaps even dysfunctional. What is required, rather, are "higher levels of coordination and control along with a meritocracy and the like that sometimes pass as individualism. Individualism, while a vital element for the first-comers, is a romantic focus for latecomers."[45]

What Levy does not take into account is that economic modernization is not the sole objective of development. Indeed, as Jacobs convincingly argues, modernization and development can easily be at cross-purposes. If some degree of coordination and control are credible requirements for modernization and development alike, there is also the problem of surplus control. The case of Korean modernization validates both the advantages and disadvantages of control-based modernization. It also suggests that at higher material levels of modernization the relative balance of these pros and cons shifts markedly in favor of greater individualism and the diminution of central control.

Kim Uchang notes that these new priorities bear striking resemblance to the goals of the Korean Enlightenment early in the twentieth century.[46] Korean postmodernism thus retrieves, on a more solid material plane, both elite and nonelite currents of cultural resistance. Far more than in Japan, postmodernism in Korea is engaged in concrete politics and public policy. While its origins lie in domestic reform traditions,[47] its dialogic reach makes it a threat to repressive regimes throughout Asia and the developing world. The next chapter tracks its collision course with reactionary economism and the cult of Asian values.

NOTES

1. David Slater, "Theories of Development and Politics of the Postmodern—Exploring a Border Zone," *Development and Change* 23, no. 3 (July 1992): 283–319, 284.

2. Edward W. Said, *The World, the Text, and the Critic* (Cambridge, Mass.: Harvard University Press, 1983), 3–4.

3. Catherine Gimelli Martin, "Orientalism and the Ethnographer: Said, Herodotus, and the Discourse of Alterity," *Criticism* 32, no. 4 (Fall 1990): 511–529, 511.

4. Slater, "Theories of Development," 283, 290.

5. Terry Eagleton, "A Spot of Firm Government," *London Review of Books* 23, no. 16 (August 23, 2001), <www.lrb.co.uk/v23/n16/eag12316.htm>.

6. Bruce Cumings, *Parallax Visions: Making Sense of American-East Asian Relations at the End of the Century* (Durham, N.C.: Duke University Press, 1999), 70.

7. Carl Boggs, *The End of Politics: Corporate Power and the Decline of the Public Sphere* (New York: Guilford, 2000), 239.

8. Richard Rorty, *Achieving Our Country: Leftist Thought in Twentieth-Century America* (Cambridge, Mass.: Harvard University Press, 1998), 91.

9. Arif Dirlik, *After the Revolution: Waking to Global Capitalism* (Hanover, N.H.: Wesleyan University Press, 1994), 91.

10. Gerald E. Caiden, "Introduction: Drawing Lessons from Korea's Experience," in Gerald E. Caiden and Bun Woong Kim, eds., *A Dragon's Progress: Development Administration in Korea* (West Hartford, Conn.: Kumarian Press, 1991), ix–xxix, xiii.

11. L. L. Wade, "South Korean Political Culture: An Interpretation of Survey Data," *Journal of Korean Studies* 2 (1980): 1–45, 23.

12. Ian Buruma, "The Quarrelsome Koreans," *New York Times Magazine* (March 27, 1988): 42–43, 76–77, 94, 42.

13. Peter McKillop and B. J. Lee, "There Will Be No Sanctuary," *Newsweek* Asian edition (June 21, 1993): 13–14, 13.

14. Masao Miyoshi and H. D. Harootunian, "Introduction," in Miyoshi Masao and H. D. Harootunian, eds., *Postmodernism and Japan* (Durham, N.C.: Duke University Press, 1989), vii–xix, xiv.

15. Lucian W. Pye, with Mary W. Pye, *Asian Power and Politics: The Cultural Dimensions of Authority* (Cambridge, Mass.: Belknap Press of Harvard University Press, 1985), 227.

16. Cited in Bruce Cumings, *Korea's Place in the Sun: A Modern History* (New York: Norton, 1997), 350–354.

17. Cumings, *Korea's Place in the Sun*, 379.

18. Norman Jacobs, *The Korean Road to Modernization and Development* (Urbana: University of Illinois Press, 1985), 17.

19. Roger L. Janelli, review of *The Korean Road to Modernization and Development*, by Norman Jacobs, *Journal of Asian Studies* 48, no. 1 (February 1989): 188–189, 189.

20. Hagen Koo, review of *The Korean Road to Modernization and Development*, by Norman Jacobs, *Korea Studies* 12 (1988): 86–88, 87.

21. John W. Murphy, "The Relevance of Postmodernism for Social Science," *Diogenes*, no. 143 (Fall 1988): 93–110, 98.

22. Gregory Henderson, *Korea: The Politics of the Vortex* (Cambridge, Mass.: Harvard University Press, 1968).

23. Bun Woong Kim and David S. Bell, Jr., "The Theory and Applicability of Democratic Elitism to Korean Public Administration," in Gerald E. Caiden and Bun Woong Kim, eds., *A Dragon's Progress: Development Administration in Korea* (West Hartford, Conn.: Kumarian Press, 1991), 19–25, 24, 22.

24. Aie-Rie Lee, "Culture Shift and Popular Protest in South Korea," *CPS* 26, no. 1 (April 1993): 63–80, 63.

25. Henderson, *Korea*, 30.

26. James B. Palais, *Politics and Policy in Traditional Korea* (Cambridge, Mass.: Harvard University Press, 1975), 3.

27. Palais, *Politics and Policy in Traditional Korea*, 280.

28. Bruce Cumings, *The Origins of the Korean War: Liberation and the Emergence of Separate Regimes—1945–47* (Princeton, N.J.: Princeton University Press, 1981), 27.

29. Carter J. Eckert, "The South Korean Bourgeoisie: A Class in Search of Hegemony," *Journal of Korean Studies* 7 (1990): 115–148, 142.

30. Paul A. Samuelson, *Hard Truths for Korea* (Seoul: Si Sa Young Uh Sa, 1992), 7.

31. Son-Ung Kim, "The Role of Social Values and Competitiveness in Economic Growth: with Special Reference to Korea," in Durganand Sinha and Henry S. R. Kao, eds., *Social Values and Development: Asian Perspectives* (New Delhi: Sage Publications, 1988), 76–92, 91.

32. Tony Emerson and Bradley Martin, "Too Rich, Too Soon," *Newsweek* Asia edition (November 11, 1991): 12–16, 12.

33. Anthony Woodiwiss, "Postmodanizumu: Japanese for (and Against) Postmodernism," *Theory, Culture and Society: Explorations in Critical Social Science* 8, no. 4 (November 1991): 111–118, 111.

34. Ezra F. Vogel, *Japan as Number One: Lessons for America* (Cambridge, Mass.: Harvard University Press, 1979).

35. Larry L. Burmeister, review of *The Korean Road to Modernization and Development*, by Norman Jacobs, *Journal of Korean Studies* 6 (1988–89): 229–234, 232; my emphasis.

36. William H. Thornton, "American Technological Culture: A Comparative Perspective," *Tamkang Journal of American Studies* 5, no. 2 (Winter 1988): 5–19, 17.

37. Takeshi Umehara, "Ancient Japan Shows Postmodernism the Way," *New Perspectives Quarterly* 4, no. 2 (Spring 1992): 10–13, 10.

38. Jacobs, *The Korean Road to Modernization and Development*, 108.

39. David J. Nemeth, review of *Research, Realpolitik, and Development in Korea: The State and the Green Revolution*, by Larry L. Burmeister, *Korea Studies* 13 (1989): 132–135, 133–134.

40. David Hulme and Mark M. Turner, *Sociology and Development: Theories, Policies, and Practices* (New York: St. Martin's Press, 1990), 65.

41. See *BBC special report*, aired in Taiwan on October 3, 1993.

42. Susan Sontag, *Against Interpretation* (New York: Dell, 1966), 277.

43. Yong-Ku Park, "A Sense of Balance Between Sensitivity and Intelligence" (trans. from Korean), *Auditorium: The Monthly Music and Performance Arts Magazine* (June 1993): 129–158.

116   Chapter 4

44. Peter L. Berger, "An East Asian Development Model?" in Peter L. Berger and Hsin-Huang Michael Hsiao, eds., *In Search of an East Asian Development Model* (New Brunswick, N.J.: Transaction Books, 1988), 3–11, 4, 6.

45. Marion J. Levy, Jr., "Confucianism and Modernization," *Society* 29, no. 4 (May–June, 1992): 15–18, 17.

46. Kim Uchang, "The Ideology of Modernization and Pursuit of Happiness," *Korea Journal* 26, no. 9 (September 1986): 41–48, 47.

47. Kim, "The Ideology of Modernization and Pursuit of Happiness," 48.

Korea and the Asian Values Debate

TOWARD A KOREAN MODEL

Culture, many believe, has moved from the periphery to the very center of social thought.[1] At the same time, however, the meaning of culture has been emptied of any concrete qualities beyond the reach of hybridization. While postcolonial critics such as Homi Bhabha celebrate this fusion as liberation from the cultural centrality of the West, globalists like John Tomlinson seize upon hybridity as the ultimate cultural shield: an a priori defense against the charge that globalization kills culture through homogenization. For Tomlinson there can be no cultural imperialism, since there is no "original" culture to kill or imperialize.[2]

This globalist hokum is a hard sell on the Rim, where politics is never far removed from active cultural volcanoes. Third Way optimism is as dangerous here as modernist optimism was in Vietnam of the 1950s and 1960s. The new cosmopolitans confuse ASEAN with the EU. They are as much out of their depth in Asian geopolitics as was a classic modernist such as Robert McNamara. The modernist model of "inside/outside" international relations, which has been as axiomatic for Rostow as for Wallerstein, can no longer contain the "fire on the Rim" that miracle economics ignited. The region's new cultural dynamics is more an "outside/outside" agonistics—a contest of raw geocultural will that could make modernist power politics, and even the Cold War, start to look good by comparison.

Of course, there are those who see none of this. Turning to the mysterious East for spiritual uplift, New Agers invert the myth that sustained modernism: its notion that there is a Western solution for most of the world's problems. If the West is bad, the East must surely be good. Globalists are more concerned with material uplift. For a while they came under the spell of Asian values economism, but the Asian Crash of 1997 killed its allure. Now they talk of "transparency," while in practice they perpetuate modernism's core/periphery schism.

It is common knowledge that transparency does not apply to globalist institutions such as the IMF, the World Bank, or the WTO—the instruments of a new economic imperialism. Nor have these new instruments displaced the older ones. The New World Order has it both ways. As Jeremy Brecher and Tim Costello point out, the old militarism is still with us:

> Despite the end of the Cold War, global military spending is more than $1,000 trillion per year [as of 1994]—nearly half of it by the United States. This is justified in large part by the need to control economic rivals and the revolts of poor and desperate peoples.[3]

Postmodernism conceivably counters such top-down unilateralism. But the idea that postmodernism is inherently liberating is every bit as naive as the idea that modernism is inherently progressive. Many recognize that reactionary modernists, ranging from Henry Kissinger to Chiang Zemin, apply advanced technology toward a frightful array of nonliberatory goals. But few recognize the supporting role that postmodern and postcolonial critics have played in diverting attention from the inroads of global power structures. It is fair to say that this so-called cultural Left has been sleeping on the job.

Ironically, a long overdue wake-up call came from the cultural Right during the 1990s. The geopolitical wing of nonliberatory postmodernism found its classic expression in Samuel Huntington's concept of civilizational clash, to be treated in chapter 7. A spate of similar admonitions would follow, including *The Next War* (1996), by Caspar Weinberger and Peter Schweizer, and *The Fourth Turning* (1998), by William Strauss and Neil Howe. These dark visions are concretely realized in the "reformed" institutions of the new China. Clearly this is not the East Asia that New Agers have in mind. Rather it is the zone of an increasingly strident East Asian exceptionalism. This doctrine holds that economic dynamism can be achieved all the better when the impediments of Western "rights" and environmental consciousness are kept outside the cultural moat.

A signal challenge to that doctrine, and to the clash it bodes between Asian and non-Asian political cultures, as well as between different Asian values regimes, comes from Korea's Kim Dae Jung, as mentioned before. Kim offers Korea as his prime example, but *not* as an "exceptional" case in point. His approach stakes a claim to being as "Asian" as any Asian exceptionalism, but without a trace of exclusionary rancor. His stance toward the West has been dialogic rather than agonistic.

By some accounts East Asian exceptionalism is an idea whose time has passed; but the profound impact of this Asian values conceit on economic and political thought is undeniable. Given its close association with Confucianism, East Asian exceptionalism could be defined as the inversion of Max Weber's belief that Confucian values blunt rationality and lead to economic stagnation. This revaluation contributes to a complete inversion of orientalism as it relates to East Asia.

A similar but less strident revaluation is contained in Pacific Rim discourse—the reconfiguration of liberal thought that (spatially) ties America to the Rim while it (temporally) moves East Asia from its former position as perpetual "latecomer" to its recent vanguard status in modernization theory. From this position, as Christopher Connery observes, Japan and the East Asian NICs have been able to break out of "the West's past. In the eighties, if Japan was anywhere in time, it was in the future, with Taiwan, Singapore, Hong Kong, and South Korea at the very least in some version of the present."[4]

Connery concentrates on the made-in-America aspect of Rim discourse, but East Asian exceptionalism has finally gone its own way, declaring its independence not only from the latecomer teleology of modernization theory but from liberalism as well. Inevitably this makes for tension between Asianism and liberalism. The "Rim" concept was premised on the glowing assumption that over time there would be a convergence of political as well as economic values around the Pacific. Such "Rimism" now confronts the exceptionalism that in Minxin Pei's opinion "poses a serious ideological, intellectual, and policy challenge to those concerned with promoting *both* democracy and market economics in the world, for it suggests that the latter can thrive without the former."[5]

The war between exceptionalism and Rimism is implicit in Huntington's concept of an East/West clash, whereby Asian democracy is reduced to mere procedural formalities that buttress the Asian values of involuntary harmony and consensus. But if Huntington, as Han Sang-Jin observes, refrains from overt criticism of Asia's reactionary values,[6] he certainly does not endorse them. That full transvaluation of the Eastern pole of Huntington's dichotomy is left to Singapore's Lee Kuan Yew.

The most striking rebuttal to Lee's position also hails from East Asia—namely, from the postmodern Other of Korean oppositionalism. In defiance of Korea's reputation for hermetic authoritarianism,[7] Kim Dae Jung posits Korea as a variant of pan-Asian democracy, the very antithesis of Lee's pan-Asian authoritarianism. This model moves beyond exceptionalism by reconciling the deep roots of Korean and East Asian political culture with liberal values.[8] One of the most vital political debates of our times is thus taking shape between the irreconcilable poles of exceptionalism and postexceptionalism, here termed the Singaporean and Korean models, respectively.

The rudiments of this Other Asian model—distinct, especially, from the Japanese consensual model[9]—are supplied in Han Sang-Jin's classic study of Korea's oppositional dynamics.[10] Recently Han has updated that work to incorporate the Kim/Lee debate over the meaning and range of Asian values.[11] Following the drift of "postmodern" development theory toward diversity[12] and away from any master narrative,[13] Han declares the whole issue of Korean political development an "open question"; but elsewhere he holds out the hope that Korea is at last in a position to shift from what he terms "rush-to" modernization toward a socially and ecologically "reflexive" development.[14]

Korea's record of democratic development over the past fifteen years deserves a more affirmative response than is allowed by Han's postmodernism. Nor did this democratic turn arise ex nihilo. In the mid-1970s Lim Hy-sop noted that throughout the postwar era Koreans had taken the word democracy almost as a synonym for development.[15] Certainly we must respect the recidivist possibilities that make Han wary of naive optimism,[16] but the point is to move beyond naive optimism and naive pessimism alike.

ASIA AT THE GLOBAL CROSSROADS

Edward Said's landmark study of orientalism sparked a needful debate over the imaginative geography of East and West. Unfortunately his impact on development theory was truncated by his curious inattention to the Rim as opposed to the Middle East. It was on the Rim, after all, that the material foundations of orientalist prejudice were shaken to the core by the "Asian miracle." Now, in the wake of the Paul Krugman thesis (which likens Asian economic expansion to the input-driven dynamics of Soviet growth in the late 1950s)[17] and the Crash of 1997 (which converted countless shocked observers to Krugman's way of thinking), that "miracle" is coming to look like another imaginary construct, a product of wishful thinking not only on the Rim but throughout the West.

To fathom this inverse orientalism we should review some of the cultural conventions of early postwar modernization theory. One key assumption was that culture rates a very low priority relative to economic and political analysis. Much as "end of ideology" social science bracketed hard questions concerning advanced capitalist institutions, development theory naturalized capitalist takeoff formulas by purging culture.

This was nothing new. Said points out that the cultural factor had long been neglected by both the Left and Right in their respective treatments of imperialism.[18] But the Right was faster to retrieve that cultural factor, writing off capitalism's developmental failure as the result of cultural deficiency in the marginal regions of the world. The Left's rejoinder, in the form of dependency theory, often involved a rejection of the relevance of culture as a whole. This duplicates the centrist fallacy that Wlad Godzich associates with the whole thrust of Western thought, whereby the cultural Other is perceived as a "potential same-to-be."[19] Thus modernization would be cast as a process of continuing Westernization.

Postmodern and postcolonial writing would have us deconstruct such orientalism. Both challenge the "presence" of West-to-East and North-to-South progressivism, which is based as much on an absent Other as on an objectively "present" West. For centuries that Western "same" was venerated at the expense of the non-Western Other; but since the mid-1970s there has been a strategic reversal. The East/West fixation of postcolonial discourse misses the key point of this reversal: that the colonial thrust of capitalism has "gone native." The cult of Asian values, for example, has the social-psychological advantage of seeming authentically "Eastern" even as it reproduces the colonial function.

This puts Asian exceptionalism into apparent conflict with standard, utopian visions of globalization. Of course, the global order now taking shape is hardly the New World Order envisioned by American triumphalists in the wake of the Soviet collapse. Nor is it cast in the formal, legalist mold of the EU. Its structure owes much to the invisible logic of East Asian capitalism, where liberal democracy is subordinate to the dynamics of statist economism. Early in the 1990s Ernest Gellner speculated that for more developed economies the collective nature of the Confucian-authoritarian mode may be superior to economic systems rooted in Calvinist individualism.[20] After the 1997 Crash, however, many hold that transnational capitalism no longer requires, nor is likely to tolerate, the inefficiencies of Asia's Old Guard regimes. Post-Crash charges of crony capitalism echo the old orientalist animus of the AMP, the Asiatic Mode of Production, which for Marx and Wittfogel was as much a moral as an economic incubus. In a similar vein, Thomas Friedman (*The Lexus and the Olive Tree* [1999]) celebrates the moral force of globalization.

Many expect this force to subsume Asian politics, if only because democracy offers rising leaders a ticket for entry into the "international club."[21] By this reasoning, reactionary Asian values will finally give way to a reformism capable of eroding the authoritarian shell of Asian exceptionalism. Meanwhile, as the Asian miracle sheds its exclusivity, it becomes an exportable model for global application. Western conservatives gladly promote this corrigible and transferable version of Asian values.[22] Fukuyama, for example, sees the Asian experience as demonstrating "that capitalism is a path toward economic development that is potentially available to all countries."[23]

The Asian "miracle" has contributed to the neoliberal turn of capitalist globalization in three ways. First, it vindicated capitalist development theory in the face of dependency theory. Second, it cut economic liberalism free from much of its moral baggage, thus underwriting the conservative politics of neoliberalism. Finally, it dictated that developmental modernism be brought in for major overhaul, giving rise to postmodern development theory. Here culture is no longer dismissed as a "soft concept" that defies economic quantification and prediction.[24] Unfortunately, the amorphous nature of the new culturalism allows for an ideological pruning of "tradition" to fit the ideological needs of a power elite.

While East Asian exceptionalism helped to instate the Weberian (cultural) line of development theory, it also disconfirmed the tendency of both Marx and Weber to equate modernization with Westernization. The long contest between Weberian culturalism and either Marxist or capitalist materialism obscured the degree to which both sides supported a distinctly Western modernism. Though Marx effectively exposed the class interest lurking behind the mask of scientific social analysis, that critique now comes full circle to expose Marxism's own Eurocentric parochialism.[25] Weber, likewise, argued that it is "both inevitable and right" that we should credit the "universal significance and validity" of European development patterns.[26] The cardinal difference between these twin biases lies in Weber's concentration on the determinative force of culture as opposed to Marx's stress on infrastructure.[27]

There was also, to be sure, a Left cultural tradition rising out of the "Western Marxism" of Gramsci, Lukács, Korsch, and Frankfurt School critical theorists;[28] but in view of this cultural turn, it can be said that Frankfurt School thought is often as Weberian as it is Marxist. Anthony Giddens points out that Marcuse's conception of one-dimensional society is very much like Weber's concept of bureaucracy writ large.[29] Moreover, a rigid cultural/material divide survived on both the Right and Left of modernist development theory. Notwithstanding many radical shifts of this paradigm—ranging from Frank's dependency theory of the late 1960s to Wallerstein's world system theory of the late 1970s—modernism continued to sideline the cultural dynamics of international development.[30]

Developmental postmodernism, by contrast, has foregrounded cultural factors in an effort to explain the success of East Asia relative to Latin America and Africa. Lawrence Harrison concludes that Weber was right to treat culture as a paramount factor in development,[31] but was dead wrong about *Western* culture. Exponents of Asian values nevertheless distrust what they see as *Western* postmodernism. Raymond Lee points out that the ludic uncertainty of most postmodernism is at odds with the resoluteness of third world modernism.[32] We should add that it also collides with the modernism of Asia's established "dragons" and upcoming NICs. Some of these latter-day modernists are starting to see postmodernism, beneath its egalitarian rhetoric of difference, as a "colonial" front for Western interests.

It should also be asked if postmodernism can be globalized without contradiction. Insofar as "local knowledge" has been presented as a postmodern corrective for the international claims of modernism, there is something oxymoronic in the idea of a global postmodernism. This does not inhibit the search for a synthesis between local and global postmodernisms, or what has been dubbed "glocalization"—the "intermixing of global commodity forms with local cultural contents."[33] But in most cases the "glocal" turns out to be a subset of the global.[34]

The localist dictum not only leads us to expect profound differences between Asian and Western postmodernisms, but also between Korean, Japanese, and Chinese versions. If this explodes the idea of a generalizable non-Western model, it also precludes the blanket transfer of any general Western model, such as the IMFism that laid siege to Thailand and Korea after the 1997 Crash. Either of these cultural transfusions would sacrifice one of Weber's foundational myths in order to save another. In the non-Western case, capitalism is spared while the myth of a unique Western miracle is expunged.

Post-Crash IMFism did the reverse: It saved capitalism while tossing out the myth of the East Asian miracle. But to toss it out prematurely, before neoliberal globalism has a firm grip on the Rim, is a dangerous undertaking. The Crash stirred great anxiety on Wall Street concerning the future not only of Asian markets but global capitalism as well. Fortunately for Wall Street a tech-stock boom was under way, and nervous capital flowed in from the Rim, supplementing the already heavy Japanese investment in the American bond market. Thus the Crash was contained, as the American economy took a leading role it had not enjoyed since the oil crisis days of the 1970s.

The developing world, however, was left without a role model. The East Asian "growth first" model that had looked so promising as late as the mid-1990s was thrown into doubt. If the myth of the Asian miracle had given capitalism a new lease on legitimacy, it also created a developmental void by sabotaging the "three world" order of Cold War development theory. While the second world of socialism was rapidly decomposing, and while much of the third world was sliding into fourth world oblivion, the Asia Pacific afforded a new pattern for development. The NICs of Hong Kong, Singapore, Taiwan, and South Korea seemed to offer an approach to modernization as distinct from the first world variety as it was from the failed development programs of Latin America and Africa.

The collapse of that model cleared a path for the only available substitute:

the global extension of Western neoliberalism. The IMF and other Washington-based institutions were given the mission of taming Asian economics while leaving politics alone. This of course was an impossible task. To bail out a failing economy is to support the regime in power against its domestic challengers, which is to say against democratic as well as ecological reform. This action is justified, ironically, in the name of democracy itself, the assumption being that good economics breeds democratic reform by a kind of spontaneous generation, and without the instability of political activism.

This bracketing of reform politics is what the "Easternization of modernization" is all about.[35] Neoliberalism has sanctioned the politics of Asian values while adding its own ideological twist: the myth that Japan, Korea, and Taiwan achieved their developmental success by riding the free market wave.[36] Thus the politics of neoliberalism and Asian values are close relatives if not ideological twins. Like the East Asian model, neoliberalism amounts to a "bricolage of values bonded by an authoritarian ethos."[37] Neoliberalism moves Western democracy closer to Huntington's concept of Eastern "procedural" democracy or van Wolferen's view of Japanese "authoritarian bureaucracy."[38] It thereby brings the power elites of East and West together, while repressing the political Other on both sides.

THE KOREAN OTHER

During the Cold War it was not expedient to interpret Japan in van Wolferen's manner, but revisionist studies now meet with less geopolitical screening. Logically, the tarnished image of Japanese political development should foster a reappraisal of competing East Asian models. However, since the most notable substitute for Japanese-style exceptionalism has come from the Singapore formula, with its open preference for "soft authoritarianism,"[39] the Japanese model has escaped relatively unscathed, while the Korean alternative has scarcely been considered. Kim Dae Jung disputes the notion that "Western" democracy "is a system so alien to Asian cultures that it will not work."[40] Korea, he suggests, is the best available testing ground for Asian democracy. The supreme irony—as the work of Bruce Cumings amply testifies—is that Korea's battle for democracy had to be waged on two fronts simultaneously: against an autocratic regime, surely, but also against that regime's Cold War overlord. The presumed archetype of global democracy turned out to be its enemy.

One of the merits of Don Oberdorfer's *The Two Koreas: A Contemporary History* is the way it connects those two fronts—albeit somewhat ambiguously. Robert Kagan points out that Oberdorfer tends to reverse Cumings's orientation, even going so far as to cast Reagan and his advisors as the clandestine heroes of Korea's democratic success.[41] That idea is too farcical for comment. Fortunately *Two Koreas* goes on to make the cardinal point that Reagan's "wholehearted embrace" of Chun Doo Hwan, "the leader whom the Carter administration had held at arm's length," evoked "a sense of betrayal among Koreans who had previously admired the United States."[42] Reagan's actions thus ensured that the democratic revolution, the culmination of long and determined domestic opposition, was at the same time a declaration of independence on the part of the Other Korea against America's invasive role on the peninsula.

Like all Americans in Korea at the time, I felt that change in an almost visceral way, though the streets of this Other Korea were still relatively safe for foreigners. Even the rock-throwing protesters at street demonstrations never targeted me or any American I knew. They understood, I think, that there was also an "other" America, which was not represented by Reagan's policies. At that moment, moreover, they could identify with us as fellow "have nots," for the only "haves" at a Korean "demo" were those with gas masks.

In his speeches of the time, Kim Dae Jung was the Other Korea's most commanding voice. But his dissent did not arise ex nihilo. Kim was as much a product of Korean political culture as were Park, Chun, and Roh. Larry Wade, accordingly, has long opposed theories of a monolithic political culture in Korea.[43] Nothing explains Korea's postcolonial brutality so well as the threat posed by the rising opposition.[44] By the criteria advanced by Seymour Lipset—that a basic prerequisite of democratization is a system open to cross-pressures[45]—Korea of the 1980s was ready for democracy.

Nevertheless, the vortex still rules Korean studies. From this centrist perspective the democratic turn of today's Korea must be either an illusion or an exogenous import. Aie-Rie Lee, as mentioned in the previous chapter, considers Korea's oppositional politics a radical departure from what she considers the deferential nature of the Korean people traditionally.[46] She forgets that the Japanese failed for decades in their effort to crush the resistance of these supposedly passive Koreans.

Full democracy cannot be implanted in Asia from the West, least of all by a neoliberal globalism that itself poses a grave threat to democracy. A successful democratic revolution must be rooted in the political culture it would mobilize. Nor can democratization depend heavily upon formal institutions that are likely to execrate real dissent, as opposed to Japan's pro forma variety. In support of such cultural oppositionalism, Hak-Kyu Sohn (*Authoritarianism and Opposition in South Korea* [1989]) focuses on diffuse, "extra-institutional" factors in the making of Korean democracy.

But just as institutional pressure could never alone achieve a democratic revolution, so too that revolution is not likely to be permanently blocked by institutions alone. From a Gramscian perspective, top-down, state-centered repression is not sufficient in itself to maintain hegemonic power. In Korea's case it is obvious that the authoritarian center is now having to listen to the margins. Kim Young Sam's "New Korea" program was able to achieve at least partial success because Korea's state-society relationship had already been substantially transformed.

No single person had more to do with that transformation than Kim Dae Jung. Even the outgoing President Rho, on the occasion of Kim Young Sam's presidential victory, telephoned Kim Dae Jung to say that "history well knows" his contribution to the nation's democratization.[47] While the "Korean model" foregrounded in this study is primarily oppositional, the Japanese model offers little more than a spurious, showpiece opposition. Worse still, the Singaporean model measures its success by a lack of opposition.

Korea has long been described as "the next Japan,"[48] but that is no longer the accolade it once was. While Japan's economy has been mired in a chronic slump, revisionist studies have demythologized the progressive image of Japanese politics. It is time to stop measuring Korean development by a Japanese yardstick. Indeed, as Sang Joon Kim observes, the Korean transition from authoritarianism does not fit neatly into any of the familiar patterns set by the Philippines, Taiwan, or East European countries.[49] Dong-Hyun Kim adds that Korea is a ponderously complex society whose economic successes are best understood "in relation to its own internal dynamics."[50] That is all the more true where Korean *political* development is concerned.

The salient question is whether the Korean model is so unique that it holds little didactic or even dialogic value for other developing countries. In his landmark *Foreign Affairs* article of December 1994, Kim Dae Jung credited Korea's own reform, yet traced the roots of this dynamism to pan-Asian values. It follows that many elements of the Korean model are unexceptional enough to be applied elsewhere, especially in Asia. To do so, however, puts these "other" Asian values on a collision course with both Singapore authoritarianism and the Japan model that Park so ruthlessly imposed on Korea.

Many still regard that cultural transplant as an heroic venture. Fukuyama explains its mixed success and failure in terms of "trust"—the communal value that Fukuyama finds sorely lacking in Korea as opposed to Japan. In his view Korea's patrilineal family orientation causes the Korean *chaebol* to resemble "a Chinese family business writ large rather than a Japanese corporation, or *kaisha*."[51] The low-trust aspect of Korean culture, we are told, makes it impossible for Korea to capitalize on economies of scale in the Japanese manner.[52] Fukuyama's *Trust* depicts everything native to Korea as an obstacle to development, while Korea's principal achievements are treated as imports. Thus Korean democracy is reduced to a byproduct of authoritarian industrial policy modeled upon Japan. It is considered a developmental liability that Koreans, like many Westerners, possess "a strong individualistic streak."[53]

Not surprisingly, the hero of Fukuyama's low-trust scenario is none other than President Park. Park alone had the clout to suppress the Other Korea in the interest of authoritarian "development," much as Chiang Kai-shek suppressed the Other Taiwan. It is ironic, given Fukuyama's politics, that his laudatory view of Park is in accord with Marx's view of state power as the best instrument for supplanting the Asiatic mode of production.[54] Park's distinction is to have streamlined Korean industrialization by duplicating, as best he could, the Japanese industrial methods he had observed in the prewar period.[55] He was applying to Korea a Japan model that the Japanese themselves would not have accepted in the postwar era.

In his 1963 book, *The Country, the Revolution, and I*, Park's "I" wears an emperor's clothes. His view of the ideal Asian government would be one that spawns millionaires and then tightly controls them[56]—exactly what Deng had in mind for China, and what Jiang has brought to fruition. This effectively reverses the Marxist line of causality. As Foster-Carter points out, Park's state "seems to have been more the creator than the creature of a ruling class."[57] Meanwhile, his regime tried to suppress all cultural traits that might retard his strategy of forced-march modernization. And in Fukuyama's view this was all for the best.

Granted, it could have been worse. Park's program of deculturalization fell short of its mark—short, that is, of the Japanese fascism he aspired to. By refuting Singaporean Asian values, Kim Dae Jung was also exorcising the Park legacy. This brand of modernism, as recycled by Fukuyama, fails to register the hidden cost of involuntary social harmony. East Asian modernization has usually been purchased in the hard currency of repression. The driving force behind the "Asian miracle" has been an illiberal mechanics of trustful and untrustful conformism, corresponding to the Japanese and Singaporean models, respectively. As Kim Dae Jung renders it, Korea's oppositional model turns the myth of Asian values on its head, replacing its authoritarian agonistics with an activistic, translocal dialogics.

THE NEW BALANCING ACT

At first sight it would appear that Kim was elected president at the worst possible time, in the midst of Korea's devastating financial crash. Saddled with a crisis he had no part in creating, Kim's options seemed few. Clearly he saw no alternative but to follow IMF guidelines, opening Korea up in a way he had never intended: by surrender to globalist fiat, complete with a corporate fire-sale. At times Kim deliberately seemed to court that image, inviting George Soros for "consultation" soon after taking office. He was just as fast in lifting the ban Kim Young Sam had placed on anonymous black market accounts.[58] Having campaigned against the triumvirate of *chaebols*, bureaucracy, and the ruling party, and against the humiliating IMF dictates that Kim Young Sam accepted, Kim Dae Jung immediately ratified those IMF agreements and made his peace with the power structure. Meanwhile, he used his opposition credentials to win concessions from the unions they had earlier refused.[59] It would be a tragic irony if such "IMFism" were to be the administrative legacy of one of the greatest oppositional leaders of modern times, but it would be even worse if he were remembered as the man who saved crony capitalism.

In some ways, though, the timing of his presidency has been auspicious. Faced with chronic food shortages in North Korea—an estimated minimum of 10 percent (2.4 million) of the North's population having died of starvation between 1995 and 1999[60]—Kim has initiated the most promising North/South dialogue since the Korean War. He may also prove indispensable in the task of restoring a viable balance of power in East Asia. In a recent interview he identifies the present crisis with the instability that characterized the region in the late nineteenth century. He believes that just as European stability requires NATO, a strong U.S. presence will be needed for East Asian stability in coming years.[61] Astonishingly, he let it be known in another interview, and in his Nobel Prize acceptance speech, that North Korea's Kim Jong Il had come over to the same position.[62]

Kim Dae Jung's goal, in other words, is the kind of reunification that would bode well for the whole region. Any hope Kim has of uniting the two Koreas hinges upon the deep cultural bonds between the two nations; yet a much broader geopolitics is always the silent partner in North/South negotiations. Reunification could put a bigger and better buffer between China and Japan, but it could also draw these ancient antagonists into hegemonic competition. In that case Japan will have no choice but to rapidly rearm, providing a semblance of balance but little real stability.

Regional stability depends in large part on what happens inside China. Along with the United States, Japan has gambled heavily on the hope that an affluent China will become a liberal democratic member of the Rim community (as well as a lucrative emerging market). Toward that end, Japan pumped in U.S.$23 billion in aid to China between 1979 and 2000, but as of September 2000 was threatening to freeze a $161 million soft loan due to the incursion of Chinese naval and intelligence ships into Japanese waters.[63] As he headed for Beijing to protest this latest provocation, the Japanese foreign minister Yohei Kono must have wondered why the Chinese so often bite the hand that feeds them. Similarly, despite years of financial assistance from Japan, the North Koreans practice a foreign policy of "feed me or else" extortion.[64] Clearly foreign aid and diplomatic overtures are no substitute for balance-of-power realism.

America and Japan, meanwhile, perpetuate a late–Cold War balancing act designed to counter Soviet rather than Chinese power. Insofar as one of the prime beneficiaries of this anachronistic policy is the Chinese military, the result is a growing regional *im*balance. The empirical basis for such commercial and diplomatic favoritism is found not in China itself but in South Korea and Taiwan, where economic "miracles" preceded and reputedly *caused* political reform. Alternative reasons for that reform are simply ignored, as are the contrary cases of authoritarian NICs such as Indonesia, Malaysia, and Singapore.[65] Despite fifty years of communist rule, China is regarded as just another repository of Confucian or "Asian" values, subject to the same democratic teleology that supposedly turned the political tide in Taiwan and Korea. The next chapter takes a closer look at the wisdom of betting on this "reverse domino" effect.

NOTES

1. Mike Featherstone, *Undoing Culture: Globalization, Postmodernism and Identity* (London: Sage, 1995), 3.

2. John Tomlinson, *Globalization and Culture* (Chicago: University of Chicago Press, 1999), 143–147.

3. Jeremy Brecher and Tim Costello, *Global Village or Global Pillage: Economic Reconstruction from the Bottom Up* (Boston: South End Press, 1994), 184.

4. Christopher Connery, "Pacific Rim Discourse: The U.S. Global Imaginary in the Late Cold War Years," in Rob Wilson and Arif Dirlik, eds., *Asia/Pacific as Space of Cultural Production* (Durham, N.C.: Duke University Press, 1995), 30–56, 34.

5. Minxin Pei, "The Puzzle of East Asian Exceptionalism," *Journal of Democracy* 5, no. 4 (October 1994): 90–103, 92.

6. Sang-Jin Han, "Economic Development and Democracy: Korea as a New Model?" *Korea Journal* 35, no. 2 (Summer 1995): 5–17, 6.

7. Sang Joon Kim, "Characteristic Features of Korean Democratization," *Asian Perspective* 18, no. 2 (Fall–Winter 1994): 181–196, 182.

8. Kim Dae Jung, "Is Culture Destiny? The Myth of Asia's Anti-Democratic Values," *Foreign Affairs* 73, no. 6 (November–December 1994): 189–194, 191.

9. Sang-Jin Han, *Korean Society and Bureaucratic Authoritarianism* (Seoul: Literature and Intelligence, 1988, title translated from Korean), 252.

10. Han, *Korean Society and Bureaucratic Authoritarianism*, 263.

11. Han, "Economic Development and Democracy."

12. Stephen Haggard, *Pathways from the Periphery: The Politics of Growth in the Newly Industrializing Countries* (Ithaca, N.Y.: Cornell University Press, 1990).

13. Heng Chee Chan, "Paradigm Shift, Paradigm Found?" *Far Eastern Economic Review* (November 4, 1994), 36.

14. Sang-Jin Han, "Modernization vs. Risk in Korean Society," *Korea Focus on Current Events* 3, no. 4 (July–August 1995): 55–69, 65.

15. Lim Hy-Sop, "Continuity and Change of Development Values in Korea," *Korea Journal* 15, no. 10 (October 1975): 38–43, 40.

16. Han, "Economic Development and Democracy," 15.

17. Paul Krugman, "The Myth of Asia's Miracle," *Foreign Affairs* 73, no. 6 (November–December 1994): 63–78.

18. Edward Said, *Culture and Imperialism* (New York: Alfred A. Knopf, 1994), 5.

19. Wlad Godzich, *The Culture of Literacy* (Cambridge, Mass.: Harvard University Press, 1994), 263.

20. Ernest Gellner, "The Mightier Pen? Edward Said and the Double Standards of Inside-out Colonialism," *Times Literary Supplement*, no. 4690 (February 19, 1993): 3–4, 3.

21. David Potter, "Democratization in Asia," in David Held, ed., *Prospects for Democracy: North, South, East, West* (Cambridge, UK: Polity Press, 1993), 355–379, 364.

22. Aidan Foster-Carter, "Explaining Korean Development: Some Issues of Ideology and Method," *Papers of the British Association for Korean Studies* 3 (1992): 19–35, 29.

23. Francis Fukuyama, *The End of History and the Last Man* (New York: Avon Books, 1992), 193. This implicit Western universalism was contradicted several chapters later. Here Fukuyama hedged his bet by noting that "Asia's economic success has led to a growing recognition that that success was not simply due to the successful borrowing of Western practices, but owed much to the fact that Asian societies *retained* certain traditional features of their own cultures—like a strong work ethic" (238). Three years later, in *Trust: The Social Virtues and the Creation of Prosperity* (1995), Fukuyama moved close to Vogel's exceptionalism by enshrining the mystique of tradition within his cultural Ur-value of "trust."

24. William J. O'Malley, "Culture and Industrialization," in Helen Hughes, ed., *Achieving Industrialization in East Asia* (Cambridge, UK: Cambridge University Press, 1988), 327–343, 327.

25. Steven Seidman, "Postmodern Social Theory as Narrative with a Moral Intent," in Steven Seidman and Daniel G. Wagner, eds., *Postmodernism and Social Theory: The Debate over General Theory* (Cambridge, UK: Blackwell, 1992), 47–81, 66.

26. Max Weber, in W. G. Runciman, ed., *Weber: Selections in Translation*, trans. by Eric Matthews (Cambridge, UK: Cambridge University Press, 1978), 331.

27. Although neither Marx nor Engels ever explicitly argued that only economics is determinative in history (Carlos Antonio Aguirre Rojas, "Between Marx and Braudel: Making History, Knowing History," *Review: Fernand Braudel Center* 15, no. 2 [Spring 1992]: 175–219, 197)—and in private letters Engels often differentiated between mechanical and dialectical modes of material determinism (Luc Ferry and Alain Renaut, *French Philosophy of the Sixties: An Essay on Antihumanism*, trans. by Mary H. S. Cattani

[Amherst: University of Massachusetts Press, 1990], 156)—Marx's patent economism in *Capital* all but guaranteed the domination of *homo economicus* in Marxist thought.

28. Russell Jacoby, "Western Marxism," in Tom Bottomore, ed., *A Dictionary of Marxist Thought* (Cambridge, Mass.: Harvard University Press, 1983), 523–526, 523.

29. Anthony Giddens, *Central Problems in Social Theory: Action, Structure, and Contradiction in Social Analysis* (Berkeley: University of California Press, 1979), 146.

30. Raymond L. M. Lee, "The Fragmentation of Modernity," *Current Sociology* 42, no. 2 (Summer 1994): 1–57, 43.

31. Lawrence E. Harrison, *Who Prospers? How Cultural Values Shape Economic and Political Success* (New York: Basic Books, 1992), 6–7.

32. Lee, "The Fragmentation of Modernity," 1.

33. Lee, "The Fragmentation of Modernity," 33.

34. William H. Thornton, "Mapping the 'Glocal' Village: The Political Limits of 'Glocalization.'" *Continuum* 14, no. 1 (April 2000): 79–89.

35. Nicholas Eberstadt, "Some Comments on Democracy and Development in East Asia," in Thomas W. Robinson, ed., *Democracy and Development in East Asia: Taiwan, South Korea, and the Philippines* (Washington, D.C.: AEI Press, 1991), 261–271, 261.

36. Alice H. Amsden, *Asia's Next Giant: South Korea and Late Industrialization* (New York: Oxford University Press, 1989), 4.

37. For Lee's definition of East Asian modernization see, "The Fragmentation of Modernity," 20.

38. Karel von Wolferen, *The Enigma of Japanese Power: People and Politics in a Stateless Nation* (New York: Alfred A. Knopf, 1989), 33.

39. Fareed Zakaria, "Culture Is Destiny: A Conversation with Lee Kuan Yew," *Foreign Affairs* 73, no. 2 (March–April 1994): 109–126, 109.

40. Kim, "Is Culture Destiny?," 191.

41. Robert Kagan, "What Korea Teaches? Models, Principles, and the Future of Democracy in Asia," *New Republic.* (September 3, 1998), <www.tnr.com/archive/0398/kagan030998.html>.

42. Don Oberdorfer, *The Two Koreas: A Contemporary History* (Reading, Mass.: Addison-Wesley, 1997), 136, 138.

43. Larry L. Wade, "South Korean Political Culture: An Interpretation of Survey Data," *Journal of Korean Studies* 2 (1980): 1–45, 44–45.

44. Harmon Zeigler, *Pluralism, Corporatism, and Confucianism: Political Association and Conflict Regulation in the United States, Europe, and Taiwan* (Philadelphia: Temple University Press, 1988), 122.

45. Lipset cited in John Chung Hwan Oh, "The Future of Democracy and Economic Growth in Korea," *Korea Observer* 25, no. 1 (Spring 1994): 47–63, 49–50.

46. Aie-Rie Lee, "Culture Shift and Popular Protest in South Korea," *CPS* 26, no. 1 (April 1993): 63–80, 77.

47. Larry L. Wade and Sung Jin Kang, "The Democratic Breakout in South Korea: An Informal Game-theory Account," *Asian Perspective* 17, no. 2 (Fall–Winter 1993): 39–70, 67.

48. Julian Weiss, *The Asian Century: The Economic Ascent of the Pacific Rim—and What It Means for the West* (New York: Facts on File, 1989), 117.

49. Sang Joon Kim, "Characteristic Features of Korean Democratization," 183.

50. Dong-Hyun Kim, "Development Experience and Future Direction of the Korean Government," *Korea Observer* 25, no. 2 (Summer 1994): 173–192, 179.

51. Francis Fukuyama, *Trust: The Social Virtues and the Creation of Prosperity* (New York: Free Press, 1995), 135.

52. Fukuyama, *Trust*, 144.

53. Fukuyama, *Trust*, 136.

54. David Hulme and Mark M. Turner, *Sociology and Development: Theories, Policies, and Practices* (New York: St. Martin's Press, 1990), 44.

55. Fukuyama, *Trust*, 129.

56. Amsden, *Asia's Next Giant*, 14.

57. Foster-Carter, "Explaining Korean Development," 27.

58. François Godment, *The Downsizing of Asia* (London: Routledge, 1999), 81.

59. Godment, *The Downsizing of Asia*, 102–103.

60. "Mass Starvation in North Korea," *Newsreview* (February 27, 1999): 11.

61. "Asia Tonight," *CNN* Live. Interview with President Kim Dae Jung following his summit meeting with North Korea, aired in Taiwan at 7:00 P.M. Friday, August 18, 2000.

62. Frank Ching, "Korea Fallout: U.S.-China Tensions," *Far Eastern Economic Review* (September 14, 2000), <www.feer.com/_0009_14/ p34eoa.html>; and Kim Dae Jung, "The Nobel Lecture given by the Nobel Peace Prize Laureate 2000, Kim Dae-Jung," available online by the Nobel Foundation at <www.nobel.no/eng_lect_2000k.html>.

63. "Japan and China Eye Each Other Warily—As Usual," *Economist* (September 2–8, 2000), <www.economist.com/editorial/freeforall/current/as8660.html>.

64. "North Korea Turns Extortion into Foreign Policy," *Asian Wall Street Journal* Editorial (October 22–23, 1999): 10.

65. Thomas W. Robinson, "Democracy and Development in East Asia—Toward the Year 2000," in Thomas W. Robinson, ed., *Democracy and Development in East Asia: Taiwan, South Korea, and the Philippines* (Washington, D.C.: AEI Press, 1991), 279–291 284.

Chapter 6

Selling Democratic Teleology: China as Reverse Domino

THE REVERSE DOMINO EFFECT

Before leaving office in 1974, Willy Brandt predicted that "Western Europe has only 20 or 30 more years of democracy left in it; after that it will slide, engineless and rudderless, under the surrounding sea of dictatorship."[1] Brandt's words come back to haunt as the dream of a liberal New World Order gives way to global crisis. Irwin Stelzer ties that crisis to the "simultaneous explosion of economic growth in still-authoritarian China and economic collapse in increasingly democratic Russia."[2] So much for the classic dictum of Seymour Lipset (set forth in his 1959 article, "Some Social Requisites of Democracy") that democracy and capitalist development are natural allies. Neither fascism nor communism was able to subvert the core institutions of democracy so profoundly as does today's multinational capitalism.

The latent incompatibility of global capitalism and democracy was already noted in the mid-1970s in an unusually candid report from the Trilateral Commission titled *The Crisis of Democracy*. The authors, including Samuel Huntington, derogated the "ungovernability" of democracy in the face of expanding government activity combined with declining government authority. These proto-globalists could endorse the now conventional linkage of democracy and capitalism only because their distrust of democracy was exceeded by their distrust of all the alternatives.[3]

If few today question the moral standing of democracy, its economic value for developing countries remains controversial. The current democratic crisis is viewed according to where one stands on globalization. On the one hand there is Michael Lind, a defender of liberal nationalism, who holds that "multinational democracy is neither."[4] On the other there is David Held, who sets

133

up a tendentious either/or: either democracy will be pushed to the level of world governance, or it will implode into a meaningless national ritual. Held recognizes that

> beneath the surface of democracy's triumph there is an apparent paradox: while the idea of "the rule of the people" is championed anew, the very efficacy of democracy as a national form of political organization is open to doubt. Nations are heralding democracy at the very moment at which changes in the international order are compromising the viability of the independent democratic nation-state. As vast areas of human endeavor are progressively organized on a global level, the fate of democracy is fraught with uncertainty.[5]

That uncertainty belies the liberal democratic triumphalism of the early 1990s—the globalism that Francis Fukuyama tagged the "end of history" and a host of multinational celebrants were pleased to call the New World Order.[6] From this perspective all advanced countries are converging on a single ideological axis[7]—the first dominant ideology to achieve such a comprehensive grip on the developed world. Despite the manifest disorder of today's regional or civilizational uni-multipolarity, as Huntington terms it,[8] this democratic-capitalist teleology has emerged in the 1990s as the foreign policy equivalent of the Cold War's domino theory.[9] To get the dominoes in line, a then president-elect Clinton called upon America "to lead a global alliance for democracy as united and steadfast as the global alliance that defeated communism."[10] His assumption was that little force would be needed to support this alliance. If the developing world had not entirely bought the liberal-capitalist line, it soon would.

CHINA: FROM BILLIARD BALL
TO DOMINO

The most telling case in point is America's China policy. In keeping with traditional realism's "billiard ball" approach to world affairs, where the domestic structure of a geopolitical partner is bracketed out of policy consideration, the Nixon/Kissinger genre of realism made it obligatory for American leaders to keep quiet about Chinese repression. All that changed after the collapse of the Soviet Union. Extant China policy, and the realist strategy behind it, faced a rationalization crisis. Both, however, were soon adapted to the futuristic norms of the "New World Order"—an order of liberal capitalist "dominoes." The legitimacy of "constructive engagement" with China would henceforth be based on a political projection whereby, in the words of former Vice President Dan Quayle, democratic reform is a simple "reality" waiting to happen. Even in the absence of a concerted business lobby pushing for China's no-strings-attached MFN status,[11] this "development first" teleology proved decisive in securing repeated MFN ratification.[12] It also cemented the case for mammoth loans on the most charitable terms from the U.S. Export-Import Bank, the World Bank, and the IMF. Through most of the 1990s, republicans and democrats alike condensed this teleology into thirty-second sound bites that went largely uncontested. President Clinton echoed Quayle in a 1997 press conference where he declared that freedom was as "inevitable" in China as the fall of the Berlin Wall had been in Germany.[13] And despite hints during his campaign that major policy changes would follow his election, George W. Bush now toes the same line—essentially holding that capitalism is not just conducive to Chinese democracy, but virtually guarantees its advent.[14] Except for the Republican far Right, defiantly represented by William Kristol and Robert Kagan,[15] there is little difference between the democratic and Republican positions on "free" trade with China.[16]

This bipartisan corporatism manages to ignore the worst human rights setback since Tiananmen: the crackdown on dissent that began in October 1998. Thomas Friedman is on solid enough ground when he looks toward the raw democratic potential of China's information explosion. Perhaps he is even justified in calling it a post-Marxist cultural revolution; but he moves into the realm of science fiction when he concludes that while "Tiananmen marked the end of the student-led democracy movement in China, it also marked the end of the Chinese Communist dictatorship."[17]

Friedman celebrates democracy in the abstract while ignoring the terroristic repression of a whole generation of actual democratic reformists. His focus is locked on China's democratic future, which he can divine because (and he tells this in all seriousness) he got the inside word from members of the faculty of Fudan University in Shanghai. These fortunetellers assured him that despite some setbacks in human rights (!), a democratic victory is close at hand. That of course depends upon the type of democracy one has in mind. Shortly after the Tiananmen massacre, Wang Huming of Fudan's International Politics Department declared that "To carry out democracy, the majority of the people must know [i.e., be told] what their interests are."[18] Wang's point was that only intellectuals such as his Fudan colleagues were capable of comprehending how, as Graham Fuller puts it, "the national leadership has been right on track for the last forty years."[19]

Friedman's position could well have been scripted in 1989, a time when communist governments were falling like bowling pins, and China looked like the next pin in line. As a newly appointed party chief, Jiang Zemin was still a dark horse from Shanghai, and no match for the task of restoring party legitimacy after Tiananmen. Since 1989, however, such doubts have all but vanished. The material gains of the past decade work against democracy by funding the CCP power structure, enabling Premier Zhu Rongji to garner more power for the political center against a recalcitrant periphery. As one wry observer put it, "Mao Zedong centralized, Deng Xiaoping decentralized, and Zhu is recentralizing."[20] Such a reversal will not produce the kind of vertigo that might be expected in the general public; for, as Lucian Pye points out, "even profound changes . . . may have little impact on the Chinese psyche because the people's sense of identity is not rooted in the political sphere."[21]

The CCP certainly hopes to keep it that way. Its slogan, "to get rich is glorious," aims to keep personal identity and social consciousness focused on money as opposed to politics.[22] The present drift is indeed toward political lassitude.[23] Under these circumstances the National People's Congress (NPC), which technically has the power to confirm or reject CCP nominations for senior executive posts, may have gained a "legitimate role"—as PRC apologist Minxin Pei claims[24]—but, in the absence of grassroots political will, that is rather like having a gun with no ammunition.

THE EMPIRE STRIKES BACK

Chinese opposition politics, however, can take a deceptively apolitical shape. The recent persecution of members of the seven-year-old Falun Gong religious movement is a clear case in point. On the surface, no movement could be less political than this, but in China no organization reputed to have more members than the CCP itself can be considered apolitical.[25] It makes no difference that Li Hongzhi, the movement's exiled leader (now living in Queens, New York), denies any political aims and certainly has never advocated the overthrow of communist rule. His consistent message has been one of personal "cultivation."[26] Indeed, faced with rising unemployment and social dislocation, the government had tacitly endorsed this kind of religious personalism. While the CCP was highly distrustful of such organized religions as Catholicism (with its close ties to Taiwan) and Tibetan Buddhism, the Falun Gong seemed innocuous, concentrating on nothing more subversive than the physical and spiritual exercises of traditional "*qigong*." The group's condemnation of drinking, smoking, and corruption, as well as homosexuality,[27] would ordinarily find favor with a government whose greatest fear is social disorder.[28]

That approbation evaporated in April 1999 when the Falun Gong punctuated its call for official recognition with a ten-thousand-member demonstration in front of central government headquarters. As Erik Eckholm notes, this action too well illustrated the organization's ability to mobilize its huge membership from different provinces.[29] Eckholm reminds us that during the Cultural Revolution Mao sent the army in to disperse his own Red Guards when their local units began to form broader organizations.[30]

Meanwhile the crackdown continues on other religions: Catholicism, Tibetan Buddhism, and the Protestant "house churches" that illegally serve 30 to 40 million clandestine worshipers.[31] The irony is that the general population's cynicism about politics is precisely what renders these religious currents political in the minds of nervous party functionaries, many of whom have reason to fear a religious reaction against corruption: the government itself admitted that in 1998 U.S.$14.2 billion in public funds—one-fifth of the central government's total revenue for that year—had been mysteriously mislaid.[32]

Tellingly, Falun Gong leaders who never saw themselves as enemies of the state began getting sentences of up to eighteen years in one-day trials—even more severe than those given to China Democracy Party leaders.[33] Most Falun Gong members were middle-aged or elderly. They no doubt had their share of resentment over being deprived of social security and health benefits that formerly came with their "iron rice bowls"; but their political demands were light as compared to activist students, intellectuals, or workers.

Why, then, did the government decide to treat this mole hill as a mountain? One possible answer is the very timing of these religious outpourings: June 1999 marked the ten-year anniversary of the Tiananmen movement and October was the fiftieth anniversary of the regime's founding. A larger historical factor, moreover, is noted by Father Benoit Vermander (director of Taipei's Ricci Institute): the rise of religious sects is associated in Chinese history with social upheavals.[34] In these all too "interesting times," the Chinese government hopes to hide the malady by suppressing the symptoms.

Another factor is again external to the Falun Gong itself: their stress on harmony between man and nature is suspiciously in line with the rising current of environmentalism. The government was sensitive to this issue after the summer floods of 1998 underscored state complicity in a development model that promotes deforestation and all but guarantees flooding. However, there is nothing special about this eco-sensitivity. Almost any new and popular idea can set the government on edge. As Steven Mufson observes, the root of the problem is that the party no longer stands for anything except raw power.[35] This produces the supreme paradox of a communist party that looks askance at all values except those of raw, undemocratized capitalism.

All this runs counter to the standard vision of Chinese democratic teleology, which by 1996 began to shift the onus of Tiananmen to the conveniently deceased Deng, thereby exonerating the next generation of Chinese elites.[36] Seth Faison points out that Jiang is not only

> stronger than ever, having won the added title of president in 1993, but the party has also remained firmly in control, without ever changing its intensely secretive and outdated mode of governing. Virtually no moves have been made to dilute its auto-cratic powers; party leaders still reach decisions in private, without more than a cur-sory pause to consider public opinion.[37]

Friedman cannot comprehend this reversal, because he imagines prosperity and authoritarianism to be like oil and water. Perhaps he should take a closer look at such repositories of Asian values as Singapore, Indonesia, and Malaysia. China affords an even more egregious example. After Tiananmen its celebrated liberalization has joined hands with a resolute neoconservatism—the belief that China needs strict authoritarianism to ensure rapid growth and stability.[38] All too easily this rearguard doctrine coexists with the commercial futurism of China's other power elite: its informational avant-garde. The two have struck a curious alliance that pushes democracy beyond China's reach.

DEVELOPMENT AS FREEDOM
(FROM DEMOCRACY)

As the editors of the *New Republic* remark, Deng's principal legacy was a disjunction between economic and political development. They see that breach as his "distinctive contribution to the taxonomy of twentieth-century tyranny."[39] Many think this mode of development inherently Chinese, but in that case Taiwan's democratic transition requires some explaining. Linda Chao and Ramon Myers distinguish what they call the "inhibited political center" of Taiwan's early authoritarianism from the "uninhibited political center" of the PRC.[40]

Much of that difference can be explained by the fact that Taiwan's authoritarianism was actually an occupation. "Mainlanders" (those who came to Taiwan with the retreating nationalist government) imposed a stark ethnic division of labor and opportunity on the island. They pulled all the strings, but at the price of being permanently viewed as outsiders. Their brutality was so much on display during the February 28 (1947) pogrom that to call their authority "inhibited" is not just a distortion. It is black humor. Any restraint they exercised was owing to their insecure minority status.

The demographics of the situation dictated that this power elite, being small and lacking real legitimacy, would eventually have to make concessions to the "Taiwanese" majority, which by the late 1980s comprised between 85 to 90 percent of the population.[41] In sum, the special case of Taiwan neither proves nor disproves the exceptionalism of Chinese politics. It definitely does not prove that democracy will naturally develop out of economic prosperity (i.e., that Taiwan's democratic achievement of the late 1980s was due to its having reached an economic level that all but guaranteed a democratic "takeoff"). The ethnic factor and the problem of legitimacy were just as decisive as Taiwan's economic success.

A common variant of the democratic takeoff theory is "developmental authoritarianism," which holds that (1) late-industrializing nations need authoritarian rule to spark their economies, but (2) after that initial phase these regimes inhibit capitalism and naturally perish.[42] The "Asian values" thesis kicks in to extend the legitimacy of authoritarian regimes indefinitely. Chinese values are said to revolve around family and community and thus to preclude democratic individualism. Dissidents such as Fang Lizhi are as much at war with this rationalization as they are with the CCP itself.[43]

Western scholars abet Asian values authoritarianism insofar as they accept the argument that, regardless of politics, stable macroeconomic policies are the key to successful development. The World Bank's *The East Asian Economic Miracle* (1993) fell into this trap by laying inordinate stress on "getting the fundamentals right."[44] In fact, such "fundamentalism" would put the Asian values thesis in serious doubt where China is concerned. As Richard Hornik observes, "China's government appears no more capable of imposing fiscal and monetary discipline—the supposed advantage of authoritarianism—than a corrupt democracy."[45]

This accords with Amartya Sen's denial of any conflict between political freedom and economic performance. Sen locates an "instrumental" value in the full panoply of human rights at all economic levels.[46] Nor is this view the least bit foreign to Chinese political thought. The intellectual thrust of the May 4 (1919) movement also made common cause with ordinary people.[47] This volatile linkage gives an egalitarian twist to the word "democracy," putting its meaning close to "an equal sharing of wealth,"[48] but also suggesting an upward flow of information and ideas.

That grassroots element found its champion during the 1980s' democratic movement in Fang Lizhi, now in exile in the United States. The classic confrontation between China's two democratic concepts—top-down and bottom-up—came in a famous debate between Fang and the reformist Vice Premier Wan Li. Wan insisted on the primacy of the party and hence the top-down mode of "democracy."[49] But the fact that he felt compelled to debate this point with Fang suggests that prior to Tiananmen democracy was still an open question in China. Once even Chairman Mao slipped into the May 4 mode, after a famine that killed millions was found to have been the result of gross misinformation. Mao credited the informational value of democracy, without which "you have no understanding of what is happening down below."[50] Today even Prime Minister Zhu Rongji distrusts Chinese economic data.[51]

Like the transplanted KMT (Nationalist Party) in Taiwan, today's CCP has its worst nightmare in ethnicity. The salient question is whether, in the face of an economic slowdown, massive social dislocation, and increasing access to global information, the CCP can maintain the one ingredient of power that the early KMT lacked: legitimacy. To assure broad support, the party must seek in nationalism the cohesion that communism no longer provides.[52] For the moment this is no problem, given the nature of the Chinese press: all workers in the news media are on the government payroll as "state cadres."

The United States, moreover, is always there to inspire unity in its capacity as most-hated-nation[53]—a helpful but ironic function for a "strategic partner." As of October 1997, the United States and China hailed this unlikely "partnership" in euphoric terms. But in April 1999, China's vociferous opposition to NATO's bombing in Kosovo, coupled with Washington's refusal even to comment on that opposition, told another story. Chinese foreign ministry spokesman Zhu Bangzao wondered publicly about Washington's indifference, while other countries, notably Japan and Taiwan, were doubtless relieved that the "partnership" had come to nothing.[54] The mass demonstrations that followed the bombing bear witness to the party's success in reinstating Mao-era standards of journalistic uniformity.[55] Internal Party documents, however, reveal that the United States was chosen for this post–Cold War role as early as 1992.[56]

Needless to say, this "strategic" use of the United States poses a problem so long as trade relations between the two "partners" are conducted on a purely bilateral basis. The obvious solution is to put commercial relations on automatic pilot via multilateral trade organizations such as the WTO. Whatever its economic impact, the political effect of China's entry into the WTO will be to reduce the international cost of nationalistic war dances, not to mention human rights violations.

TWIN ELITES:
THE UNDERTOW EFFECT

That reactionary turn would be consistent with a moderate degree of democratization. Limited democratic reforms could even be in the party's interest when a constituency clearly leans toward the conservative precepts of the old PRC. Accordingly, the CCP is experimenting with carefully monitored local elections to reestablish its grip on rural society.[57] In any broader sense the democratic prospect is bleak. Even Wei Jingsheng, China's leading dissident-in-exile, now tends to equivocate on the question of democracy's immediate feasibility. In March 1999 he is reported to have stated that the China Democratic Party was founded prematurely. He concluded that priority should have been given to free speech and a free press rather than democracy per se;[58] but in June he was again saying that the "best way to avoid a violent catastrophe is to immediately institute democratic rule."[59] This equivocation simply underscores the fact that nobody knows what the democratic prospect is. All that can be said with assurance is that it is not a teleological "given."

David Potter notes the importance of a "break-up of overwhelming concentrations of economic and political power" as a corrective for authoritarianism in general.[60] But this breakup is happening only on the economic side. Paradoxically, rising commercial affluence is producing an undertow effect by pumping fresh revenue into the flagging political order. The result is a massive "reactionary modernization" similar to that of Indonesia, Malaysia, and Singapore.[61] This makes for a deadlock, if also for a dangerous symbiosis, between economic and political power structures.

If any exogenous force can break that deadlock, it is the fifth column of global communications. Such resistance, however, must be directed as much against the new economic order as the old political one. As in most countries where affluence reinforces authoritarianism, the contest in China is between two privileged orders: the CCP old guard and the new plutocrats. An implicit conflict between the two simmered under Deng, but recently has gone public in an unlikely way: a law suit and war of words between market reformist Ma Licheng (coauthor of the best-selling *Crossed Swords*) and his Marxist antagonists. Wisely, Jiang and the central party leadership are sitting this one out. Jiang is reported to have said that he does not support either side.[62] The notion that one of these sides is reactionary and the other democratic is patently false. This fallacy supports a post–Cold War version of the same growth-first formula that set the tone of Cold War development policy.

"LORD ONLY KNOWS": THE WTO QUESTION

Once again the enabling assumption is that human rights and democracy are the inevitable products, rather than prerequisites, of development in third world countries and even NICs. The U.S./Chinese WTO agreement of November 1999 would have been impossible without this widely held and largely unexamined assumption. Winston Lord (former U.S. ambassador to

China and assistant secretary of state for East Asian and Pacific affairs) observes that the U.S./China accord was "welcomed not only by the Clinton administration but also by leading Republicans, not only by U.S. business but also by Human Rights Watch and Hong Kong's democracy advocate Martin Lee."[63]

Lord adds himself to that list, for reasons that are left extremely underexposed. "Lord only knows" why this vocal critic of China's repressive policies[64]—the best and the brightest so far as U.S. Asian policy goes—is turning against the thrust of his own argument. Often that argument fits the pattern of moral realism, as defined in chapter 8. Lord argues, for example, that to champion "freedom reflects not only American international standards and universal aspirations. It . . . serves Washington's national security. Can anyone doubt that a more open, democratic and lawful China would be a more peaceful and positive player on the world stage?"[65] So too he sometimes sounds like Amartya Sen: "A freer society is in China's self-interest, too. In the age of information, . . . freedom is essential for development." He grants that China's entry into the WTO "could feed the tendency, already familiar in the business community, to mute concerns over human rights in China." And against those who "assert that the dramatic opening of the Chinese economy will lead inexorably to political reform," he charges that this "attitude sells out U.S. interests—and Chinese ones as well."[66] We are left to wonder just whose interests that leaves. Who is served by an institution that pays no heed to labor rights, social justice, environmental sustainability, and, needless to say, democracy?

Xiao Qiang, the executive director of Human Rights in China, rules out the standard argument of trade advocates that China's entry will encourage not only commercial rule of law but political reform and respect for human rights:

Sadly, . . . there is little evidence to support such claims. Nothing in the U.S.-China agreement . . . would require the Chinese government to take such steps, and Beijing has given no indication that it intends to do so. In all the overheated optimism about the WTO deal, hardly anyone has mentioned the fact that WTO entry has not achieved a marked improvement in human rights in any other country. Burma, Cuba, Pakistan, Nigeria and Indonesia have all been WTO members since its 1995 founding. Yet these states have not become paragons of human rights. . . . [Moreover] the WTO terms will entail significant economic pain for many Chinese workers. . . . At a time when unemployment is already at a record high and there is no comprehensive unemployment insurance system in place, workers' rights to assemble, form independent unions, and voice grievances with public policy must be protected. . . . The international community has put a great deal of effort into bringing China into the WTO. It is shameful that no similar effort has been expended on insisting China play by the rules on human rights.[67]

Gordan Chang, a lawyer for an American firm in Beijing, reminds us that China has a long history of ignoring its international agreements: "Ask the elderly Falun Gong practitioners who were dragged by their hair from Tiananmen Square this month [November 1999] . . . about Beijing's adherence to the United Nations International Covenant on Civil and Political Rights, which it signed last year."[68] Robert Herzstein (former U.S. undersecretary of commerce for international trade) does not believe China will alter its behavior where WTO rules are concerned: "China does not have the habits, culture or legal institutions needed to restrain its own officials from improperly controlling or influencing business deals."[69]

Likewise, the International Trade Commission (ITC) has concluded that China's entry will not, as WTO advocates insist, dramatically open markets and reduce the U.S. trade deficit.[70] Some even expect the deficit to grow after China comes in: "After all, the United States would also have to lower its own trade barriers, eliminating remaining tariffs and restrictions like environmental regulations, or risk being penalized."[71]

Others caution potential investors that the WTO will not cut Chinese red tape. Vast areas of the Chinese economy will still be so mired in top-heavy bureaucracy that no firm can expect to prosper without special protection from the government. And then there is the question of *which* government; for the opening of China's markets over the past two decades has been matched by the fragmentation of its economy into zones of local protectionism. In the words of economist Alwyn Young, "China has moved from having one central plan to having many."[72] These zones pose obstacles not only for foreign companies seeking trade advantages under WTO auspices, but also for the creation of giant Chinese companies that could generate competitive economies of scale.[73] China's WTO entry offers just the excuse Beijing needs to crack down on local enclaves that pose a political as well as economic challenge to the central regime. Much as we saw in the case of Japan, globalization works against the cause of Chinese decentralization. Rather it buttresses the center against the margins. It is little wonder that the CCP looks favorably upon the WTO.

For many foreign firms, the WTO's vaunted benefits will never materialize. Dealing with the central government will be no big improvement over haggling with local authorities. Government favoritism is usually extended only to export-driven companies that support import substitutions and introduce new technological processes, especially those with military application.[74] Those lacking government protection cannot expect fair treatment under the Chinese legal system. With or without the WTO, and the interprovincial uniformity it is expected to foster, foreign businesses will face years of feckless litigation when commercial disputes erupt.[75] Pervasive fraud (much of it by

Chinese business partners) already threatens the China investment boom.[76]
Clearly it would be in China's own long-term interest to stem trade violations
and graft, but failing that, the WTO's 135-nation bureaucracy is hardly the
best remedy. There is no substitute for the kind of unilateral action that the
WTO would in fact preclude.[77]

CHINA'S PLACE IN A
NEW MORAL REALISM

The push to get China into the WTO is energized by the hope that increased
"engagement" could eventually have reciprocal economic benefits for
America as a whole—not just for a small group of investors. But "engagement" also has a geopolitical motive: to draw China into the free trade zone
that presumably promotes peace and democracy as two sides of the same
"strategic" coin. It is assumed that democracies that trade with one another
do not wage war on one another. What is overlooked is that China, or rather
the CCP, has its own strategic agenda. Its leaders are of the opinion that economic and technological backwardness caused the fall of the Soviet empire,[78]
and they intend to buttress their own reactionary politics and military options
by way of economic dynamism.

Thus far they are succeeding. For two decades China's exports have grown
on average 15 percent a year, a figure that exceeds even the Japanese trade
record during the "miracle" years between 1953 and 1973.[79] However, the
social cost of China's boom has been far greater than Japan's. As many as
100 million migrants grub for work on the margins of society, stripped of
welfare benefits which are tied to a regular employer (if a state-owned enterprise) or an official place of residence.[80] Not only has the economic "miracle" failed to bring China into the "third wave" of democratization. It has
produced the very archetype of political nondevelopment.

This does not prevent futurists such as Minxin Pei from envisioning the
birth of a democratic trend in the passing of the old revolutionaries. Shortly
after Deng's death, an *Asiaweek* editorial declared that his "last great service
to his nation may be posthumous: to take upon himself the sins of Tiananmen
so the slate can be wiped clean for future generations." The editorial goes on
to say that his proto-democratic reforms are so potent that all "his successors
need to do is to allow them to flower."[81] In the same teleological vein, Pei
regards the current drift toward decentralization (despite Zhu's recentraliza-
tion efforts) as proto-democratic "federalism."[82] Though he admits that "little has been achieved thus far in the way of *actual* democracy," he insists
that the "institutional foundations for *genuine* democracy" are fast taking

shape—one of these foundations being the "maturation of the rule of law."[83] That would be astonishing news to countless imprisoned dissidents. But their suffering is merely in the present. Pei is seeing past them to a glorious democratic future, though he grants that the present reform process is moving at an "uneven pace."[84]

Just how "uneven" it is may be beyond the imagination of most supporters of unqualified "engagement"; and I say that in their moral defense. The teleology of engagement holds that democratization will occur naturally in China.[85] But it also depends on two other assumptions: that democratization and human rights reform will come fairly soon, and meanwhile the conditions of their absence are tolerable under accepted global standards, including two international human rights agreements recently signed by China.

In 1992, prior to his China policy reversal,[86] Bill Clinton charged President Bush with "coddling dictators from Baghdad to Beijing."[87] At that time he certainly did not find conditions in China tolerable. Nor has there been any improvement in those conditions since then. Clinton's initial stance represented a timely post–Cold War embrace of new ethical possibilities in America's China policy[88]—a vital link in what I term the "new moral realism."[89]

From a moral realist standpoint, the error of both American and British China policy has been their excessive "engagement" with the CCP establishment as opposed to the Chinese people. This is why Wei Jingsheng has called Britain's policy a signal "disgrace."[90] Realism in general trusts other nations about as far as their interests extend and is always ready to back rhetoric with force, or at least hard bargaining. The new moral realism is not averse to hard bargaining, but it differs by implanting ethics in realism, uniting "idealist" concerns with realist power politics. It is thus able to "engage" the interests of Wei Jingsheng—most notably his demand for democracy as China's "fifth modernization"[91]—while guarding against the interests of Jiang Zemin.[92]

This moral realist gambit concurs with Denny Roy's observation that American policymakers now have wider opportunity "to implement liberal principles and institutions" abroad. To make "the spread of democracy the central principle of American grand strategy represents a step towards convergence between the oft-contradictory impetuses of national interests and national ideals."[93] However, on the side of strategy, Robert Manning (director of Asian studies at the U.S. Council on Foreign Relations) speaks of the need for a "new realism" in U.S.-China relations, one that no longer ignores the Chinese military buildup in order to counter a defunct Soviet Union.[94] By the same token, this new realism no longer has the Soviet Union as an excuse for ignoring Chinese human rights violations. The new moral realism that I posit amounts to the union of Roy's idealism and Manning's new realism.[95]

While Clintonesque "engagement" has no place in this moral realism, neither does a policy of categorical disengagement, which would just as surely void the possibility of economic sanctions and other peaceful means of hard diplomacy. To expose the U.S.-China "strategic partnership" as a sham is not to say the two nations have no common interests. It is obvious after September 11, 2001, that both would be ill served by the spread of Islamic fundamentalism,[96] and both (although China often forgets this) have a big stake in curtailing the spread of weapons of mass destruction. By voluntarily stanching that proliferation, China could reap tremendous global prestige, not to mention the "peace dividend" of regional security. Likewise, as Orville Schell argues, China would gain world respect if it would renounce the use of force in its disputes over Taiwan's self-determination, Tibet's autonomy, and Hong Kong's democratization.[97] In short, China's interest would be better served by a less truculent realism.

So too, American policy cannot afford to neglect the moral element in the new realism. This must include concern for the economic welfare *and* political development of China's 1.3 billion population. That expansive sense of engagement is the very antithesis of current efforts to placate the CCP. This misguided accord is not redeemed by highly selective expressions of concern for Chinese democratization. Even Wei Jingsheng, the darling of neoliberal pundits, resents the U.S. State Department's use of his and Liu Niachun's release (Liu's coinciding with the eleven- and twelve-year prison sentences given to three other democratic activists: Xu Wenli, Wang Youcai, and Qin Yongmin) as an example of China's "positive steps in human rights."[98] This reservation does not prevent Wei's de facto co-optation by globalists. The major media pay no heed to the warning of Liu Binyan, at Princeton, that except "for people who listen to foreign broadcasts, nobody in China has ever heard about Wei Jingsheng."[99] Few know or care that as a representative voice of Chinese democratic dissent, Wei falls short of his rival expatriate Wang Xizhe, whose socialist views ensure his relative anonymity in the West.[100] Like Wang, most Chinese are appalled by party corruption yet unready to forfeit what they see as the better elements of socialism.

Wei is heard to the extent that he is a pawn in the emerging globalist chess game. The privileged pieces on this geo-commercial chessboard are the post-industrial traders of information that Robert Reich calls "symbolic analysts."[101] Once they would have been labeled "capitalist roaders," but today both party reactionaries and democratic dissidents require their communicative support. Chinese democracy will have to find its own voice, somewhere between Wei and Wang, in the interstices of this highly privileged discourse.

My point is not that globalists like Friedman are dead wrong about the global democratic prospect, but simply that their teleological confidence works against the democracy they foresee. To treat democratization as an inevitable byproduct of commercial relations serves those who would relax pressure on the PRC by unlinking trade and human rights. Fang Lizhi warns that every time China releases a political prisoner or joins a UN discussion on human rights, it is because of such pressure.[102]

There is also the danger that less-experienced Chinese dissidents, ignoring the admonitions of moderates like Fang, could fall under the spell of a global teleology that ignores the hard realities of local political culture. Just such media saturation set the stage for the unnecessary tragedy of Tiananmen. Reform under Deng Xiaoping had proceeded on a tightrope that local reformers well understood but outside supporters could scarcely grasp. While global communications kept the world apprised of events in Beijing, it also flooded local reformists with first-world delusions of immediate democratic prospects. That global agenda upset the delicate balance of authority and resistance at the local level.

Under the panoptic gaze of CNN, the first world could "read" Tiananmen as a scripted spectacle: the future according to Francis Fukuyama. This vision of harmony in the making—the making of the "end of history"—came to be believed by many of the protesters themselves. What CNN viewers took as a logical step in a liberal-democratic teleology, the CCP saw as a high-tech Trojan horse: first-world values implanted in the heart of the second.

Along with the BBC and Hong Kong radio and television broadcasts, the major source of this implantation was the Voice of America (VOA), which reached an estimated 60 to 100 million Chinese during the 1989 crisis. The VOA took the same cheerleading role that Radio Free Europe played forty years ago in Budapest, egging on the Hungarians to a tragically futile revolt. Ironically, China's martial law crackdown created an informational void that enormously increased foreign influence in those crucial days. After May 20, students and other protesters turned by default to the foreign press, while more and more protest signs appeared in English.[103]

Local knowledge, however, is not the only area where global mediation falls short. It has more programmatic defects. Friedman fails to grasp that more is being packaged in the global media than democratic ideals. There is also the structured inequality that Leslie Sklair calls the "culture-ideology" of consumerism, and Roland Axtmann sees as the ideological prerequisite of global capitalism.[104] The media's democratic trappings, while significant, must be viewed as a silver lining on this otherwise dark cloud. The communicative process that transmits democracy also transforms it—selling it, but also selling it out.

NOTES

1. Quoted in Michael J. Crozier, Samuel P. Huntington, and Joji Watanuki, eds., *The Crisis of Democracy: Report on the Governability of Democracies to the Trilateral Commission* (New York: New York University Press, 1975), 2.

2. Irwin Stelzer, "A Question of Linkage: Capitalism, Prosperity, Democracy," *National Interest*, no. 35 (Spring 1994): 29–35, 29.

3. Crozier et al., *The Crisis of Democracy*, 30, 102, 159.

4. Michael Lind, "In Defense of Liberal Nationalism," *Foreign Affairs* 73, no. 3 (May–June 1994): 87–99, 95.

5. David Held, "Democracy, the Nation-State and the Global System," in David Held, ed., *Political Theory Today* (Stanford, Calif.: Stanford University Press, 1991), 197–235, 197.

6. For the most part Fukuyama qualifies as a model democratic teleologist. As he puts it, "a remarkable convergence of political and economic institutions has taken place around the world. . . . Today virtually all advanced countries have adopted, or are trying to adopt, liberal democratic political institutions" (Francis Fukuyama, *Trust: The Social Virtues and the Creation of Prosperity* [New York: Free Press, 1995], 1). Since for Fukuyama the force behind this convergence is technology-driven capitalism (*Trust*, 2), it follows by his logic that to promote capitalism in a country like China is to promote liberal democracy. At times, however, Fukuyama gets cold feet, retreating from teleology to the more contingent realm of politics (e.g., Francis Fukuyama, *The End of History and the Last Man* [New York: Avon Books, 1992], 220).

7. Fukuyama, *Trust*, 1.

8. Samuel P. Huntington, "The Lonely Superpower," *Foreign Affairs* 78, no. 2 (March–April 1999): 35–49, 36.

9. Thomas L. Friedman, "The Reverse Domino," *New York Times* Op-Ed (March 19, 1999), <www.nytimes.com/library/opinion/friedman/031999frie.html>.

10. Quoted in Robert W. Tucker, "Realism and the New Consensus," *National Interest*, no. 30 (Winter 1992–93): 33–36, 35.

11. James Mann, *About Face: A History of America's Curious Relationship with China, from Nixon to Clinton* (New York: Alfred Knopf, 1999), 231.

12. Henry S. Rowen, "The Tide Underneath the Third Wave," in Larry Diamond and Marc F. Plattner, eds., *The Global Resurgence of Democracy* (Baltimore: Johns Hopkins University Press, 1996), 307–319, 317.

13. Mann, *About Face*, 235.

14. Lawrence F. Kaplan, "Trade Barrier: Why Trade Won't Bring Democracy to China," *New Republic* (July 9, 2001), <www.thenewrepublic.com/070901/kaplan 070901.html>.

15. Murray Hiebert, "Pushing Bush to the Right," *Far Eastern Economic Review* (May 31, 2001), <www.feer.com/_0105_31/p021region.html>.

16. Kaplan, "Trade Barrier."

17. Thomas L. Friedman, "While We Were Sleeping," *New York Times* Op-Ed (March 26, 1999), <www.nytimes.com/library/opinion/friedman/032699frie.html>.

18. Quoted in Graham E. Fuller, *The Democracy Trap: The Perils of the Post-Cold War World* (New York: Dutton, 1991), 234.

19. Fuller, *The Democracy Trap*, 234.

20. Enzio von Pfeil, "China's Need for Law," *Far Eastern Economic Review* 162, no. 12 (March 25, 1999): 55.

21. Lucian W. Pye, "Chinese Democracy and Constitutional Development," in Fumino Itoh, ed., *China in the Twenty-First Century: Politics, Economy, and Society* (Tokyo: United Nations University Press, 1997), 205–218, 209.

22. Pye, "Chinese Democracy and Constitutional Development," 205.

23. Liu Kang, "Is There an Alternative to (Capitalist) Globalization? The Debate about Modernity in China," *Boundary 2* 23, no. 3 (Fall 1996): 193–218, 198.

24. Minxin Pei, "Is China Democratizing?" *Foreign Affairs* 77, no. 1 (January–February 1998): 68–82, 74–75.

25. George Melloan, "China's Unspoken Goal Is to Destroy America's Power," *Asian Wall Street Journal* (May 11, 1999): 10.

26. Erik Eckholm, "A Quiet Roar: China's Leadership Feels Threatened by a Sect Seeking Peace," *New York Times* International (November 4, 1999), <www.nytimes.com/library/world/asia/110499china-falon.html>.

27. Erik Eckholm, "China Sentences 4 in Spiritual Group to Long Jail Time," *New York Times* International (December 27, 1999), <www. nytimes.com/library/world/asia/122799china-falunggong.html>.

28. Jonathan Mirsky, "Jumping into the Sea," *New York Review of Books* 42, no. 11 (June 22, 1995): 52–54, 52.

29. Eckholm, "China Sentences 4."

30. Eckholm, "A Quiet Roar."

31. John Pomfret, "China Girds for a Battle of the Spirit," *Washington Post* (January 10, 2000), <www.washingtonpost.com/wp-srv/WPlate/2000-01/10/110l-011000-idx.html>.

32. See "Chinese Communists Cracking Down," *New York Times* AP Breaking News (September 18, 1999), <www.nytimes.com/aponline/i/AP-Purging-China.html>.

33. Eckholm, "China Sentences 4"; Eckholm, "A Quiet Roar."

34. Benoit Vermander, "China's Masses Seek a Creed, Not a Revolution," *Asian Wall Street Journal* (April 28, 1999): 10.

35. Steven Mufson, "The Real Deal: Chinese Communism Doesn't Mean Much Anymore," *Washington Post* (November 21, 1999): BO1.

36. For example, see "China's Next Reform: The Emperor is Dead! Long Live . . . Democracy?" *Asiaweek* Editorial (March 7, 1996), <www.asiaweek.com/asiaweek/97/0307/ed1.html>.

37. Seth Faison, "Eye of the Tiger: What Jiang Zemin Tells Us About China," *Foreign Affairs* 18, no. 1 (January–February 1999): 140–145, 140–141.

38. Yongnian Zheng, "Development and Democracy: Are They Compatible in China?" *Political Science Quarterly* 109, no. 2 (Summer 1994): 235–259, 236.

39. "Destructive Engagement," *New Republic* Editorial (March 10, 1997), <www.enews.com/magazines/tnr/textonly/031097.html>.

40. Linda Chao and Ramon H. Myers, *The First Chinese Democracy: Political Life in the Republic of China on Taiwan* (Baltimore: Johns Hopkins University Press, 1998), 8–9.

41. Shelley Rigger, "Mobilization Authoritarianism and Political Opposition in Tai-

wan," in Garry Rodan, ed., *Political Oppositions in Industrializing Asia* (London: Routledge, 1996), 300–322, 311.

42. Garry Rodan, "Theorising Political Opposition in East and Southeast Asia," in Garry Rodan, ed., *Political Oppositions in Industrializing Asia* (London: Routledge, 1996), 1–39, 2.

43. Lizhi Fang, "A Distant View of Tiananmen," interview, *Newsweek* Asian edition (July 18, 1994): 48.

44. Quoted Richard Hornik, "Bursting China's Bubble," *Foreign Affairs* 73, no. 3 (May–June 1994): 28–42, 29.

45. Richard Hornik, "Bursting China's Bubble," *Foreign Affairs* 73, no. 3 (May–June 1994): 28–42, 29.

46. Amartya Sen, *Development as Freedom* (New York: Alfred A. Knopf, 1999), 150, 151.

47. Jonathan Mirsky, "The Prodigal Sons," *New York Review of Books* 41, no. 11 (June 9, 1994): 36.

48. Perry Link, "The Old Man's New China," *New York Review of Books* 41, no. 11 (June 9, 1994): 31–36, 31.

49. Orville Schell, *Discos and Democracy: China in the Throes of Reform* (New York: Pantheon Books, 1988), 217.

50. Mao quoted in Sen, *Development as Freedom*, 182.

51. Gerald Segal, "Does China Matter?" *Foreign Affairs* 78, no. 5 (September–October 1999): 24–36, 25.

52. Yongnian Zheng, "Nationalism, Neo-Authoritarianism, and Political Liberalism: Are They Shaping Political Agendas in China?" *Asian Affairs* 19, no. 4 (Winter 1993): 207–227, 210–211; Gerald Segal, "China's Changing Shape," *Foreign Affairs* 73, no. 3 (May–June 1994): 43–58, 43.

53. Robert Kagan, "China's No. 1 Enemy," *New York Times* Op-Ed (May 11, 1999), <www.nytimes.com/yr/mo/day/oped/11kaga.html>.

54. Bruce Gilley and Shawn W. Crispin, "Limited Engagement," *Far Eastern Economic Review* 162, no. 16 (April 22, 1999): 12–14, 12.

55. Weiguo Zhang, "China's Puppet Journalists," *Asian Wall Street Journal* (June 3, 1999), 10.

56. Richard Bernstein and Ross Munro, *The Coming Conflict with China* (New York: Alfred A. Knopf, 1997), 20.

57. Merle Goldman, "In Rural China, a Brief Swell of Electoral Waters," *Washington Post* Editorial (February 21, 1999): B02.

58. Erling Hoh, "Freedom's Factions: Wei Jingsheng Fails to Rally Exiled Dissidents," *Far Eastern Economic Review* 162, no. 2 (March 4, 1999): 26–27, 26.

59. Jingsheng Wei, "China Must Embrace Democracy," *Asian Wall Street Journal* (June 4–5, 1999): 10.

60. David Potter, "Democratization in Asia," in David Held, ed., *Prospects for Democracy: North, South, East, West* (Stanford, Calif.: Stanford University Press, 1993), 355–379, 376.

61. Kanishka Jayasuriya, "Understanding 'Asian Values' as a Form of Reactionary Modernization," *Contemporary Politics* 4, no. 1 (1988): 77–91, 83.

62. Susan V. Lawrence, "War of Words," *Far Eastern Economic Review* (May 6, 1999): 27–29, 28.

63. Winston Lord, "WTO: Proceed Without Illusions," *Asian Wall Street Journal* (November 22, 1999): 10.

64. For example, "Former U.S. Envoy Criticizes China," *New York Times* AP Breaking News (May 18, 1999), <www.nytimes.com/aponline/i/AP-Taiwan-China-US.html>.

65. Lord, "WTO," 10.

66. Lord, "WTO," 10.

67. Qiang Xiao, "China's Human Rights Struggle," *Asian Wall Street Journal* (December 10, 1999): 10.

68. Gordan G. Chang, "Why Trade Will Win," *New York Times* Op-Ed (November 15, 1999), <www.nytimes.com/yr/mo/day/oped/15chan.html>.

69. Robert Herzstein, "Can China Honor Its WTO Promises?" *Asian Wall Street Journal* (November 16, 1999): 12.

70. William R. Hawkins, "Don't Ask 'How,' But 'Why' Should China Be in the WTO," (November 4, 1999), <ic.voxcap.com/issues/issue316/item7086.asp>.

71. James V. Feinerman, "The Clinton Oversell," *New York Times* Op-Ed (November 27, 1999), <www.nytimes.com/yr/mo/day/oped/27fein.html>.

72. Quoted in Bruce Gilley, "Local Powers Handicap Economic Revolution," *Far Eastern Economic Review* (July 12, 2001), <www.feer.com/_0107_12/p019region.html>.

73. Bruce Gilley, "Breaking Barriers," *Far Eastern Economic Review* (July 12, 2001), <www.feer.com/_1007_12/p016region.html>.

74. Scott Seligman, "Getting Things Done in China," *Asian Wall Street Journal* (April 13, 1999): 12; William H. Wurster, "Trading with China: The Reality," *Foreign Policy Research Institute E-Notes* (December 1, 1999), distributed exclusively via fax and email; contact fpri@fpri.org.

75. Claude E. Barfield, "The China WTO Deal: Sweet and Sour," *Asian Wall Street Journal* (November 17, 1999): 8.

76. Peter Humphrey, "Looking before You Leap into China," *Asian Wall Street Journal* (November 4, 1999): 12.

77. Steven Greenhouse, "Union Leaders, Sensing Betrayal, Will Try to Block Agreement," *New York Times* International (November 17, 1999), <www.nytimes.com/library/world/asia/111799china-us-labor.html>.

78. Joseph Y. S. Cheng, "China's ASEAN Policy in the 1990's: Pushing for Regional Multipolarity," *Contemporary Southeast Asia* 21, no. 2 (August 1999): 176–204, 181.

79. "China and the WTO: The Real Leap Forward," *Economist* 353, no. 8146 (November 20, 1999): 25–27, 25.

80. Jeffrey Henderson, "Danger and Opportunity in the Asia-Pacific," in Grahame Thompson, ed., *Economic Dynamism in the Asia-Pacific: The Growth of Integration and Comparativeness* (London: Routledge, 1998), 356–384, 380.

81. "China's Next Reform."

82. Minxin Pei, "'Creeping Democratization' in China," *Journal of Democracy* 16, no. 4 (October 1995): 65–79, 77.

83. Pei, "'Creeping Democratization' in China," 77; my emphases.

84. Pei, "'Creeping Democratization' in China," 77.

85. Daniel Byman and Roger Cliff, with Phillip Saunders, "US Policy Options Toward an Emerging China," *Pacific Review* 12, no. 3 (1999): 421–451, 433.

86. Mann, *About Face*, chap. 16.

87. Patrick E. Tyler, "Who's Afraid of China?" *New York Times Magazine* (August 1, 1999), <www.nytimes.com/library/magazine/home/19990801mag-china-threat.html>.

88. William H. Thornton, "The New Moral Realism," plenary speech presented at the UN/RIT conference on social justice at the Rochester Institute of Technology, Rochester, New York, July 20–23, 2000.

89. William H. Thornton, "The New Moral Realism"; "Analyzing East/West Power Politics in Comparative Cultural Studies," *CLCWeb: Comparative Literature and Culture: A WWW Journal* 2, no. 3 (September 2000), <http://clcwebjournal.lib.purdue.edu/clcweb00-3/thornton00.html>.

90. Quoted in Nicholas J. Wheeler and Tim Dunne, "Good International Citizenship: A Third Way for British Foreign Policy," *International Affairs* 74, no. 4 (October 1998): 847–870, 864.

91. Jingsheng Wei, "The Missing Modernization," *New York Times* Op-Ed (December 5, 1997), <www.nytimes.com/yr/mo/day/oped/05wei.html>.

92. Dan Wang and Juntao Wang, "Jiang Zemin Shows His True Colors," *New York Times* Op-Ed (July 27, 1999), <www.nytimes.com/yr/mo/day/oped/27dan.html>.

93. Denny Roy, "Current Sino-U.S. Relations in Strategic Perspective," *Contemporary Southeast Asia* 20, no. 3 (December 1998): 225–240, 234.

94. Robert A. Manning, "Shaping China's New Nuclear Doctrine," *Asian Wall Street Journal* (June 8, 1999): 10.

95. Thornton, "The New Moral Realism"; "Analyzing East/West Power Politics."

96. Bates Gill, "Limited Engagement," *Foreign Affairs* 78, no. 4 (July–August 1999): 65–76, 68.

97. Orville Schell, "China's Dysfunctional Public Relations Barrage," *New York Times* Op-Ed. (September 2, 2000), <www.nytimes.com/yr/mo/day/oped/02sche.html>.

98. "The Limits of China's Reform," *New York Times* Editorial (December 24, 1988), <www.nytimes.com/yr/mo/day/editorial/24thu1.html>; and Jingsheng Wei, "China's Diversionary Tactics," *New York Times* Op-Ed (December 24, 1998), <www.nytimes.com/yr/mo/day/oped/24wei.html>.

99. Quoted in Hoh, "Freedom's Factions," 26.

100. Hoh, "Freedom's Factions," 26.

101. Robert B. Reich, *The Work of Nations: Preparing Ourselves for 21st Century Capitalism* (New York: Alfred A. Knopf, 1991), 177.

102. Fang, "A Distant View of Tiananmen," 48.

103. James Lull, *China Turned On: Television, Reform, and Resistance* (London: Routledge, 1991), 190–192.

104. Leslie Sklair, *Sociology of the Global System* (Hemel Hempstead: Harvester Wheatsheaf, 1991), 76; Roland Axtmann, "Collective Identity and the Democratic Nation-State in the Age of Globalization," in Ann Cvetkovich and Douglas Kellner, eds., *Articulating the Global and the Local: Globalization and Cultural Studies* (Boulder, Colo.: Westview Press, 1997), 33–54, 35.

Chapter 7

Getting Past Huntington and Fukuyama: Cultural Realism in East/West Power Politics

HUNTINGTON AND
CULTURAL REALISM

The cultural premise of America's China policy, as treated in the previous chapter, is a vision of all-embracing consumerism. The United States is betting everything on the old modernist notion that substantive cultural difference—the kind that could profoundly impact international relations—is on the wane. Oddly, this dismissal of indigenous political culture as a serious policy consideration comes at a time when cultural theory more than ever stresses the significance of cultural difference, and when IR scholarship more than ever embraces cultural theory.

Nothing has done more to "enculturate" IR than the recent work of Samuel Huntington, who sees culture as supplanting ideology as the shaping force of global politics.[1] Whereas the standard postmodern culturalist celebrates "difference" as an unequivocal virtue, Huntington's cultural politics is marked by multipolarity and civilizational strife.[2] Nevertheless, he partakes in the broad cultural turn that has become synonymous with postmodernism in foreign affairs. In the words of one skeptic, culture is the unavoidable "fad sweeping the literature on international relations, security studies, and international economics."[3] Political realists hope it is only a fad, since their reputation hangs in the balance. It was on their watch that culture was marginalized in the first place.[4]

This chapter seeks a rapprochement with realism in its effort to explore the place of culture in East/West power politics. It undertakes to preserve the

153

strategic potency of realism while putting culture back on Asia's geopolitical map. This requires that classical realism and neorealism alike be revised in favor of a new "cultural realism":[5] a post–Cold War melding of geopolitical strategy and geocultural negotiation, or what Joseph Nye has called "hard power" and "soft power."[6]

The distinguishing mark of classical realism has been the subordination of all factors that lie outside a rational calculation of "interest" qua power.[7] This is supposed to render politics "autonomous" by purging realism of "irrational" elements such as religion and moral valuations. Neo- or structural realism, as developed by Kenneth Waltz in the late 1970s, begins with that same purgation but moves further toward what is considered a scientific geopolitics, one in which the basic balancing act of realism operates systemically and without any necessary conscious intent.[8]

> It also operates without reference to culture. As Francis Fukuyama sees it, realism treats nation-states like billiard balls, whose internal contents, hidden by opaque shells, are irrelevant in predicting their behavior. . . . International politics, then, is not about the interaction of complex and historically developing human societies, nor are wars about clashes of values. . . . [Nonetheless the] earlier generation of realists like Morgenthau, Kennan, Niebuhr, and Kissinger allowed some consideration of the internal character of states to enter into their analyses, and could therefore give a better account of the reasons for international conflict than the later academic school of "structural" realists. The former at least recognized that conflict had to be driven by a *human* desire for domination, rather than from the mechanical interaction of a system of billiard balls.[9]

In *The Clash of Civilizations*, Huntington points the way toward a revised realism where "internal contents" count as much or more than external mechanics. *Clash* implants culture or "civilization" in the very heart of realism, if only negatively, by way of a sweeping cultural agonistics. The stress Huntington gives to intractable conflict undermines the democratic trajectory of his previous book, *The Third Wave*, where he granted the problem of a geopolitical rent between East and West, yet clung to his modernist optimism.[10] As late as 1991, then, it could still be said that he broadly concurred with democratic optimists such as Fukuyama, Rueschemeyer, and Di Palma[11] on the thrust of liberal democratic globalization. Two years later, however, that optimism had disappeared from his incendiary *Foreign Affairs* article, "The Clash of Civilizations?" His subsequent book, which dropped the question mark, details the ethnic and civilizational factors that fracture nations even as they threaten to culturally fuse whole regions, such as East Asia, against the West.

Thus Malcolm Waters, writing in 1995, should have qualified his linkage of Huntington with Fukuyama's liberal democratic teleology;[12] for by 1993 Huntington had clearly taken his cultural turn. This shift was all the more dramatic because his previous work was so often the epitome of cultural myopia. Thirty years before, in *Political Order in Changing Societies*, he famously overlooked the moral and cultural weaknesses of Soviet modernism, namely, the destabilization that was sure to erupt in a system built on the hard politics of lies, militarism, and ethnic repression.[13]

Huntington's newfound culturalism is all the more significant in view of his credentials as a Cold War realist. *Political Order* argued that it was simply unrealistic to press third world countries to become instant democracies when they lacked any semblance of democratic traditions. Hence, strong central authority must first be established. This cultural critique already harbingered Huntington's cultural turn of the 1990s, though *Political Order* was primarily read as a case for the realist suspension of Wilsonian idealism in foreign affairs. Walden Bello points out that *Order* quickly became the handbook for a whole generation of development-minded officials in organizations such as the State Department, the Agency for International Development, and the U.S.-dominated World Bank.[14]

In *Clash*, Huntington easily disposes of the noncultural competition within realism by noting that by their pristine logic Western Europe (either by classical realist design or neorealist structural reflex) would have coalesced with the Soviet Union against the United States in the late 1940s.[15] Likewise, in the post–Cold War world, the core states of non-Western regions should logically unite against America and the West. This has been attempted, but the centripetal force it requires is disrupted by the constant factionalism that stems from deep cultural or civilizational distrust.[16]

While this study credits the contribution of Huntington's culturalism, it rejects the fatalism of his "Atlanticist" retreat from Asian cultural politics.[17] His cultural agonistics leaves as little room for the art of diplomacy as does neorealism. By rejecting that retreat and neorealist positivism alike, it is possible to keep diplomacy in the geopolitical game and in that respect to move closer to classical realism. What distinguishes this study is its focus on culture as an integral factor in geopolitical reality. In the tradition of Vico's verum-factum principle (whereby we know history or culture far better than nature, insofar as we create the former), cultural realism has as much claim to objectivity as does a more "scientific" neorealism.

One element that will be salvaged from Huntington's cultural retreat is his recoil from any attempt to impose Western values and institutions as a blueprint for global development. Since most "globalism"[18] follows this orientalist blueprint in all but name,[19] this study is in that sense anti-globalist. Especially it opposes what Huntington calls "Davos Culture": the convergent interests and values of the small global elite that controls virtually all of the world's dominant international institutions.[20]

However, in place of Huntington's cultural agonistics, my weapon of choice against Davos globalism is a realism built on cultural dialogics. For me this involves a post-Bakhtinian commitment to cross-cultural engagement, including political engagement. In such a dialogics, cultural identities take shape very much as do individual voices: "in response to and in anticipation of other voices."[21] This makes for a fluid identity, but hardly a vacuous one. As Caryl Emerson convincingly argues, Bakhtin's dialogics kept the self intact, since a prerequisite for engaging a unique Other is the assertion of one's own uniqueness.[22] Thus the twin acts of taking a stand and interacting are wedded to the twin processes of identity formation and political action. (It should be stressed, however, that in previous studies such as *Cultural Prosaics* I depart from Emerson by extracting from Bakhtin the ingredients of a political counter-discourse that she would not countenance.)

This approach avoids the cultural relativist trap of holding that on all issues one cultural perspective is as good or just as another, an attitude that has permitted such pressing global issues as human rights and the environment to be labeled "Western" and hence "imperialist." These agonistic labels are designed to block communication and freeze geopolitical discourse in an East/West or South/North mode. The dialogic reach of cultural realism equips it to cross those agonistic lines to deal with transnational issues that have no place in classical realism or neorealism.

One such issue is global ecology. The rise of environmental consciousness has given third world regimes a source of blackmail, "with countries (not all of them very poor) demanding to be paid to carry out environmental measures which are actually in their own interest as well as everyone else's."[23] Global ecology is at once a local and transnational concern, such that neither classical realism nor neorealism is equipped to handle it; whereas cultural realism is perfectly suited to the task. As with all realism,[24] one of cultural realism's primary concerns is security. But in an increasingly global age, security can no longer be restricted to "national interest" in the limited sense. And just as there is now a place for "green" issues within realism, so too there is a growing "realo" wing within Green parties. These groups recognize that although the state has often worked against the environment, its powers are "needed to match the scale of ecological problems . . . [and to] counter corporate power."[25]

These eco-realists have come to appreciate the solicitude for the individual state that all realists share. The environmental recklessness of international organizations like the World Bank and GATT is a matter of record. Between 1976 and 1986, the World Bank funneled U.S.$600 million into deforestation/

resettlement programs in Indonesia alone. The result was massive erosion that "degraded the soil to the point where it could not sustain subsistence agriculture or even absorb water."[26] John Dryzek points out that in 1991 "a GATT committee declared that the United States' ban on imported tuna caught in ways that caused the deaths of large numbers of dolphins contravened the GATT. If a state wishes to guarantee by law or regulation that its food imports do not contain unsafe levels of pesticides, then that, too, will be a violation of free trade."[27]

Meanwhile, environmentalism has taken what is in effect a postmodern turn. Its goals are no longer closely tied to an empirical and hence material frame of reference, exclusive of the moral and aesthetic concerns that are now embraced by "post-environmentalism."[28] The result of these various trends is a remarkable fit between the new (as opposed to "neo") realism and the new ecology. Clearly this is part of a broad postmodern turn from mere survival values to well-being values, and from achievement motivation to postmaterial motivation.[29]

Once realism takes this postmodern turn, however, it must confront the dark side of culturalism: the agonistic realities that killed the New World Order in its infancy. At that point it faces the stark choice of Huntingtonesque retreat into cultural insularity or the development of a more "engaged" realism, as treated in the next chapter. What Huntington's *Clash* gives us is the negative realism of cultural disengagement. In the post–Cold War world that *Clash* so well describes, but declines to ethically engage, a more affirmative posture is required.

CONFRONTING EAST/WEST AGONISTICS

This more dialogic cultural realism bypasses both poles of the East/West incommensurability argument, as propounded by Huntington on the Western side and Singapore's Lee Kuan Yew on the side of Asian values. Fortunately there are dialogic alternatives to both. We have already contrasted Lee's "Singapore model" of authoritarianism with the democratic voice of Kim Dae Jung. The coexistence of economic and political development in Kim's "Korean model" would free American foreign policy from the burden of choosing between the false antipodes of stability and social justice. That blighted choice was thought necessary during the Cold War, when the West had to worry about driving third world regimes into Moscow's camp.[30]

The always dubious rationale for treating oppressive regimes as full strategic partners died with the Cold War. With it died, also, the rationale for a virulent strain of realism that helped produce—in terms of genocide, ethnocide, and environmental apocalypse[31]—the most destructive century in recorded history. Many, unfortunately, did not get the message. On March 9, 1991, in the wake of the Gulf War, President Bush declared, "By God! We've kicked the Vietnam Syndrome once and for all. . . . The specter of Vietnam has been forever buried in the desert sands of the Arabian peninsula."[32] By retreating from post–Cold War global imperatives, the "Vietnam syndrome" was indeed an invitation to trouble, and no realist should lament its passing. Unfortunately, the cultural sensitivity that attended that syndrome is also put at risk by the return of the old power politics.

What is needed, in the absence of a New World Order, is a *via media* between Fukuyama's dialogic liberalism and Huntington's undialogic realism. Huntington's agonistics stems from his still-modernist habit of treating whole civilizations as reified systems. It must be granted that the agonistic worldviews of Hobbes and Huntington are in many ways closer to global reality, and especially Asian reality, than are some dialogic alternatives (e.g., the Grotian notion of a salutary society of nations).[33] Here my objective is simply to keep dialogics in the game by charting a course that is "in but not of" agonistics. The last effective metatheory of global peace, based largely on a nuclear balance of terror, could not survive the passing of the Cold War. And its heir apparent, Fukuyama's posthistorical vision of a New World Order, never materialized. History refused to go away.

That is not to say that Fukuyama's liberal globalism is a feckless illusion. Rather, it is intertwined with its theoretical opposite, realism. Too often globalism turns out to be little more than a front for vested interests, while "realism" becomes a euphemism for the purchase of stability or geopolitical advantage at any price. Theoretical distinctions between the two then evaporate. For example, the opposition one would expect between Clinton's manifest globalism and Kissinger's nominal realism all but vanishes where China is concerned.

The operative theory behind America's post–Cold War China policy—democratic and republican—has been a market-obsessed economism that even Fukuyama could not endorse.[34] This vision of unproblematic economic growth rests on the expansion and empowerment of the middle classes, which are expected in turn to demand political reform. Proponents of such economic prioritization often point to the development patterns of South Korea and Taiwan. However, as Kanishka Jayasuriya counters, Singapore and Malaysia could just as well be spotlighted in support of the opposite case. Both sing the praises of authoritarian Asian values, despite the fact that each is "dominated by a party with strong middle class support. . . . Hence, those who suggest that Asian middle classes will demand greater liberalization are likely to be sorely disappointed. The Asian values ideology serves only to provide a comfortable canopy for this middle class."[35]

The unilateral privileging of economic over political liberalization in the Singapore model differs from Japanese economism in that the Japanese people have more clearly given their consent to these priorities. In that sense the authority behind the Japan model could be called top-down by consent. It is the more forceful removal or manipulation of consent that distinguishes the Asian values model from the Japanese. In Singapore's case this repressive turn had its debut in 1963 with the People's Action Party (PAP) Operation Cold Store, involving the arrest of one hundred opposition leaders. Since that time all Singaporeans have been subject to constant political surveillance.[36] But for the most part PAP has operated through the less direct means of intense media control and a unilateral scripting of tradition. If "other" Asian values have been politically dormant in Japan, they have been forcefully suppressed in Singapore, Malaysia, and Indonesia, and virtually crushed in Myanmar and the PRC. Here the de facto motto might go beyond "growth first" to "growth only." This dictum was spelled out by Deng Xiaopeng, and its place in post-Deng CCP ideology is hardly less secure.

By no means, however, does this development strategy stop at the boundary of Asian values. It is a potent factor throughout the third world, or what is increasingly (metaphorically more than geographically) called "the South," where authoritarianism is primarily an instrument for suppressing the unrest that is bound to erupt from gross inequality. Speaking before the UN General Assembly in 1974, Secretary of State Henry Kissinger asserted that the "notion of the Northern rich and the Southern poor has been shattered."[37] Indeed, many countries that fall under this "Southern" rubric did make impressive gains prior to the 1980s in terms of per capita GDP. Only on closer analysis, with attention shifted to the actual distribution of gains, does the "Southern" argument strike home. As the South Commission reported in 1990, inequalities

> tended to widen as the economy grew and became more industrialized. . . . Increasingly, the rich and powerful in countries of the South were able to enjoy the life-style and consumption patterns of developed countries of the North. But large segments of the population experienced no significant improvement in their standard of living, while being able to see the growing affluence of the few.[38]

Consequently, the stage is set for what Jayasuriya (generalizing a term that Jeffrey Herf applied to Nazi Germany) calls "reactionary modernism"[39]—a condition of radical divorce between economic and technical modernization, on the one hand, and political (liberal democratic) modernization on the other. Where cultural or civilizational friction reaches the proportions described by Huntington's *Clash*, we can expect reactionary modernism to be the rule rather than the exception in developing countries. In India, for example, Hindu fundamentalism is less a threat to material modernization than to the secular state and the whole democratic apparatus. Countries such as Algeria, Nigeria, and Sudan have reverted to military authoritarianism, while Egypt, Peru, and Russia have shifted to repressive state controls. Elsewhere, as in Guatemala, Argentina, Uruguay, and (until very recently) Chile, the ongoing veto power of the military has reduced democracy to a stage prop.[40]

THE NEW SINO-GLOBALISM

It is no accident that Clinton's development strategy, built on the assumptions of vintage modernization theory, bore remarkable resemblance to Kennedy's Alliance for Progress. Both lay stress on the cultivation of the middle classes as the alpha and omega of development. Castro saw that the Alliance for Progress was doomed to fail.[41] But at least Kennedy's naiveté can be defended on the grounds that, apart from the experience of fascism, which could be dismissed as a twentieth-century aberration—reactionary modernization had not yet made its full global debut. Clinton had no such excuse.

As Richard Rorty argues in *Achieving Our Country* (1988), American society is itself being split into a cosmopolitan upper crust and a downwardly mobile remainder. America's "vital center" is decomposing even as American foreign policy strives to create new "vital centers" around the world. This might be a harmlessly quixotic enterprise except that extant power elites are imagined to be the vanguard of these proto-democratic "centers." Growth of any kind is imagined to be progress. One of the chief architects of Clinton's China policy, Anthony Lake, a self-described "centrist," so closely equated U.S. interest with Chinese economic growth that he pressed the United States not to expose Chinese exports of nuclear materials to third world clients.[42]

Whether judged by a Wilsonian or realist standard, Kissinger's present stance on China is equally odious. In 1987 he was encouraged by China's ambassador to the United States to found the American China Society, through which he became one of the Chinese government's most powerful defenders. He is credited with personally persuading former House Speaker Newt Gingrich to drop his support for Taiwan independence, and for convincing the Clinton administration to disconnect the issues of trade and human rights.[43] Whatever argument might be made for these policies from a globalist perspective, there is no reconciling them with any form of realism, not at a time when China is the paramount source of Asia's growing *im*balance of power, a fact that is only compounded by the prospect of Korea's reunification.[44]

This raises the question of the purity of Kissinger's realist credentials even during the Cold War. Legend has it that his policies dislodged the illusion of monolithic communism from American foreign policy. In fact, Kissinger was inclined toward a highly ideological reading of world affairs. Daniel Patrick Moynihan points out that Secretary of State Kissinger warned that America must "face the stark reality that the [Communist] challenge is unending."[45] The context of this eschatological utterance was America's by then obvious failure in the Vietnam War. The domino theory, the most commonly stated rationale for escalating the war in the first place,[46] was being justly discredited by a new brand of culturalism (e.g., Walker Conner's case for the salient political role of ethnic heterogeneity in Asian political cultures).[47] At this of all times, Kissinger blew second wind into America's Cold War ideology by naturalizing its communist adversary.

Kissinger did, however, recognize the limits of the domino theory as applied to Vietnam[48] and China, which he perceived as a nationalistic entity vis-à-vis the Soviet Union and North Vietnam alike. He was aware that China secretly condoned U.S. operations in Laos, despite (or even because of) its negative impact on North Vietnam.[49] He favorably cites André Malraux's belief that China's support of North Vietnam was an "imposture," for the historical animosities between China and North Vietnam ran too deep.[50] In global balance-of-power terms, it was no secret that China feared the possibility of Vietnam becoming a Soviet satellite state, thus completing the encirclement of China.[51]

If Kissinger's early China policy can be credited with promoting a global balance of power, it now lives on as an effete mockery of realism; for, as was said, China is fast becoming the major agent of Asian instability. By any "realist" logic, the fall of the Soviet Union and the concomitant rise of China should have prompted an immediate shift in Kissinger's position on the latter. This naturally raises suspicions that his refusal to budge an inch in that direction is related to the operations of the firm he founded, Kissinger Associates, which assists corporate clients in setting up business ties in China. Thus Kissinger the arch-realist has become, in actual practice, a closet globalist (if not, like his protégé Haig, a mere opportunist; see further comments on Haig in the conclusion).

THE POST–COLD WAR CULTURAL IMPERATIVE

With the end of the Cold War, culture has emerged as a linchpin of world affairs,[52] and any political theory that ignores this factor is at risk of being marginalized. Fukuyama has managed to keep his version of globalism in the game by taking a modest cultural turn, blurring the stock association of economism with rationality and culture with irrationality.[53] Perhaps it would be fair to call his position a cultural globalism, as far removed from unalloyed globalism as cultural realism is from traditional realism.

Kissinger, however, holds fast to the tablets he brought down from the mountain. His hard-line realism treats culture as local color, style, or sentiment rather than political substance. In his Washington years he perpetuated Cold War logic by putting containment in an older realist package: the classic balance of power that tries to reduce international relations to a cold calculation of interest. Moynihan wryly notes that Kissinger's "realism" put him out of touch with the inner substance of political reality.[54]

Where East Asia is concerned, responses to this cultural challenge range from globalist denial to militant agonistics. Huntington's thesis, for example, comes under fire from the collection of papers contained in *Techno-Security in an Age of Globalization: Perspectives from the Pacific Rim*, edited by Denis Simon (1997). One reviewer, Steven Rosefielde, points out that these papers comprise a national security paradigm consistent with

> Lester Thurow's and Francis Fukuyama's notions about the global triumph of capitalism and the end of history. . . . Traditional international security concerns, it is intimated, have become obsolete. Imperialism is dead, great nations are war averse, economic systems don't matter (because there is only capitalism), and Huntington's clash of civilizations is a mirage. What really matters today, the authors variously contend, are technological threats . . . and other lower intensity quarrels.[55]

At the opposite pole there is the all-too-cogent realist manifesto of Richard Bernstein and Ross Munro (*The Coming Conflict with China* [1997]). But these authors misconstrue their own position. In a *Foreign Affairs* article they attempt to distinguish their approach from Huntington's, on the ground that theirs is strictly geopolitical rather than cultural or civilizational.[56] That distinction runs aground on several points. First, it is granted that part of the reason for China's new assertiveness is its traditional view of itself as Asia's preeminent power.[57] That is a deeply ingrained *cultural* viewpoint, entirely consistent with Huntington's thesis.

Second, Bernstein and Munro conclude that China will not go the route of democracy, despite its rising affluence, because it lacks a tradition of limited government, individual rights, independent judiciary, and so forth.[58] These, however, are culture-based absences. Likewise, China's habit of treating opposition as treason is cultural-based and, so it seems, not the least bit incompatible with China's burgeoning techno-nationalism. Bernstein and

Munro, in short, are not the classical realists they imagine themselves to be. However unwittingly, they are cultural realists.

One reason why their warning is not being heeded is likewise culture-related. Americans view Asia as a far more alien place than Europe. Even if they see China as a budding superpower, they are not inclined to regard Chinese regional power as posing so serious a threat to their culturally defined interests as would an equivalent military threat on the European side. This bias skews Americans' sense of global priorities. As Fareed Zakaria argues, two facts are paramount for today's geopolitics: Russian weakness and Chinese strength: "China . . . is surging economically, bulking up its armed forces and becoming more assertive by the day."[59]

Early in May 1998 India shocked the world by conducting three nuclear tests. It was generally assumed that this action was aimed almost exclusively at Pakistan. But for Henry Sokolski, a top Defense Department official for nuclear nonproliferation issues in the first Bush administration, it amounted to "an act of impatience with failed American efforts to stop China and North Korea from developing and spreading strategic weapons." Sokolski quotes the *Times of India*'s comment that "by the time the Clinton Administration wakes up to the danger posed by the China-Pakistan-North Korean axis, it will be too late for India."[60] This view gains credibility in the light of India's former conciliation toward Pakistan. Despite friction over Kashmir, the two antagonists had renewed ministerial contacts and, guided by Indian Prime Minister Inder Kumar Gujral, were seeking more economic cooperation.[61] The United States, however, was sluggish in revising policies formed when Pakistan was a Cold War ally and India a leader of "nonaligned" nations and a major recipient of Soviet economic and military aid.[62]

By the 1990s, if not before, that mentality was worse than dated. In combination with Clinton's China policy it contributed to renewed militarism in South Asia and an even greater distrust of the United States on India's part. Finally some regional advisors awakened to this fact and prevailed on Bush to partially amend current policy:

This new realism in Washington . . . extends to a keener recognition of what Stephen Cohen of the Brookings Institution describes as "a unique nuclear triangle," with India's old foe China constituting the third side. India argues that its strategic focus must primarily remain in China—which it fears has hegemonic ambitions in the region—and only after that on Pakistan. This explains its efforts to develop a long range ballistic missile and a second strike capability through a submarine-based nuclear-strike force. It also explains its insistence on a nuclear arsenal too large for just deterring Pakistan.[63]

This policy revision, welcome as it is, does not amount to a realism fit for post–Cold War circumstances. India and the United States may be back on talking terms, but a security gained by nuclear proliferation on all sides, so as to achieve parity, is a poor substitute for security through nonproliferation and conflict abatement. A realism fit for our times must address the prime mover of the region's insecurity, which is America's corporate-sponsored China policy. Instead, the United States is positioning itself to rake in profits from all sides. Such rank commercialism is neither "realist" nor trust-inspiring.

The United States faces a similar crisis of trust in Southeast Asia, where wariness toward American designs is hardly new, but had to be tempered during the Cold War. That latent resistance found a home with ASEAN, which from 1967 to 1989 was the only regional political organization in Asia.[64] ASEAN's simmering regionalism gave impetus to the more globally attuned APEC, which was founded in 1989 under Western auspices. The United States and Australia sought to circumvent trade barriers by transforming APEC from a mere consultative group into a formal trading bloc. Asian governments rightly saw this as an attempt to saddle them with U.S. free-trade policies. Indeed, a key figure in the U.S. strategy was Fred Bergsten, who by no accident had also been a lobbyist for the GATT and NAFTA.

ASEAN, which leaned heavily toward state-assisted capitalism, reacted by shortening the timetable for its own AFTA (ASEAN Free Trade Area) trade bloc. Another anti-Western shock came when Mahathir Mohamad, Malaysia's prime minister, proposed an East Asia Economic Group (EAEG) under the aegis of Japan, with China and Korea invited but with the United States, Australia, and Canada pointedly excluded. Still another blow was struck when the Philippines shut down the American naval base at Subic Bay, to the tune of an anti-Western diatribe from the Philippine senate president Jovito Salonga: "Today we have summoned the political will to stand up and end 470 years of foreign military presence in the Philippines."[65]

Meanwhile, thought was being given in the early 1990s to an ASEAN-type NEA (Northeast Asian) unity. Like AFTA in the south, one NEA goal was a trade bloc that would exclude the United States, Australia, and Canada. The idea had obvious economic merit: coupled with China's huge and affordable workforce and Russia's abundant natural resources, the capital and technology of Japan and South Korea could be expected to turn the NEA region into an Asian "mega-tiger." What killed this notion was the enormous distrust that every NEA nation felt toward every other. By 1994 the idea had all but disintegrated.[66] Gilbert Rozman points out that the prospect of NEA regionalism "brought to the forefront true civilizational divides."[67] Fearing that Japan would turn NEA cooperation into its own "flying-goose" cartel, China upgraded her diplomatic relations with Moscow, thus putting Tokyo on edge.

Increasingly, however, the United States took the brunt of Chinese invective,[68] a clear signal of China's new geopolitical ambition. The question was how NEA neighbors would react. NEA multilateralism might be dead, but a sinocentric coalition was a distinct possibility. It was not good news for the United States when, in the middle of Clinton's first term, China's vice premier Zhu Rongji got a warm reception on his trip to Tokyo, or when Japan's Morihiro Hosokawa reciprocated with a visit to Beijing. Then Korea's president Kim Young Sam was well received by both.[69] But again the old distrust worked against this trend. In the April 1997 Moscow summit between Jiang Zemin and Boris Yeltsin, both pledged support for regional resistance to the hegemony of any state. Ostensively that meant the United States,[70] but it put other NEA nations equally on guard.

This was the geopolitical context of the June 2000 summit between North Korea's Kim Jong Il and the South's Kim Dae Jung. Some believe a North/South reconciliation could prove a threat to regional stability.[71] More plausibly, Bruce Cumings sees Kim Dae Jung as the pivotal figure in a promising peace process. That initiative gained momentum during the Clinton years but was quickly sabotaged by Bush. One of Kim's dialogic achievements, in keeping with his "sunshine" policy toward the North, was the rapport he established with China and Japan alike.[72] Such "soft" diplomacy is as necessary for security on the Korean peninsula as on the whole Pacific Rim. It is unfortunate that Bush, in his meeting with Kim soon after taking office, failed to grasp the fact that soft and hard realism complement each other, and indeed require each other. Secretary of State Colin Powell showed a better grasp of that fact when he announced his intention to "pick up where President Clinton and his administration left off" on Korea.[73] Within twenty-four hours Bush had countered that statement, exposing a deep but largely unreported rift within his cabinet.[74]

There is no question that the United States has a vital role to play in the region as a balancing agent. That task, however, requires both diplomatic subtlety (a big problem for Bush) and close attention to the cultural minutia of "real" as opposed to abstract or ideological realism. To follow Huntington in his concentration on civilizational fault lines is already to bypass those details. This would reproduce in cultural geopolitics the monolithic scale that encumbered domino theory logic, and with the same catastrophic results. Not only would it do a disservice to legitimate U.S. security concerns, but to the interests of all Asian nations under China's expanding shadow. Without outside support, weaker Rim countries will be pushed into a politics of accommodation where the center holds all too well, while stronger countries will be forced into a costly and perilous arms race.

That is fine, of course, for U.S. corporate interests that anticipate selling arms to both sides. It is a sad fact that this mounting "fire on the Rim" carries a made-in-America label. Deservedly mistrusted, the United States can no longer expect the unqualified welcome it enjoyed in most parts of the region during the Cold War. Nor can it come to the Rim uninvited. Its most urgent challenge in Asia and throughout the developing world is the winning back of trust. Cold War amoralism is obsolete, but the corporate venality that replaced it has proved even less trust-inspiring. Only a culturally informed moral realism, as treated in the next chapter, can meet this post–Cold War imperative.

NOTES

1. Samuel P. Huntington, "The Erosion of American National Interests," *Foreign Affairs* 76, no, 5 (September–October 1997): 28–49, 39.

2. Samuel P. Huntington, *The Clash of Civilizations and the Remaking of World Order* (New York: Simon and Schuster, 1996), 21.

3. Michael J. Mazarr, "Culture and International Relations: A Review Essay," *Washington Quarterly* 19, no. 2 (Spring 1996): 177–197, 177.

4. Yosef Lapid, "Culture's Ship: Returns and Departures in International Relations Theory," in Yosef Lapid and Friedrich Kratochwil, eds., *The Return of Culture and Identity in IR Theory* (Boulder, Colo.: Lynne Rienner, 1996), 3–20, 3.

5. As here employed, the term "cultural realism" carries a double meaning, at once geopolitical and epistemological. Its concern with the emic channels of local knowledge owes much to postmodern realism as opposed to mainstream postmodern theory. The politics of postmodern realism is congruent with Bakhtinian cultural dialogics rather than the epistemological anarchy of deconstructive or Foucaultian theory (see Thornton, *Cultural Prosaics: The Second Postmodern Turn* [Edmonton: Research Institute for Comparative Literature/University of Alberta, 1998], chap. 6). The latter powerfully influenced Edward Said, but (for reasons that are not surprising to a postmodern realist) could not be sustained where Said turned his attention to the particulars of cultural politics. Said's *Covering Islam*, as Bryan Turner points out, is built upon a solidly realist epistemology (see Turner's *Orientalism, Postmodernism and Globalism* [London: Routledge, 1994], 6). On its geopolitical side, cultural realism is a manifestation of what Yosef Lapid and Friedrich Kratochwil call, in their anthology of that title, *The Return of Culture and Identity in IR Theory* (1996). The term "cultural realism" has been applied specifically to Chinese cultural politics by Alastair Johnston (1995), who argues that a tradition of realpolitik lies beneath China's cloak of Confucian-Mencian moderation. This inclines China to be much faster than most states to use force in territorial disputes. Johnston considers this cultural proclivity to be heightened by improvements in China's military capabilities—a point I fully endorse. Here, however, I broaden the application of "cultural realism" to the whole issue of East/West geopolitics. This approach would qualify rather than dismiss the standard realist concern with balance-of-power relations. Johnston's insights, for example, lend cultural depth to the realist admonitions of Bernstein and Munro (*The Coming Conflict with China* [1997]) concerning China's destabilizing impact on the current Asian bal-

ance of power. Globalists tend to overlook the inertia of the bureaucratic and authoritarian tradition that traces to the Qin dynasty, and the isolationism that traces to the Ming. In this study cultural realism is equally concerned with traditional and emerging relations between political cultures.

6. Joseph S. Nye, "The Changing Nature of World Power," *Political Science Quarterly* 105, no. 2 (Summer 1990): 177–192, 181.

7. Hans Morgenthau and Kenneth W. Thompson, *Politics Among Nations: The Struggle for Power and Peace* (6th ed.) (New York: Alfred A. Knopf, 1985), 5.

8. Michael Sheehan, *The Balance of Power: History and Theory* (London: Routledge, 1996), 194; Steven Forde, "International Realism and the Science of Politics: Thucidides, Machiavelli, and Neorealism," *International Studies Quarterly* 39, no. 2 (June 1995): 141–160, 142.

9. Francis Fukuyama, *The End of History and the Last Man* (New York: Avon Books, 1992), 248, 256.

10. Samuel P. Huntington, *The Third Wave: Democratization in the Late Twentieth Century* (Norman: University of Oklahoma Press, 1991), 310.

11. Dietrich Rueschemeyer, Evelyn Huber Stephens, and John D. Stephens, *Capitalist Development and Democracy* (Chicago: University of Chicago Press, 1992); Giuseppe Di Palma, *To Craft Democracies: An Essay on Democratic Transitions* (Berkeley: University of California Press, 1990).

12. Malcolm Waters, *Globalization* (London: Routledge, 1995), 118–119.

13. Charles Lane, "TRB from Washington: Disorderly Conduct," *New Republic* (November 24, 1997), <www.thenewrepublic.com/archive/11/112497/trb112497.html>.

14. Walden Bello, *People and Power in the Pacific: The Struggle for the Post-Cold War Order* (London: Pluto Press, 1992), 33.

15. Huntington, *The Clash of Civilizations*, 24.

16. Huntington, *The Clash of Civilizations*, 185.

17. See Huntington, *The Clash of Civilizations*, 312.

18. Here defined as the ideology of those who "are in the habit of praising the current process of globalization" (Mohamed A. Salih, "Global Ecologism and Its Critics," in Caroline Thomas and Peter Wilkin, eds., *Globalization and the South* [New York: St. Martin's Press, 1997], 124–142, 137).

19. Waters, *Globalization*, 3.

20. Huntington, *The Clash of Civilizations*, 57.

21. Don Bialostosky, "Dialogic Criticism," in G. Douglas Atkins and Laura Morrow, eds., *Contemporary Literary Theory* (Amherst: University of Massachusetts Press, 1989), 214–228, 214.

22. Caryl Emerson, "Keeping the Self Intact During the Culture Wars: A Centennial Essay for Mikhail Bakhtin," *New Literary History: A Journal of Theory and Interpretation* 27, no. 1 (Winter 1996): 107–126, 110.

23. Max Beloff, "Utopia Undone," *Times Literary Supplement* (January 26, 1996): 5–6, 5.

24. Howard H. Lentner, *International Politics: Theory and Practice* (Minneapolis/St. Paul: West Publishing, 1997), 39.

25. John S. Dryzek, *Democracy in Capitalist Times: Ideals, Limits, and Struggles* (New York: Oxford University Press, 1996), 35–36.

26. Bello, *People and Power in the Pacific*, 53.

27. Dryzek, *Democracy in Capitalist Times*, 81.

28. Klaus Eder, "The Institutionalisation of Environmentalism: Ecological Discourse and the Second Transformation of the Public Sphere," in Scott Lash, Bronislaw Szerszynski, and Brian Wynne, eds., *Risk, Environment and Modernity: Towards a New Ecology* (London: Sage Publications, 1996), 203–223, 214–215.

29. Ronald Inglehart, *Modernization and Postmodernization: Cultural, Economic, and Political Change in 43 Societies* (Princeton, N.J.: Princeton University Press, 1997), 77.

30. Bilahari Kausikan, "Asia's Different Standard," *Foreign Policy*, no. 92 (Fall 1993): 24–41, 27.

31. Bello, *People and Power in the Pacific*, chap. 7.

32. Quoted in Ngô Vĩnh Long, "Vietnam in the New World Order," in Phyllis Bennis and Michel Moushabeck, eds., *Altered States: A Reader in the New World Order* (New York: Olive Branch Press, 1993), 397–406, 397.

33. Sheehan, *The Balance of Power*, 11–12.

34. Francis Fukuyama, *Trust: The Social Virtues and the Creation of Prosperity* (New York: Free Press, 1995), 34.

35. Kanishka Jayasuriya, "Understanding 'Asian Values' as a Form of Reactionary Modernization," *Contemporary Politics* 4, no. 1 (1998): 77–91, 88.

36. Beng-Huat Chua, *Communications Ideology and Democracy in Singapore* (London: Routledge, 1995), 16, 44.

37. Henry A. Kissinger, "A Common Response to the Challenge of Development," an address by U.S. Secretary of State, Henry A. Kissinger, to the Sixth Special session of the UN General Assembly on April 15, 1974. *U.S. Policy Statement Series–1974*, 3.

38. Quoted in Caroline Thomas, "Globalization and the South," in Caroline Thomas and Peter Wilkin, eds., *Globalization and the South* (New York: St. Martin's Press, 1997), 1–17, 5.

39. Jayasuriya, "Understanding 'Asian Values,'" 82–84.

40. Timothy M. Shaw and Fahimul Quadir, "Democratic Development in the South in the Next Millenium: What Prospects for Avoiding Anarchy and Authoritarianism?" in Caroline Thomas and Peter Wilkin, eds., *Globalization and the South* (New York: St. Martin's Press, 1997), 36–59, 49.

41. Arthur M. Schlesinger, *The Cycles of American History* (Boston: Houghton Mifflin, 1986), 147.

42. Jacob Heilbrunn, "The Great Equivocator," *New Republic* (March 24, 1997), <www.thenewrepublic.com/textonly/032497/txtheilbrunn032497.html>.

43. John B. Judis, "China Town," *New Republic* (March 10, 1997), <www.thenew republic.com/textonly/031097/txtjudis031097.html>.

44. "Japan and China Eye Each Other Warily—As Usual," *Economist* (September 2–8, 2000), <www.economist.com/editorial/freeforall/current/as8660.html>.

45. Quoted in Daniel Patrick Moynihan, *Pandaemonium: Ethnicity in International Politics* (Oxford: Oxford University Press, 1993), 145.

46. Gabriel Kolko, *Anatomy of a War: Vietnam, the United States, and the Modern Historical Experience* (New York: New Press, 1985), 75.

47. Frank Conner, "Ethnology and the Peace of South Asia," *World Politics* 22, no. 1 (October 1969): 51–86; and, specific to Vietnam, see Frances FitzGerald, *Fire in the Lake: The Vietnamese and the Americans in Vietnam* (New York: Vintage Books, 1972).

48. Henry A. Kissinger, *Years of Upheaval* (Boston: Little, Brown, 1982), 82.

49. Kissinger, *Years of Upheaval*, 58.

50. Cited in Henry A. Kissinger, *White House Years* (Boston: Little, Brown, 1979), 1052.

51. Kolko, *Anatomy of a War*, 419.

52. Joel S. Kahn, *Culture, Multiculture, Postculture* (London: Sage, 1995), x.

53. Fukuyama, *Trust*, 37–38.

54. Moynihan, *Pandaemonium*, 145–146.

55. Steven Rosefielde, review of Denis Fred Simon, ed., *Techno-Security in an Age of Globalization: Perspectives from the Pacific Rim* (1997), *Journal of Asian Studies* 56, no. 3 (August 1997): 750–751, 751.

56. Richard Bernstein and Ross H. Munro, "The Coming Conflict with America," *Foreign Affairs* 76, no. 2 (March–April 1997): 19–32, 21.

57. Bernstein and Munro, "The Coming Conflict with America," 22.

58. Bernstein and Munro, "The Coming Conflict with America," 26–27.

59. See Fareed Zakaria, "Let's Get Our Superpowers Straight," *New York Times* Op-Ed. (March 26, 1997), <www.mtholyoke.edu/acad/intrel/zakaria.htm>.

60. Henry Sokolski, "A Blast of Reality," *New York Times* Op-Ed (May 13, 1998), <www.mtholyoke.edu/acad/intrel/sokolski.htm>.

61. International Institute for Strategic Studies, *The Military Balance—1997/98* (London: Oxford University Press, 1997), 146.

62. Paul Kennedy, *The Rise and Fall of the Great Powers: Economic Change and Military Conflict from 1500 to 2000* (London: Fontana Press, 1989), 507.

63. Maseeh Rahman, "Nukes? Okay!" *Far Eastern Economic Review* (August 9, 2001), <www.feer.com/2001/0108_09/p023region.html>.

64. François Godement, *The New Asian Renaissance: From Colonialism to the Post-Cold War*, trans. by Elisabeth J. Parcell (London: Routledge, 1997), 281.

65. Quoted in Bello, *People and Power in the Pacific*, 3.

66. Gilbert Rozman, "Flawed Regionalism: Reconceptualizing Northeast Asia in the 1990s," *Pacific Review* 11, no. 1 (1998): 1–27, 1, 4.

67. Rozman, "Flawed Regionalism," 22.

68. Rozman, "Flawed Regionalism," 20.

69. "Time for Focus: America Needs to Attune Its Interests to Asia's," *Asiaweek* (April 20, 1994): 18–19, 19.

70. Elizabeth Wishnick, book review of Hafeez Malik, ed., *The Roles of the United States, Russia, and China in the New World Order* (1994), *Journal of Asian Studies* 56, no. 4 (November 1997): 1049–1050, 1049.

71. "Japan and China Eye Each Other Warily—As Usual."

72. Bruce Cumings, "Périls sur la détenté asiatique," *Le Monde diplomatique* (May 2001), <www.monde-diplomatique.fr/2001/05/CUMINGS/15203.html>.

73. David E. Sanger, "Bush Tells Seoul Talks with North Won't Resume Now," *New York Times* International (March 8, 2001), <www. nytimes.com/2001/03/08/world/08/KORE.html>.

74. Jane Perlez, "Washington Memo: Divergent Voices Heard in Bush Foreign Policy." *New York Times* (March 2, 2001), <www.nytimes.com/2001/03/12/12DIPL.html>.

Chapter 8

Back to Basics: Human Rights and Power Politics in the New Moral Realism

In moving beyond Huntington and Fukuyama, moral realism abandons their simple solutions to the problem of cultural relativism: complete cultural incongruity or global convergence, respectively. Minus these easy answers, there is no evading the hard question of universal rights and wrongs. The moral realist must take at least a qualified affirmative stand on behalf of certain rights, those that Michael Walzer (*Thick and Thin* [1994]) has dubbed "thin," by contrast to the obese locationality of postmodern culturalism. This takes us across ethnic and civilizational boundaries, and not just by way of a postmodern "hybridity" that would again evade hard questions. To accept cultural realism while refusing this ethical crossing would be to retreat into the Huntingtonesque agonistics that the last chapter sought to overcome.

"Singapore School" Asianists, inadvertently supported by many postcolonial culturalists, will charge that even to raise the question of transcultural rights is an act of Eurocentric imperialism. But this ignores the ironic observation of the Japanese legal scholar Inoue Tatsuo that the rejection of human rights by Asian values is premised on another Western concept: that of state sovereignty.[1] The real issue is not so much where values come from but where they are going. Alongside Dirlik's argument that there is history after Eurocentrism,[2] we must conclude that there is a place for rights discourse after Eurocentrism.

But what place? The most convenient forum for a post-Western discourse would be the United Nations—would be, that is, if the United Nations were not mired in its own rights crisis. No UN secretary-general has had a problem quite like Kofi Annan's. In the wake of Rwanda and Kosovo, UN peacekeeping credibility is caught between the growing need to intervene in "internal" crises and the patent constraints of the UN charter. Although support for human rights is mandated in the charter's preamble, Annan is less than convincing in his argument that "Nothing in the UN charter precludes a recognition that there are rights beyond borders. What the charter does say is that 'armed force shall not be used, save in the common interest.'"[3]

That, of course, is the snag: Who is to define this "common interest"? In a world divided by resurgent nationalism and culture clash, Annan advances the notion that "intervention must be based on . . . universal principles."[4] This was the heart of his opening address at the UN General Assembly that convened just as a UN-sanctioned peacekeeping force was landing in East Timor. Many are alarmed by recent attempts to draft a "universal" formula for intervention, whether under UN or NATO auspices. Robert Madsen, for instance, blames the Kosovo formula for prompting former ROC President Lee Teng-hui's inflammatory state-to-state proclamation of July 9, 1999.[5]

Madsen does not do justice to Lee, but his concern over universals is well justified. One could say that Annan's universalism is off the mark by about two centuries, as he is applying an early modern formula to a postmodern dilemma. Universal norms don't square with our new world disorder—the world as described, for example, in Robert Kaplan's *The Ends of the Earth*. Nevertheless, Annan is very much on target, and in rough accord with Kaplan's entropic worldview, when it comes to the changing nature of war. Today 90 percent of war casualties are civilian, as opposed to 15 percent at the opening of the century.[6] Under these straits the United Nations must offer more than a buffer between clearly defined combatants.[7] But on what basis can it do so?

Annan suggests that an adequate basis is already at hand: the Universal Declaration of Human Rights. Half a century after its ratification by the UN General Assembly, the declaration has become, as Michael Ignatieff puts it, "the major article of faith of a secular culture that fears it believes in nothing else."[8] The declaration circumvents the horizontal authority of states and sanctions natural rights on the basis of an unnamed vertical authority.[9] This seemingly dated metaphysics is exactly what postmodernists usually rail against. Their silence regarding the declaration would seem to be a tacit admission that they have no substitute for this essentialism of last resort.

While the declaration may stand for timeless values, its very existence was an accident of fleeting political circumstance. It emerged as a reaction to Nazi genocide,[10] and baldly contradicts the Westphalian tenet of nonintervention that prevailed in international law prior to 1945.[11] This puts it at odds with Article 2.7 of the UN Charter, which strictly proscribes intervention across national boundaries. This statist principle—a veritable escape clause for rogue governments[12]—would be reaffirmed in 1965 with Resolution 2625, the Declaration on the Inadmissibility of Intervention in the Domestic Affairs of States and the Protection of Their Independence and Sovereignty.[13] It would be further entrenched with the General Assembly's 1970 Declaration of Principles of International Law Concerning Friendly Relations Among States, which Richard Falk describes as "a kind of Faustian bargain that meant consigning restive minorities to oppressive regimes in exchange for an agreed principle of order."[14]

The Universal Declaration, by contrast, was a manifestation of the same liberal moment that spawned Japan's "Tokyo spring" in the early occupation years of 1946 and 1947. The "great reversal" that followed in Japan was emblematic of a general Cold War deliberalization.[15] Clearly the declaration could not have been ratified much later than it was. Peter Baehr points out that the Soviet Union, torn between its wish to cover up its own human rights record and its desire for intervention in cases of fascism and Western colonialism, abstained in the vote of December 1948.[16] Ignatieff adds that the Chinese seat on the drafting committee, later to be occupied by a Maoist, was still held by a compliant Confucian. The most important accident of timing, however, was the fact that nascent decolonialism could still play into universalism by turning Western rights discourse against the Western powers themselves: "The descent of so many . . . newly independent states into dictatorship or civil war had not yet occurred. It was still possible to believe that winning independence and freedom as a state would be enough to guarantee the freedoms of the individuals inside it."[17] With the rise of the Asian "miracle" economies and the advent of radical Islamism, the Declaration's core principle—the universality of human rights—would lose its global thrust.

In sum, the postwar call for "universal" human rights was an experiment that could never be replicated. The Declaration would stand as the meager but enduring antithesis to Cold War realism. Its force was limited so long as the Cold War persisted, but the fall of the Soviet Union opened unprecedented opportunities for human rights diplomacy. The United Nations had a chance to greatly expand its operations,[18] while the United States had the opportunity to bring its foreign affairs "in from the cold." This could produce not only a post–Cold War "peace dividend" in terms of reduced military spending, but also a moral dividend, as less doctrinaire realists began to reconsider their position on human rights in the absence of a first-order military adversary.

In a sense the clock was turned back to 1949, when the terms of the realist/

idealist schism had been limned in a debate between Hans Morgenthau and William T. R. Fox. Morgenthau set the mold for postwar realism by defining national interest as national security, and national security as the defense of both territorial integrity and basic institutions. Fox countered with a simple question: Which institutions *are* basic to a democracy such as America's? As he put it, "The camel's nose of moral principle is already under the tent when one admits that it is territorial integrity *plus* basic institutions which must 'in the national interest' be protected."[19]

With the Cold War behind, pragmatic realists could afford to get back to "basics." Moreover, they could expect the full blessing of the military-industrial complex, which was facing its worst downsizing since the end of World War II. In lieu of a major ideological foe, a moral mission of global scope could be worth billions in defense contracts—this at a time when the military joint chiefs are gaining unprecedented access to high-level policy sessions.[20] The resulting militant idealism gives material impetus to a Third Way amalgam of realism, idealism, and commercial globalism.

One ersatz version of this post–Cold War synthesis was the Clinton Doctrine, as it emerged in Kosovo. Although this precedent did collide with the Powell Doctrine, which demands crystal clear objectives and an equally clear exit strategy before military engagement is considered, Kosovo was hardly an unambiguous case of interventionist élan. Clinton kept the war in the air, and even refrained from using the Apache helicopters that were sitting unused in Macedonia.[21] Retroactively, however, Clinton put a more aggressive spin on what he had done. In his June 1999 "victory lap" tour of the Balkans, he stated axiomatically that if "somebody comes after innocent civilians and tries to kill them because of their race, their ethnic background or their religion, and it's within our power to stop it, we will stop it." Just in case anyone missed the fact that Kosovo had been an intranational affair, Clinton added that his doctrine would apply "whether within or beyond the borders of a country."[22]

China and Russia did not need that clarification. Their veto in the UN Security Council would ensure that such action could be undertaken only by NATO, not the United Nations. For his part Clinton quickly retreated from his dramatic moral stance by having his national security advisor Samuel Berger announce that the United States has neither the capacity nor the responsibility to come to the aid of every people in trouble.[23] Americans could thus feel good about their moral mission without having to fear entanglement in places like Rwanda, Sierra Leone, Kashmir, Sri Lanka, or, most emphatically, Tibet or Taiwan. The real goal of the Clinton Doctrine, in Robert Manning's view, is precisely this low-risk mode of intervention: a foreign policy legacy on the cheap.[24]

Nevertheless, Kosovo sets a precedent that is not lost on China or on hardcore realists such as George Kennan. Too easily this idealism could entrap the United States in a model of "reconstructive" humanitarianism that actually upholds what Clinton claimed to stand for on his victory tour.[25] In a recent interview, Kennan flatly asserts that the United States should "withdraw from its public advocacy of democracy and human rights."[26] These matters should not impinge upon diplomatic relations, for the State Department and White House "have more important things to do."[27] This is especially the case, Kennan holds, where China is concerned, for no matter what we do the Chinese are not going to "become like us."[28] Such cultural realism concurs with Huntington's contention that the world is at once "becoming more modern and less Western."[29]

One may object—against both Huntington and Lee Kuan Yew—that to encourage human rights at the "ends of the earth" does not require the non-Western Other to become "like us"; for the West no more has a monopoly on freedom and democracy than the East has a patent on authoritarianism. Amartya Sen points out that Chinese, Indian, and Arabic cultures have their own traditions of tolerance.[30] Missing this point, critics like Bernstein and Munro lend support to the myth of an insurmountable East/West divide by extrapolating future democratic impossibility from the failure of past democratic reforms: "China, whether under the emperors or under the party general-secretaries, has always been ruled by a self-selected and self-perpetuating clique that operates in secret and treats opposition as treason."[31] Ergo, it must be so.

Lucian Pye counters that since 1908 every one of the eleven Chinese constitutions have included unqualified provisions for freedom of speech, press, and assembly. The "repeated inclusion of such guarantees of freedom in each successive constitution points to the unrealized aspirations of thinking Chinese. No outsiders, and certainly no Westerners, imposed these human rights values on the Chinese."[32] Similarly, as we have seen, President Kim Dae Jung of Korea outlines an East Asian approach to liberal democracy that closely resembles the views of former ROC President Lee Teng-hui;[33] and likewise Megawati Sukarnoputri, Indonesia's president after Abdurrahman Wahid's fall,[34] speaks of "a democracy operating within Indonesian traditions."[35] Most notably, Sen distinguishes the equity and pragmatism of what he calls the "Eastern strategy" from the quasi-traditional dictates of so-called Asian values.[36]

Cold War realism coupled two pernicious assumptions: first, the notion that human rights and democracy are inherently Western, and second, the modernist "growth first" dictum that puts political development on hold.[37] These presuppositions allowed for the continued support of repressive and environ-

mentally catastrophic regimes such as Suharto's. It is little wonder that auto-
crats like Singapore's Lee and Malaysia's Mahathir Mohamad tie their
legitimacy to a bogus reading of Asian values, whereby an indigenous label
is pasted on authoritarian development programs.

Kennan's argument for nonintervention, apart from such extreme cases as
the Holocaust or Milosevic's ethnic cleansing in Kosovo, which Kennan sees
as a threat to Western civilization,[38] rests on the premise that the United States
"has, as a rule, nothing to do with the origins of the ways in which regimes in
other continents oppress elements in their own populations."[39] The following
examples tell a very different story.

WHAT KENNAN OVERLOOKS

Kennan long ago repudiated his early Cold War militancy,[40] yet now he seems
to forget the fruits of the policy he helped to formulate. From World War II
to the close of the Cold War the United States intervened militarily more than
200 times.[41] Nor was U.S. economic influence any less invasive.

The foreign policy priorities of Pax Americana were harbingered early in
the century by the support lavished on the ruthless Mexican dictator Porfirio
Díaz, who won respect in Washington and London for his commercial relia-
bility.[42] The postwar Truman Doctrine only shifted these priorities by weighing anti-communism into the balance. William Robinson argues that
postcolonial capitalism, not the Cold War per se, was the driving force behind
postwar foreign policy.[43] Trilateral Commission veteran Samuel Huntington
admitted as much when he advised that Cold War intervention must be sold
to the American public "in such a way as to create the misimpression that it
is the Soviet Union that you are fighting. That is what the United States has
been doing ever since the Truman Doctrine."[44] In fact, the two motive
forces—commercial and geopolitical—would be blood brothers in the containment model of intervention that Kennan launched under the name "Mr.
X" in the July 1947 issue of *Foreign Affairs*. The following year Kennan
pridefully noted that with 6.3 percent of the world's production, the United
States held 50 percent of the world's wealth. The "real task" of U.S. foreign
policy, he declared, was "to maintain this position of disparity."[45]

An infamous case in point was American hegemony in Guatemala, where
the terms United Fruit and United States were almost synonymous in the
early postwar years. Efforts to liberalize the country and curtail United
Fruit's monopoly powers were met with charges of communist insurrection.
With generous U.S. support, and backed by U.S.–piloted F-47 fighters, Colonel Rodolfo Castillo (a graduate of U.S. military training at Fort Leaven-

worth) invaded his own country in 1954 to "liberate" it from the democratically elected reform government of Jacobo Arbenz Guzmán. The planners of the operation included the U.S. ambassadors to Guatemala, Costa Rica, and Nicaragua; and, not surprisingly, recently released documents implicate the CIA as well.[46] Allen Dulles (whose brother, John Foster Dulles, had once represented United Fruit legally) was "then the number one man at the CIA. . . . [He] cabled . . . his congratulations on a job well done. Allen Dulles had previously been on United Fruit's board of directors, and a year after the invasion his seat was occupied by another CIA man, Walter Bedell Smith."[47] The terroristic dictatorships that followed were deemed ideologically and commercially commendable.

That political/economic balance shifted in Indochina, where America had no United Fruit equivalent to protect. Greg Lockhart points out how the American phase of the Vietnam War had a déjà vu quality. Like the French phase, it marked the failure of a divide-and-rule strategy that was doomed from the first.[48] America's involvement began with an act of treachery: the stabbing of a World War II ally in the back. After Japan occupied Vietnam in 1940, Ho Chi Minh returned to Vietnam to form the Vietminh Party and to fight both the Japanese and the French, who continued to administer the territories under Japanese auspices, much as the Vichy operated under the Nazi shadow in France. In April 1945 an Office of Strategic Services (OSS) advisory mission was established to help the Vietminh fight the Japanese.

In August, after the Japanese surrender, Ho announced the formation of the Democratic Republic of Vietnam (DRV), which by September was under attack in Saigon by the French. America was thus forced to choose between two allies. That choice was effectively made in 1950 when the United States recognized the French-sanctioned government of the puppet Emperor Bao Dai, known to all Vietnamese nationalists as a collaborator with both the French and Japanese. By 1951 over U.S.$500 million in military aid had been extended to France, along with ninety F-8F "Bearcat" fighters.[49] A report dated February 26, 1950, from the National Security Council defined the conflict almost completely in terms of anti-communist containment.[50] As Frances FitzGerald aptly puts it, "the United States was attempting to fit its global strategies into a world of hillocks and hamlets."[51]

Late in 1945, French army intelligence reported nearly "universal" popular support for Ho Chi Minh. Again in 1955 the CIA predicted that if general elections were held in 1956, as promised in Geneva, Ho was sure to win. In short, the escalations that had begun in 1945 and 1960 were bound to face popular resistance. In 1968, as in 1952, even the most obtuse observer had to recognize that heightened intervention was futile. The respective "Vietnamizations" of 1953 and 1973 came too late to dent the outcome: "At the root of a great double tragedy was the fact that successive French and American governments juggled an imperial lie. For thirty years Western powers wilfully ignored the national unity of independence which Ho Chi Minh's government first constituted in 1945."[52] Even as U.S. policymakers refused to acknowledge this unity at the national level, they imagined an international communist unity that removed America's options. David Halberstam holds that America's initial involvement in Vietnam traces directly to its sense of having lost China to a communist monolith.[53]

To lend a democratic veneer to U.S. operations, American planners considered it imperative that their local puppet be a civilian, a Vietnamese equivalent of Korea's Syngman Rhee, though hopefully more tractable; but given the scope of his family's venality, Ngô Dinh Diêm could better be compared to Ferdinand Marcos. He raked in U.S. funds while all but ignoring U.S. proposals. This inspired W. W. Rostow, early in 1963, to make the radical suggestion (in keeping with his brand of modernization theory) that Washington would be better off sponsoring military rather than civilian puppets. "Benevolent authoritarianism," Rostow concluded, was the best ticket for third world development.[54] Henry Cabot Lodge and Robert McNamara likewise endorsed the idea of military rule in Vietnam.[55] That principle was applied not only in Vietnam, with the Nguyên Khanh coup that eliminated Diem, but in Chile, with the 1973 ouster of Salvador Allende by General Augusto Pinochet. Declassified documents reveal that President Nixon had instructed the CIA to organize just such a military coup.[56]

A similar "realism" was applied toward the Suharto regime in Indonesia. Suharto had enjoyed sustained U.S. support since the CIA-backed overthrow of Sukarno in 1965. Much as America had condoned attacks on Bangladesh by Pakistan in 1971, U.S. assistance for Suharto was not reduced in 1975 when Indonesia invaded East Timor, which at that moment was gaining its long-awaited independence from Portugal. President Ford and Secretary of State Kissinger departed from a state visit to Indonesia just a day before the invasion.[57] Twelve hours before the annexation Kissinger gave Suharto a green light with his statement that "the U.S. understands Indonesia's position."[58] His advice to Jakarta was unambiguous: "Do it quickly."[59] In clear violation of American law, 90 percent of the weaponry used in the invasion was supplied by the United States.[60] When this was pointed out to Kissinger, he angrily retorted that he knew what the law was, but his concern was with U.S. national interest.[61]

Much to his embarrassment, Suharto was unable to "do it quickly." The Timorese bravely defended themselves with weapons left behind by the Portuguese. The war continued deep into the next American administration,

when that presumed paragon of human rights, Jimmy Carter, secretly supplied Suharto with the Bronco counterinsurgency planes that he badly needed
to win the war in the mountains. The U.S. ambassador to the United Nations,
Patrick Moynihan, succeeded in blocking UN diplomatic intervention,[62] thus
killing the last real hope of local resistance.

It is estimated that between 1977 and 1979 about a third of East Timor's
population died as a result of Jakarta's invasion. That would put the mortality
rate much higher than that of Pol Pot's better known genocide of the same
period in Cambodia. The American ambassador to Indonesia withheld this
vital information from the Congress and the American press.[63] Even conservative estimates put the death toll at over 200,000, or nearly a third of the
Timorese population, by the early 1990s. That figure includes those executed
after their surrender.[64] As in Iran, where the same "realism" was used to
secure stability under the Shah, the result was not only heinous repression but
the very instability that authoritarianism was supposed to stanch.[65]

This paradox was recycled in the recent terrorism of anti-independence
militias in East Timor, as record numbers of voters risked their lives to get to
the polls for a referendum on their belated independence. More than 15,000
Indonesian troops stood by as the terror escalated.[66] Indeed, one of the few
remaining foreign reporters, Allen Nairn, bore witness that militiamen who
picked him up were taking orders from a uniformed colonel in the National
Police. In the midst of this conflagration, the U.S. commander in chief of
the Pacific was in Indonesia giving assurances of continued U.S. support to
Indonesia's military.[67] The Nobel Peace laureate José Ramos-Horta, who
charges unequivocally that the terror was preplanned by Indonesia, equates
American and UN faith in Indonesia with trusting Hitler to protect the Jews.[68]
In fact, the violence that followed the independence vote had been amply predicted by Indonesian officials themselves. The East Timorese had naively
assumed the international community would not just supervise their election
but secure its results; and they were not incorrect in thinking this possible,
given the dependence of Indonesia on international support for its continued
economic recovery.

Once again, however, the United States sent signals that Indonesia had
nothing to fear. First the Clinton administration refused to discuss the formation of a peacekeeping force in advance of the elections, and then it procrasti-
nated for days after violence had erupted.[69] Samuel Berger was left to evade
the question of why the United States would take action in Kosovo but not in
East Timor, where there was a much stronger case for intervention: Kosovo
was a province of Serbia while Jakarta never had a legitimate claim to East
Timor.[70]

GETTING IDEALISM OUT
OF QUARANTINE

This cursory review of American interventionism suffices to turn Kennan's argument on its head. The United States not only obstructed local progressive movements throughout the Cold War era, but is presently the major player in the global financial incursion that indirectly funds militarism from the killing fields of East Timor to those of Chechnya and Xinjiang. Meanwhile a new "lean and mean" version of American corporatism—new in having been stripped of its prior social responsibilities—has become the prototype for multinational capitalism.[71] International engagement is thus a virtual given. The question is not whether to intervene across national boundaries, but where, when, and toward what ends.

It was assumed throughout the Cold War that stability and development required the sacrifice of liberal idealism so far as foreign policy was concerned. The above examples, however, throw us back to the question of "basics" posed earlier by William Fox: Which institutions are "basic" to a democracy such as America's? Hard experience proves that the realist divorce of foreign policy and domestic "basics" is usually as counterproductive as it is morally reprehensible. Chalmers Johnson calls this "blowback"—"shorthand for saying that a nation reaps what it sows."[72]

Unfortunately Johnson's remedy—a standard Left retreatism—bears remarkably close resemblance to Huntington's retreatism on the Right. Moral realism counters both. It is not averse to "hard" geopolitical means when the alternative is heinous oppression or genocide; but its strong preference is for dialogue and leadership by example. Its "soft power" goal is to close the gap between ends and means, between "us" and "them," and hence between progressive domestic values and foreign affairs. From this vector it is clear that political development should be assigned at least as much importance as economic development.

This foreign/domestic and realist/idealist convergence nevertheless has its limits, both material and ethical. That is why it can better be described as a morally concerned realism than a strategically informed idealism. Samuel Berger was correct in that sense: America's material resources can be stretched only so far. Priority must be given to those cases where assistance and/or intervention can make a real difference. It behooves us, likewise, to recognize the limits of America's moral right to judge which direction another society should take. Current foreign policy must abandon the one-size-fits-all universalism of developmental modernism.

Somewhere in the middle, between the ethical absolutism of the Declaration of Human Rights and the "anything goes" amorality of mainstream postmodernism, which matches in that respect the amorality of classical realism, a new moral realism must be forged. If postmodernism is not to forfeit all standards of judgment, a new ethical course must be charted within postmodernism. This "second turn" postmodernism, as I term it in *Cultural Prosaics: The Second Postmodern Turn*, would allow for selective humanitarian intervention.

One approach to ethical realism, that of "Yale School" legal realists, argues for human rights on the basis of internationally shared "super values." The Yale School, however, has been duly criticized for the cultural provinciality of its major "super value," human dignity. The meaning of dignity varies markedly in different cultural contexts and can shift substantially over time.[73] Any credible response to this criticism must begin with a radical "thinning down" of these putative "super values." It must be conceded that only a small number of human rights issues will be "thin" enough, and hence broad enough, to stand the test of cultural pluralism that is basic to postmodern thought.

It is on this very "thin" tightrope, balanced between transnational super values and discrete cultural values, that Michael Walzer's *Thick and Thin* marks his own "second postmodern turn." Walzer has long appreciated the communicative limits or "thickness" of cultural particularity, as set forth by Clifford Geertz's *The Interpretation of Cultures* (1973). However, after pondering a film clip of a 1989 protest march in Prague, Walzer also recognizes the "thinness" embedded within "thickness." Realizing that he immediately (albeit incompletely) comprehends the meaning of signs carried by culturally remote demonstrators, Walzer faces the stark limits of his own postmodern relativism.

Words like "truth" and "justice," he finds, retain an inexplicable (by current theoretical fashion) degree of transferability when the issues at stake are elemental or "thin." By supporting the "thinner" meanings of those signs, Walzer vicariously joins the Prague march. That dialogic commitment distinguishes his realism from the cultural retreatism of a Kennan or Huntington. Their geopolitical realism would put an end to humanitarian intervention, while doing nothing to blunt the inroads of commercial globalization or its local surrogate, "glocalization."[74] America's chief cultural export would thus be a corporatism that (to borrow the words of a Noam Chomsky title) puts "profits over people" and answers to no authority other than the pro-corporate strictures of NAFTA, GATT, or the WTO.[75] Building on Hayek's idealized model of the market as a neutral mechanism of collective choice—a model that takes neoliberalism for reality itself[76]—the new corporatism casts globalization in its own image.[77]

That image has never been so graphically conveyed as when *Fortune* mag-

azine invited the CEOs of the world's top multinationals to join the Chinese
Communist Party leadership in celebrating the fiftieth anniversary of the
PRC. More than 200 CEOs quickly signed up, along with the communications magnates of Time Warner, CNN, and NBC.[78] In the words of Representative Nancy Pelosi, "The spectacle of U.S. C.E.O.s kowtowing to the
Chinese Communist leaders is grotesque but not new. This time, however,
when the C.E.O.s stand in Tiananmen Square with the Beijing regime to
'celebrate' 50 years of killing and repression, they will have blood on the
soles of their shoes."[79]

When Clinton first ran for the presidency he looked to Pelosi for guidance
on the China question. Soon, however, many of those same "Fortunati" con-
vinced Clinton to reverse his China policy.[80] This power structure has likewise dictated Clinton's Indonesian policy, as was evident in his long-delayed
response to the East Timor crisis. State Department spokesman Jaime Rubin
unabashedly expressed the need to give first consideration to American business interests in Indonesia.[81] What United Fruit was to America's Nicaraguan
policy of the 1950s, multinationals like Nike, Texaco, Chevron, and Mobil
are to Indonesian policy today. This would seem to support William Robinson's thesis, previously mentioned, that Cold War exigencies were never the
prime mover of U.S. foreign policy. The main impetus behind that policy was
the "defense of a budding post-colonial international capitalism under U.S.
domination."[82]

There is a big difference, however, between the thrust of corporate influence during and after the Cold War. As is clear in the case of East Timor,
today's transnational corporations (TNCs) are prone to prevent rather than
foster intervention. Minus the threat of Soviet communism, and with China
opened to trade across ideological boundaries, there is no pressing need to
intervene on behalf of capitalist expansion. The capitalist world order is
vexed, rather, by those who would intervene for nonmaterial reasons. They,
not the Chinese Communist Politburo, are now the most vocal critics of the
worldview advanced by the CEOs on Fortune's anniversary guest list.

Corporate priorities were never fully realized under Clinton, who remained
half-pledged to the principle of moral interventionism. The resulting conflict
of commitments left his administration without a consistent strategy beyond
crisis-to-crisis reaction to the latest polls.[83] The Clinton Doctrine was boldly
applied to Burma, while U.S.-China policy was essentially turned over to the
Commerce Department. It was here that Clinton ironed out internal conflict
by abandoning idealism in favor of something closer to a new dollar diplomacy.[84] For all his nationalist bluster, G. W. Bush is following much the same
course and indeed is expanding the range of foreign policy "incorporation"
by squeezing out the last vestiges of liberal idealism from his "new realist"

agenda. By this standard many of Clinton's interventions would have been precluded.[85] Yet in terms of increasing corporate empowerment there is a marked continuity between the two administrations.

Selective moral interventionism is not a lost cause, however. Its case is all the more potent because its humanitarian bent cannot, after the Cold War, be so easily quarantined within the innocuous boundaries of "idealism." Cold War priorities allowed realists like Kennan and Kissinger to dismiss idealism categorically, but now a new strain of realism is beginning to embrace moral issues. If George Lakoff is right in his contention (*Moral Politics* [1997]) that American politics is basically about morality, then this hybrid realism—dubbed by its critics "smorgasbord" realism—could pose a formidable challenge to Bush's more streamlined corporatism.[86] The front line of foreign policy debate in years to come will not be between idealism and realism, but moral and amoral realism.

China policy will again be the locus of this debate. It is surprising that so few China analysts, and even fewer foreign policymakers, evince any awareness of the moral realist option. A case in point is Patrick Tyler's recent study of America's China policy since Nixon (*A Great Wall: Six Presidents and China* [1999]). Tyler accepts the conventional wisdom that realist "engagement" with China is the only sensible policy available. To this day Kissinger toes that same line.[87] He not only recycles the one-China dictum of the early 1970s (as capsulated, for example, in Resolution 2758 of the 1971 UN General Assembly), but accepts a virtual mandate for reunification on PRC terms. Behind that acceptance is the assumption that China is rapidly rising to first-rank economic and military status and must be "engaged" (i.e., appeased) at all costs. In a recent issue of *Foreign Affairs*, the late Gerald Segal put an iconoclastic question to that assumption: "Does China Matter?" His paradigm-breaking answer was *not that much*. The Middle Kingdom is still a middling power, and could be dealt with more effectively through a policy of "constrainment" than "engagement."[88]

Granted, it is hardly in the United States' interest to alienate one-fourth of the world's population by closing either the diplomatic or trade doors to the PRC. Neither, however, is it in China's interest to slam those doors shut on the United States. As one China analyst puts it, "China is playing a weak hand well, while the West is playing a strong hand poorly."[89] Kissingeresque realism gives away all its bargaining chips by failing to weigh that second factor—China's even greater need for good relations with the United States[90]—into the balance. Such quasirealism operates on the basis of a Cold War logic that gives no quarter for moral considerations.

Though it is framed in the inordinately "thin" terms of universal values, Kofi Annan's call for a broader definition of national interest is a step in the right direction. It gets us "back to basics" by way of a new realist/idealist hybridity. National interest, when closely tied to moral "basics," leaves ample room for issues such as human rights within the realist agenda. Heretofore these concerns were sequestered within a legalist paradigm that only confused the issue of intervention.[91] No realist basis alone could justify U.S./ NATO actions in Kosovo or the Australian initiative in East Timor; but neither could moral grounds alone suffice. Only the combined critical mass of both grounds can support such actions.

In coming years moral realism will extend to environmental and social justice issues around the world. Patrick Tyler is probably right in *Great Wall*: even presidents like Carter and Clinton, who took strong idealist stands during their campaigns, end up as foreign policy realists. But it should be added that the nature of realism is fast changing in the post–Cold War era. Kennan and Kissinger no longer have the last word on the subject. Walzer is no less a realist, yet his rapprochement with "thin" concerns like human rights puts him close to the views of Joseph Nye and Peter Baehr on the American tradition of a foreign policy "typified by a combination of ethical principles and national interests."[92] Rarely, Nye stresses, have Americans "accepted pure *realpolitik* as a guiding principle."[93]

The Cold War bifurcation of ethics and interests, advanced by Kennan and Kissinger as a prerequisite of sound policy, reached its zenith in the rhetoric of Reagan's UN ambassador, Jeane Kirkpatrick.[94] While criticizing the Carter administration for withholding support from allies who grossly violated human rights, Kirkpatrick followed Ernest Lefever in defending ties with "authoritarian" (tractable) regimes as opposed to "totalitarian" (intractable) ones.[95] Idealists like Sidney Schanberg protested that to forfeit America's humanitarian tradition is to sap "our strength as a moral nation."[96]

The end of the Cold War spawned a euphoric sense that the realist/idealist debate could be retired to the national archives. Many thought that without the Soviet menace global problems would largely take care of themselves. Instead, the collapse of the Cold War balance of powers brought global chaos. One measure of this tumult, John Harris notes, was seen in the UNICEF (UN International Children's Emergency Fund) budget allocations. In 1990 UNICEF spent 4 percent of its budget on emergencies, whereas by 1994 that figure had jumped to 30 percent. Nor was that increase nearly enough. Harris is forced to conclude that the complexity of these emergencies, "in which enormous humanitarian demands are muddled up with political and military problems, has shown up as never before the weaknesses and limitations of the United Nations Organization."[97]

That being the case, stability must be secured the old-fashioned way— through the hard politics of geopolitical realism. It does not follow, however, that humanitarian concerns must be jettisoned. Kofi Annan's call for a broader sense of national interest, like Schanberg's call for an ethical foreign policy, posits the long-term complementarity of human rights and power politics. While Kennan and Kissinger still regard humanitarian values as an unaffordable luxury, other realists are starting to appreciate the crucial role of "soft power"—Nye's term for moral force as opposed to military coercion or economic sanctions.

An apt example—noted by Huntington, as discussed in the previous chapter, and by the German journalist Joseph Joffe—is the broad acceptance of America's post–Cold War preeminence.[98] Both classic and structural realism (neorealism) would have predicted the formation of massive countervailing alliances in the early 1990s. Such reactions could still develop. Witness the strong Asian revulsion triggered by American-directed IMFism after the 1997 Crash, the massive "blowback" from U.S. policies in the Islamic world, or the smoldering European irritation over the Bush administration's denigration of a long list of international accords: Kyoto, the ABM treaty, the comprehensive test ban treaty, the biological warfare treaty, the small-arms treaty, the international criminal court, the antimoney-laundering effort, the international tobacco control convention, and so forth.[99] If he keeps at it, Bush could succeed in turning a largely French concern over American "hyperpower" into global outrage.

So far, however, the present world response can better be described as a mood swing than a balance-of-power shift. Clearly the absence of a swift and sweeping global counter to U.S. unipolarity is due to America's ample stock of moral capital. The question is how far Bush, egged on by his very undialogic National Security Advisor Condoleezza Rice, in contrast to a more politic Secretary Powell,[100] can push his minimalist realism before America's soft power reserves are depleted.

Powell's multilateralism was quickly brought out of dry dock following the September 11 attacks,[101] but only on the question of terrorism. It would be a grave error to mistake this single issue internationalism for a fundamental policy shift. Quite the contrary, it represents the Bush administration's complete forfeiture of idealist or soft power concerns. U.S. relations with Malaysia, for example, had been kept in cold storage pending Mahathir's more judicious treatment of political opponents such as Anwar Ibrahim. Now all that matters is Mahathir's stance regarding "terrorism" (as if his own domestic policies are not terroristic). Here again, as Murray Hiebert notes, there is great danger of "blowback." Future instability could flow from "U.S. moves to support unpopular regimes in Central Asia, place less stress on human rights in countries such as China, Indonesia and Malaysia or ignore attacks by Beijing on Islamic rebels in its northwest province of Xinjiang."[102]

Cold War foreign policy put liberal idealism on ice for four long decades. It was simply taken for granted that idealism and realism were irreconcilable under those circumstances. A priceless ethical opportunity arose, therefore, when the Cold War ended. Unfortunately this was also the triumphant moment of one of idealism's worst enemies: not some nefarious foreign power, but the globalized version of America's own newly dominant ideology, neoliberalism.

It is all the more imperative, after September 11, for liberals of a more idealistic persuasion to come out of seclusion—out of quarantine. They will continue to have their differences with realists, but at this critical moment they should join with moral realists against their common foe, multinational globalization, precisely as they did in the streets of Seattle against the WTO. Their common challenge will be to forge what fifteen years ago would have seemed a complete oxymoron: a moral geopolitics. To sacrifice the opportunity of this post–Cold War moment on the altar of global neoliberalism would be, in soft power terms, to lose the world by conquering it.

Moral realists recognize that hard power alone is self-defeating, not only because it foments terrorism and other forms of "blowback," but because it saps the moral energy of those who overuse it. Nothing imperils America's global stature so much as the amoral drift of U.S. foreign policy under the sway of global corporatism. There is much to be said, even in utilitarian terms, for "getting back to basics": back to a foreign policy that draws strength and direction (i.e., the strength *of* direction) from its organic bond with the nation's most basic domestic values. These are the values of the "other" America, outside the "Washington consensus" that rules the country in the name of neoliberalism, but increasingly answers to multinational interests.

If Kim Dae Jung is correct in locating a similar set of political "basics" in the Other Korea, and by extension the Other Asia, then the geopolitical imperative of moral realism is to find the point of intersection—Walzer's intercultural realm of the "thin"—between these distant Others. The idea is to replace the shifting alliances of "top-down" power structures with a deeply rooted cultural accord. In the long run this new realism, at once transnational and post-Western, can do more to promote peace and deter tyranny than any missile shield. It offers, moreover, the only available shield against corporate globalization, which is the most pressing threat to Other values around the Rim and throughout the developing world.

NOTES

1. Emran Queshi, "Pass the West, Pass Its Values," *National Post Online* (August 4, 2001), <www.nationalpost.com/scripts/printer/printer.asp?f=/stories/20010804/6372 52.html>.

2. Arif Dirlik, *Postmodernity's Histories: The Past as Legacy and Project* (Lanham, Md.: Rowman & Littlefield, 2000), chap. 3.

3. Kofi Annan, "Two Concepts of Sovereignty," *Economist* 352, no. 8137 (September 18, 1999): 49–50, 49; A. Glenn Mower, Jr., "The U.N. and Human Rights," in Burton Yale Pines, ed., *A World Without a U.N.: What Would Happen if the U.N. Shut Down* (Washington, D.C.: Heritage Foundation, 1984), 93–118, 94.

4. Annan, "Two Concepts of Sovereignty," 49.

5. Robert Madsen, "Taiwan's Kosovo Precedent," *Far Eastern Economic Review* 162, no. 39 (September 30, 1999): 28.

6. "Kofi Annan's Critique," *New York Times* Editorial (September 22, 1999), <www.nytimes.com/yr/mo/day/editorial/22wed1.html>.

7. Robert P. DeVecchi and Arthur C. Helton, "Are We Asking Too Much of the U.N.?" *Washington Post* (September 19, 1999): B01.

8. Michael Ignatieff, "Human Rights: The Midlife Crisis," *New York Review of Books* 46, no. 9 (May 20, 1999): 58–62, 58.

9. David J. Whittaker, *United Nations in Action* (London: UCL Press, 1995), 134.

10. Peter R. Baehr, *The Role of Human Rights in Foreign Policy* 2nd ed. (London: Macmillan, 1996), 5; Richard Falk, "Mission Implausible: Caught Between National Interests and Nationalism," *Washington Post* (September 19, 1999): B01.

11. Dominick McGoldrick, "The Principle of Non-Intervention: Human Rights," in *The United Nations and the Principles of International Law: Essays in Memory of Michael Akehurst* (London: Routledge, 1994), 85–119, 85.

12. Whittaker, *United Nations in Action*, 134.

13. McGoldrick, "The Principle of Non-Intervention," 89.

14. Falk, "Mission Implausible," B01.

15. William H. Thornton, "Putting the (Second) Postmodern Question to Japan: Postmodernism and Japan Ten Years Later," *Asian Profile* 28, no. 2 (April 2000): 117–124.

16. Baehr, *The Role of Human Rights in Foreign Policy*, 40–41.

17. Ignatieff, "Human Rights," 59.

18. Harold K. Jacobson, "The United Nations in Crisis," in David P. Forsythe, ed., *The United Nations in the World Political Economy* (London: Macmillan, 1989), 212–227, 212.

19. Quoted in Henry Shue, "Morality, Politics, and Humanitarian Assistance," in Bruce Nichols and Gil Loescher, eds., *The Moral Nation: Humanitarianism and U.S. Foreign Policy Today* (Notre Dame, Ind.: University of Notre Dame Press, 1989), 12–40, 19.

20. Robert D. Kaplan, "Fort Leavenworth and the Eclipse of Nationhood," *Atlantic Monthly* (September 1996), <www.theatlantic.com/issues/96sep/leaven/leaven.htm>.

21. "Clinton Doctrine," *National Review* Editorial. (June 14, 1999), <britannica.com/magazine/print?content_id=120585>.

22. Quoted in Robert Manning, "The Myth of the 'Clinton Doctrine'," *Intellectual Capital* (August 26, 1999), <www.intellectualcapital.com/issues/issue284/item6175.asp>.

23. Manning, "The Myth of the 'Clinton Doctrine'."

24. Manning, "The Myth of the 'Clinton Doctrine'."

25. On the term "reconstructive" see James Kurth, "Models of Humanitarian Intervention: Assessing the Past and Discerning the Future," *Foreign Policy Research Institute Wire: A Catalyst for Ideas* 9, no. 6 (August 2001), via email.

26. Quoted in Richard Ullman, "The US and the World: An Interview with George Kennan," *New York Review of Books* 46, no. 13 (August 12, 1999): 4–6, 6.

27. Ullman, "The US and the World," 6.

28. Kennan quoted in Ullman, "The US and the World," 6.

29. Samuel P. Huntington, *The Clash of Civilizations and the Remaking of World Order* (New York: Simon and Schuster, 1996), 78.

30. Amartya Sen, *Development as Freedom* (New York: Alfred A. Knopf, 1999), 246.

31. Richard Bernstein and Ross H. Munro, *The Coming Conflict with China* (New York: Alfred A. Knopf, 1997), 16.

32. Lucian Pye, "Chinese Democracy and Constitutional Development," in Fumio Itoh, ed., *China in the Twenty-First Century: Politics, Economy, and Society* (Tokyo: United Nations University Press, 1997), 205–218, 206.

33. Lee Teng-hui, "Understanding Taiwan: Bridging the Perception Gap," *Foreign Affairs* 78, no. 6 (November–December 1999): 9–14; William H. Thornton, "Korea and East Asian Exceptionalism," *Theory, Culture and Society: Explorations in Critical Social Science* 15, no. 2 (May 1998): 137–154.

34. John McBeth, "Choosing Sides," *Far Eastern Economic Review* (September 7, 2000), <www.feer.com/0009_07/p26region.html>; also "New Leader, New Indonesia," *Economist* 353, no. 8142 (October 23, 1999): 31–32; and "Indonesia's Presidential Surprise," *New York Times* Editorial (October 21, 1999), <www.nytimes.com/yr/mo/day/editorial/21thu3.html>.

35. Megawati Sukarnoputri, "Her Father's Daughter," interview with Megawati Sukarnoputri, *Newsweek* Asia Edition (June 22, 1998): 58.

36. Amartya Sen, "A Plan for Asia's Growth," *Asiaweek* (October 8, 1999): 62–63, 62.

37. Regarding this second assumption see Jack Donnelly, "Repression and Development: The Political Contingency of Human Rights Trade-Offs," in David P. Forsythe, ed., *Human Rights and Development: International Views* (London: Macmillan, 1989), 305–328, 306–307.

38. Kennan in Ullman, "The US and the World," 6.

39. Quoted in Ullman, "The US and the World," 6.

40. Norman Podhoretz, *The Present Danger: Do We Have the Will to Reverse the Decline of American Power?* (New York: Simon and Schuster, 1980), 17.

41. William I. Robinson, *Promoting Polyarchy: Globalization, US Intervention, and Hegemony* (Cambridge, UK: Cambridge University Press, 1996), 14.

42. Abram L. Sachar, *The Course of Our Times* (New York: Delta, 1972), 542.

43. Robinson, *Promoting Polyarchy*, 14–15.

44. Quoted in Noam Chomsky, *Profit Over People: Neoliberalism and Global Order* (New York: Seven Stories Press, 1999), 140.

45. Quoted in Robinson, *Promoting Polyarchy*, 1.

46. "America's Secret Past in Chile," *New York Times* Editorial (March 16, 1999), <www.nytimes.com/yr/mo/day/editorial/16tue2.html>.

47. Eduardo Galeano, *Open Veins of Latin America: Five Centuries of the Pillage of a Continent*, trans. by Cedric Belfrage (New York: Monthly Review Press, 1973), 127–128.

48. Greg Lockhart, *Nation in Arms: The Origins of the People's Army of Vietnam* (Sydney: Allen and Unwin, 1989), 271.

49. John Clark Pratt, "Chronology," in John C. Pratt, ed., *The Quiet American: Text and Criticism* (novel by Graham Greene) (New York: Penguin Books, 1996), x–xxv, xxi–xxiv.

50. "Report by the National Security Council on the Position of the United States with Respect to Indochina," (February 27, 1950) in John C. Pratt, ed., *The Quiet American: Text and Criticism* (novel by Graham Greene) (New York: Penguin Books, 1996), 262–264, 264.

51. Frances FitzGerald, *Fire in the Lake: The Vietnamese and the Americans in Vietnam* (New York: Vintage Books, 1972), 5.

52. Lockhart, *Nation in Arms*, 274.

53. David Halberstam, *The Best and the Brightest* (New York: Fawcett Crest, 1969), 130.

54. Quoted in Gabriel Kolko, *Anatomy of a War: Vietnam, the United States, and the Modern Historical Experience* (New York: New Press, 1985), 117.

55. FitzGerald, *Fire in the Lake*, 311.

56. "America's Secret Past in Chile."

57. Anthony Lewis, "The Fruits of 'Realism'," *New York Times* Op-Ed (September 7, 1999), <www.nytimes.com/library/opinion/lewis/090799lewi.html>.

58. Walden Bello, *People and Power in the Pacific: The Struggle for the Post–Cold War Order* (London: Pluto Press, 1992), 74.

59. Benedict Anderson, *The Spectre of Comparisons: Nationalism, Southeast Asia and the World* (London: Verso, 1998), 133.

60. Anderson, *The Spectre of Comparisons*, 133.

61. Lewis, "The Fruits of 'Realism'."

62. Anderson, *The Spectre of Comparisons*, 133.

63. Anderson, *The Spectre of Comparisons*, 134.

64. Bello, *People and Power in the Pacific*, 74.

65. "East Timor Under Siege," *New York Times* Editorial. (September 8, 1999), <www.nytimes.com/yr/mo/day/editorial/-08wed1.html>.

66. "East Timor Under Siege."

67. Allen Nairn, "U.S. Complicity in Timor," *The Nation* (September 27, 1999), <www.thenation.com/issue/990927/0927nairn.shtml>.

68. José Ramos-Horta, CNN Asian edition interview, aired on September 10, 1999.

69. John Roosa, "Fatal Trust in Timor," *New York Times* Op-Ed (September 15, 1999), <www.nytimes.com/yr/mo/day/oped/15rous.html>.

70. Ronald Steel, "East Timor Isn't Kosovo," *New York Times* Op-Ed (September 12, 1999), <www.nytimes.com/yr/mo/day/early/09129912stee.html>.

71. See Marina Whitman's apologetic for this new style of corporatism in her *New World, New Rules: The Changing Role of the American Corporation* (Boston: Harvard Business School, 1999).

72. Chalmers Johnson, *Blowback: The Costs and Consequences of American Empire* (New York: Henry Holt, 2000), 223.

73. Scott Davidson, *Human Rights* (Buckingham, Penn.: Open University Press, 1993), 36–37.

74. William H. Thornton, "Mapping the 'Glocal' Village: The Political Limits of 'Glocalization'," *Continuum* 14, no. 1 (April 2000): 79–89.

75. Ralph Nader, "Introduction: Free Trade and the Decline of Democracy," in Ralph Nader, William Greider, Margaret Atwood, David Philips, and Pat Choate, eds., *The Case Against Free Trade: GATT, NAFTA and the Globalization of Corporate Power* (San Francisco: Earth Island Press, 1993), 1–12, 1.

76. David Held, *Democracy and the Global Order: From the Modern State to Cosmopolitan Governance* (Stanford, Calif.: Stanford University Press, 1995), 245.

77. William H. Thornton, "Back to Basics: Human Rights and Power Politics in the New Moral Realism," *International Journal of Politics, Culture and Society* 14, no. 2 (2000): 315–332.

78. A. M. Rosenthal, "Partying in China," *New York Times* Op-Ed (September 18, 1999), <www.nytimes.com/library/opinion/rosenthal/091799rose.html>.

79. Quoted in Rosenthal, "Partying in China."

80. James Mann, *About Face: A History of America's Curious Relationship with China, from Nixon to Clinton* (New York: Alfred A. Knopf, 1999), 285.

81. Russell Mokhiber and Robert Weissman, "Timor: Business Interests Cause US to Move Slowly," *Corporate Watch* (September 13, 1999), <www.corpwatch.org/trac/corner/worldnews/other/435.html>.

82. Robinson, *Promoting Polyarchy*, 14–15.

83. Robert B. Zoellick, "A Republican Foreign Policy," *Foreign Affairs* 79, no. 1 (January–February 2000): 63–78, 68.

84. John B. Judis, "Beyond National Interest," *New Republic* (June 21, 1999), <www.thenewrepublic.com/magazines/tnr/archive/062199/judis062199.html>.

85. Michael T. Klare, "America's Military Revolution: Cold War Government with No War to Fight," *Le Monde diplomatique* (July 2001), <www.en.monde-diplomatique.fr/2001/07/04/america2>.

86. Jeffrey W. Legro and Andrew Moravcsik, "Faux Realism: Spin versus Substance in the Bush Foreign-Policy Doctrine," *Foreign Policy* (July–August 2001), <www.foreignpolicy.com/issue_julyaug_2001/legro.html>.

87. William H. Thornton, "Analyzing East/West Power Politics in Comparative Cultural Studies," *CLCWeb* 2, no. 3 (September 2000), <http://clcwebjournal.lib.purdue.edu/clcweb00-3/thornton00.html>.

88. Gerald Segal, "Does China Matter?" *Foreign Affairs* 78, no. 5 (September–October 1999): 24–36, 35.

89. See Robin Munro, interviewed on CNN World News (aired October 19, 1999).

90. Erik Eckholm, "China's Need for U.S. Trade May Outweigh Disputes with White House," *New York Times* International (July 30, 2001), <www.nytimes.com/2001/07/30/international/30CHIN.html>.

91. Cornelia Navari, "Intervention, Non-Intervention and the Construction of the State," in Ian Forbes and Mark Hoffman, eds., *Political Theory, International Relations, and the Ethics of Intervention* (New York: St. Martin's Press, 1993), 43–60, 52.

92. Baehr, *The Role of Human Rights in Foreign Policy*, 83.

93. Joseph S. Nye, "Redefining the National Interest," *Foreign Affairs* 78, no. 4 (July–August 1999): 22–35, 31.

94. Cynthia J. Arnson, *Crossroads: Congress, the Reagan Administration, and Central America* (New York: Pantheon, 1989), 59.

95. Baehr, *The Role of Human Rights in Foreign Policy*, 85–86; Christopher M. Gray,

"The Struggle for the Soul of American Foreign Policy," *Orbis* 43, no. 3 (Summer 1999): 497–506, 503.

96. Sidney H. Schanberg, "Memory Is the Answer," in Bruce Nichols and Gil Loescher, eds., *The Moral Nation: Humanitarianism and U.S. Foreign Policy Today* (Notre Dame, Ind.: University of Notre Dame Press, 1989), 9–11, 10.

97. John Harris, "Introduction: A Time of Troubles—Problems of International Humanitarian Assistance in the 1990s," in John Harris, ed., *The Politics of Humanitarian Intervention* (London: Pinter, 1995), 1–15, 12.

98. Joseph S. Nye, "The Power We Must Not Squander," *New York Times* Op-Ed (January 3, 2000), <www.nytimes.com/yr/mo/day/early/01030003nye.html>.

99. Matthew Rothschild, "The Lone Wolf Policy," *Progressive* (August 2, 2001), <www.progressive.org/webex/wx080201.html>.

100. Jane Perlez, "Rice on Front Lines as Adviser to Bush," *New York Times* International (August 19, 2001), <www.nytimes.com/2001/08/19/international/americas/19DIPL.html>.

101. "A General Who Paints," *Economist* (October 18, 2001), <www.economist.co.uk>.

102. Murray Hiebert, "A Flawed Policy," *Far Eastern Economic Review* (October 25, 2001), <www.feer.com/2001/0110_25/p030region.html>.

Conclusion

A Concert of "Others"

TOWARD A GLOBAL ANTI-GLOBALISM

The East Asian "miracle" constituted the most intensive capitalist restructuring of the twentieth century. In defiance of dependency theory, the "Asian tigers" seemed to be invading the very core of the capitalist world system. Japan's postwar upsurge had been less "miraculous" insofar as it was more of a restoration. Like Germany's, its takeoff began in the nineteenth century, before the world system had completely congealed.[1]

One reason both modernists and dependency theorists were unable to account for the later Asian miracle was their neglect of the vital role of geopolitics in postwar development. Through generous loans and direct foreign investment, but more especially through protracted tolerance of trade imbalances in support of export-oriented growth, the capitalist core nurtured East Asian exceptionalism as a geopolitical barrier to communism.[2] East Asian development more than held its own. The Left in general was wounded, and dependency theory was dealt an ostensive death blow. Not only Asian capitalism, but capitalism per se took the prize. That seeming victory did more to bury Soviet resolve than all of Reagan's military spending. Unfortunately it also helped to kill what was left of liberal progressivism. Neoliberalism was born out of this mythic triumph.

East Asia's admission ticket to capitalism's inner circle was provisional and costly. Its price was political stability, at a time when stability could be secured only through the device of political underdevelopment. For two decades Asian values provided nativist cover for what Frank once called, with reference to Brazil and Chile, the "development of undevelopment."[3] The coercion that required got support from a simple train of Singapore School logic: (1) Western culture is inherently democratic, (2) the East is not like the West, therefore (3) to be authentically Asian is to be authoritarian. This "self-orientalizing" syllogism, to borrow Dirlik's term, was not uniquely tied to Confucian values. It was applied with equal venom in Suharto's Indonesia, where it helped to divert attention from the Golkar Party's repression of *merdeka*, Indonesia's endemic philosophy of freedom.[4]

The myth of Asian values went almost unquestioned in developmental thinking of the 1980s, but started to come unraveled in the 1990s. Two East Asian societies—Korea and Taiwan—were fast becoming democratic, a fact that was turned to "free market" advantage as a "growth first" argument for raw economism. This was crucial for the making of neoliberal globalism, for it allowed economic liberals to have their idealism on the cheap. By treating democracy and human rights as teleological givens, the byproducts-to-be of affluence, neoliberals could claim the moral high ground of reform without the risk or inconvenience of actual reformism. Political activism would compromise the stability that in the neoliberal view makes for growth and political development, in that order.

Thus neoliberalism has reaped advantages from two antithetical systems. While nominally upholding the full range of liberal ideals, it in practice condoned the economism of Asian values. This allowed the power elites of East and West to snugly coexist for several years under the common roof of an optative New World Order.

Then the roof began to leak. An already strained accord was finally terminated by the Crash of 1997. Globalists scrambled to reconstruct the classic East/West hierarchy on neoliberal terms, with priority given to economic deregulation rather than immaterial issues such as democracy. The charge against Asian cronyism was not that it violated human rights and trashed the natural environment. Its crime was its failure to properly register the profits from these enterprises. It therefore represented an antiquated mode of capitalism that had to be purged from the *Newer* World Order of "free market" globalization. The IMF was there to enforce Western standards in everything from accounting practices to labor relations, that is, everything *but* human and ecological welfare. "Transparency" was the word of the moment, but the key point was that the West would now be in full charge of globalization. No Asian nation was in a position to retreat from the Western prescription for financial liberalization.[5]

Malaysia's Mahathir was right on that point: the West did seize upon the Crash as an opportunity to put Asian capitalism in its place. Already, as they gained confidence in the renascent Western market, neoliberals were declaring "Asian development" a contradiction in terms.[6] But Asian values had already put their indelible mark on the New World Order by discarding the liberal democratic vestments of earlier globalization. It was this illiberal (or "mean") capitalism that neoliberalism now repossessed. To that it added its own austere (or "lean") mandate, thus producing the "lean and mean" amalgam that would define globalization in the 1990s as an East/West hybrid.

If globalism has any redeeming feature, it is the fact that political progressivism can now go its own way, free from the ball and chain of economic liberalism that it has dragged about since the days of Adam Smith. Throughout the modernist era the liberal Left has been stigmatized by this unfortunate coupling of economic and political liberalism. Thus neoliberalism, which has no use for political reform except as a teleological ploy, does an unwitting favor to the Left by casting it in the role of democracy's late capitalist savior.

A signal feature of this Newer Left is its highly eclectic opposition to multinational capitalism. Corporate globalization is producing its own worst enemy by bringing old foes together with a vengeance. This lays the foundation for an opposition movement that knows no geographic boundaries and spans a wide ideological spectrum.[7] What most concerns corporate globalists, however, is that voices of resistance from the South (among the best: Eduardo Galeano on Latin America and Walden Bello on Southeast Asia) are finally getting a modest hearing in the North. Likewise the Other Asia is beginning to come into view. Across both axes of contention—North/South and East/West—multifarious Others are turning eclecticism into a potent tool of resistance.[8]

Global resistance, unfortunately, may never get past this nascent stage unless it is welded to a moral realist agenda, as treated in chapter 8. There is only one way to contain the "fire on the Rim" that globalization is fueling: by fighting fire with geopolitical fire. Idealistic intervention at critical flashpoints—the Jimmy Carter approach to fire control—has its tactical merits, but cannot lay a foundation for lasting peace and balanced growth, not to mention Sen's vision of "freedom as development."

That nonglobalist road will not be open for travel until a new oppositional alliance is in place. The post–Cold War decline of the Left has allowed global capitalism to win nearly all its battles by default. What little resistance it has met has been scattered and largely reactive. Progressive-minded reformists of all stripes have gone their separate ways, while local voices from developing or undeveloping countries have seldom been heard. The resulting sense of futility has lent credibility to Third Way policies that appropriate the language of reform while surrendering to the supposed inevitability of corporate globalization. Such tepid resistance, typified by the recent work of Anthony Giddens (*The Third Way* [1998], and *Runaway World* [2000]), could just as well have been funded by the multinationals themselves, for it ends up celebrating what it purports to critique.

Likewise, John Gray's undialogic pluralism tends to boomerang. Gray is as concerned about global capitalism as any Marxist, yet in the final analysis his critique serves his adversary by dismantling the one weapon corporate globalists might lose sleep over: anti-globalism with a global reach. French resistance in the winter of 1995 failed for lack of a global agenda. That agenda finally emerged at the November 1999 WTO convention in Seattle. It was shocking enough that environmentalists marched shoulder to shoulder with labor activists, but what most alarmed the multinationals was the sight of union protesters from the first world joining ranks with their third world counterparts. Against the Third Way doctrine of TINA (There Is No Alternative to corporate globalization), Seattle and its progeny gave global scope to the message on a Parisian protest banner: *"Le monde n'est pas une marchandise."*[9]

That message had been harbingered a few months before Seattle at an alternative conference at New Zealand's Auckland University. Organized as a retort to the September 1999 APEC meeting in Auckland, this counterconference united Maori and non-Maori activists in an unprecedented common cause: resistance to the new wave of economic regionalization and globalization. The Maoris testified

> that they had been suffering from the invasion of capital for the last 150 years. The form has changed but the results are very similar. The conference heard about U.S. domination of the Philippines, the negative effects of the North American Free Trade Agreement (NAFTA) on Canada and Mexico (and possibly the whole of the Americas in the near future), the exploitation of Bougainville (where a foreign company, in the process of mining copper, made the largest hole in the southern hemisphere), the plight of migrant workers, Mexican workers, New Zealand unions, Korean workers—all these stories added to a picture of a region in trouble as a result of APEC-type policies.[10]

It was in Seattle, however, that a global anti-globalism took definitive shape. The question was whether the syncretism of that message could be duplicated in subsequent months. Futile efforts were made to recapture its momentum, at the April 2000 World Bank meeting in Washington, the republican convention in Philadelphia in July and the democratic convention in Los Angeles in August. In a short-sighted attempt to gain support in Los Angeles, the movement turned its focus to local concerns as opposed to the global "magnet" issues of Seattle.[11]

The ultimate opposition magnet is provided by the multinationals themselves, whose borderless ravages invite global outrage. Such embryonic solidarity is anything but univocal,[12] and in that fact lies the movement's strength and weakness alike. Its strength was suggested when, just prior to the September 2000 IMF meeting in Prague, the institution's head banker revealed a plan to give poor countries a larger voice in the process of globalization.

Clearly this was an attempt to ward off the kind of North/South convergence that upended Seattle. The ploy did not assuage protest organizers, but did illustrate their ability to make IMF director Horst Koehler dance to a different tune. To his colleagues it must have seemed that Koehler was speaking in tongues when he began babbling about the need for greater openness and inclusion.[13]

Such victories, however, are largely symbolic. Anti-globalism has put on a good show, but could hardly affect the direction or pace of globalization. Subsequent protests were tainted when police violence was returned in kind, as at the Genoa G8 Summit of July 2001.[14] The corporate establishment could not have imagined how tame and politic those clashes would seem after the events of September 11. An absolute boundary has been drawn between two types of anti-globalism: the civil, dialogic form and the kind that savagely vented itself on thousands of innocent victims. If this tragedy does not awaken corporate globalists to the need to communicate with their moderate and utterly nonviolent critics, who in effect serve as canaries in the mine shaft, then more and still greater tragedies are bound to follow. In that case it could fairly be said that the savagery has two sides.

CHINA WATCH

Nowhere is globalist intransigence on more graphic display than in the politics of America's China policy. When the State Department released its annual report on human rights on February 25, 2000, China came in for the harshest criticism it had received since Tiananmen, owing largely to its October 1999 crackdown on the Falun Gong and its ongoing oppression in Xinjiang province and Tibet. Beijing, moreover, had just unveiled a far more bellicose position toward Taiwan. Many wondered how Clinton could possibly gather the needed support for congressional approval of PNTR (permanent normal trade relations), which was a necessary step toward China's full WTO admission.[15]

The House nonetheless passed the PNTR bill in May by a vote of 237 to 197. Then, in September, the Senate passed the same bill by a shocking 83 to 15. This was Clinton's biggest foreign policy victory since NAFTA in 1993.[16] Echoing a Noam Chomsky title, Senator Jim Bunning (R-Ky.) voiced his consternation that the Senate would put "profits over people" at a time when China posed an increasingly serious hazard to security and human rights.[17]

For Peter Beinart the question "is how to change troublesome governments without seeming to meddle in their internal affairs. The Clintonite answer is to involve them in international institutions, norms, and treaties, which they will join out of self interest, and whose liberal values they will gradually internalize."[18] Despite his professed view of China as a "strategic competitor," George W. Bush did a fast and predictable about-face. By the time of his July 2001 visit to Beijing, Secretary of State Colin Powell was calling China his "friend,"[19] and acting the part. Doing slapstick comedy skits onstage, he seemed to have modeled his act on Jiang Zemin's antics at Williamsburg. The Chinese applauded on cue, but many on the Rim were not laughing. This Republican reversal, like Clinton's before, is unnerving to countries under the Chinese shadow. Robyn Lim warns that the region's "growing fear of Chinese ambition . . . combined with a lack of action in Washington could result in a nuclear arms race in Asia. Signs of discontent are emerging first in Japan because it stands out as the only Asian great power which does not possess nuclear weapons."[20]

If Japan goes nuclear, Australia and Taiwan could follow. India felt it had no choice but to respond in kind to "a rising China enjoying unprecedented strategic latitude, arming Pakistan with nuclear technology and missiles, with the backing of a U.S. president prattling about 'strategic parnership' with China. . . . What Beijing hopes Japan and others will ignore is China's role in destabilizing Northeast Asia through its assistance to North Korea's missile program."[21]

To be sure, Japan is not ignoring it. In August 2000 Prime Minister Yoshiro Mori paid an official visit to India to repair relations that were strained by India's nuclear tests two years before.[22] The two countries went on to conduct joint naval exercises under the official pretext of combating piracy.[23] The message this sent to China hardly needs decoding. India, on the same pretext, stepped up its diplomacy and naval cooperation with Vietnam.

It is typical Rim policy to deal with China in this circuitous manner. U.S. plans to install a theater missile defense system have been justified as protection against North Korea rather than China. The same goes for the projected presence of U.S. forces on the Korean peninsula. As the two Koreas edge toward reunification, the half-fiction of these excuses will expand into an obvious lie, forcing Washington to "more explicitly identify China as a regional threat."[24] There is still a bipolar mind-set that evades "the fact that over the next decade it will likely be China, not Russia or any rogue, whose nuclear weapons policy will concern America most."[25]

Intelligence sources have noted a major shift in Chinese military strategy since the late 1990s toward a more offensive posture. To establish itself as a superpower, China could benefit from a military conflict large enough to put itself "on the map," but not large enough to put it at war with the United States. Its location of choice could well be the Philippines-held portion of the Spratlys, a rock formation in the South China Sea. In April 2000 Chinese media released a report declaring that Chinese holdings in the Spratlys, which formerly had been claimed as fishing facilities, are indeed for military usage.[26]

Meanwhile, China is forging new ties with a host of small Pacific nationalities. In the past two years it has actively courted Tonga, Micronesia, Samoa, Fiji, Vanuatu, Papua New Guinea, and Kiribati, while doing all it can to exclude Taiwan from any meaningful interaction with the Pacific Islands Forum, the main political body of the region. Its immediate objective is to drive a wedge between Taiwan and the five Pacific nations that still maintain active diplomatic relations with Taipei: the Solomon Islands, Nauru, Tuvalu, the Marshall Islands, and Palau. But its broader objective of supplanting U.S. power in Oceania is no secret.[27]

This maritime threat gives Japan one more reason to upgrade its military. Other reasons, closer to home, include North Korea's 1998 missile launch over Japanese territory, China's saber rattling toward Taiwan in 1995–96, and her recent naval probes near Japanese waters. Finally there is China's bellicose stance following the April 2001 Hainan incident, when a midair crash between a Chinese fighter jet and a U.S. navy surveillance plane forced the American plane to make an emergency landing on China's Hainan Island. After refusing to release the plane for three months, China gave the affair diplomatic closure by sending the United States a $1 million airport parking bill.[28]

The biggest reason for Japan's remilitarization, however, is also the most understated: the pro-China policy that took shape in Washington during the 1990s, reaching an alarming crescendo with Clinton's June 1998 visit to China. Just as China looks to the Spratlys as a world stage, Japan is looking to its planned multilateral naval operations in the Strait of Malacca. Though officially aimed at the piracy problem, Japan's participation, coupled with an unusually robust parliamentary debate over constitutional constraints on the military,[29] clearly spotlights the coming "normalization" of Japan's geopolitics.[30]

It also marks the end of Japanese political solidarity. At least half the general public breaks with the old and new power elite—the LDP old guard and the new corporate guard—by supporting a harder line toward the PRC. When China gave prompt assurances that Japanese territorial rights would not be violated in the future, the LDP was quick to release loans to China that had been frozen in August 2000. The public, however, concluded that China responds only to power politics, not to the trustful "engagement" of Japan's twenty-year loan program. A gap is thus forming between corporate Japan, which is acutely mindful of China's status as Japan's second-largest trading partner, while Japan is China's number-one partner, and a younger genera-

tion of powerbrokers in Tokyo, especially those associated with the opposition Democratic Party.[31]

THE CULTURAL DYNAMICS OF TRUST

This China policy rift calls attention to a still deeper divide within Japanese
cultural politics: the new nationalism that trails Japan's new internationalism
like a shadow, both being tied to rising security concerns. That foreign/
domestic nexus conforms to a basic axiom of the new "critical geopolitics":
just as foreign affairs cannot be divorced from domestic politics, no geopolitics is morally neutral or "simply geopolitical."[32] In the age of globalization,
security issues involve more than weaponry or production capacity. Even
some IR realists, who formerly prided themselves on bracketing the cultural
factor, have started to see that security in the post–Cold War world may
depend as much on cultural dynamics as on military-industrial force.[33] Thus
the sphere of foreign affairs gives up its realist externality in favor of the
inner/outer dialectic of cultural realism, as discussed in chapter 7. Much as
India's sense of geopolitical insecurity has reinforced its turn toward Hindu
nationalism, Japanese nationalists such as Shintaro Isihara and Shingo Nishi-
mura are gaining mainstream support as a result of Japan's growing suspicion
of American priorities.

It is strange, to say the least, for Japan to feel insecure at this of all times.
Throughout the Cold War, Japan trusted America against a very real military
superpower. Now, with America standing virtually alone in terms of military
clout, Japan's rising anxiety seems anachronistic. Perhaps it could be
explained in part by Japan's sense of being less needed by America as a geopolitical buffer. But far less American commitment would be required to produce a given measure of security when the threat to Japan is so greatly
reduced. The question therefore stands: Why so much angst?

The simple fact is that Japan feels more threatened by tomorrow's China
than it was by yesterday's Soviet Union. It would be too easy to explain this
by pointing an accusing finger solely at America's China policy. What conditions that policy, as argued in chapter 2, is the metamorphosis of liberal capitalism since the early 1980s. Liberalism has lost much of its contradictory
character—the redemptive ambiguity that saved it from the clutches of pure
corporatism. On some occasions, such as George McGovern's 1972 presidential bid, an older liberalism served to distinguish Democratic from Republican foreign policy. The advent of neoliberalism marks the erosion of the
countervailing tension that Bryan Turner locates in the cultural citizenship of
an earlier capitalist order.[34] Working together, neoconservatism and neoliber-

alism have purged most noncapitalistic elements from today's foreign policy. It follows that America can no longer be counted on where corporate interests are not directly at stake.

The case of Kissinger Associates provides a chilling example of how those interests operate where China policy is concerned. China has the advantage of having always regarded capitalism as degenerate. This allows the CCP to confidently embrace capitalism and even to invite private entrepreneurs into its ranks. It trusts their amoral motivations far more than it trusts real Marxists—witness the crackdown on orthodox Marxist editors who warned the party against such membership reform.[35] Most especially the CCP trusts everybody connected with Kissinger Associates, which is uniquely positioned to lobby for a commercially-inspired China policy. Ex-Secretary of State Lawrence Eagleburger, a former president of Kissinger Associates, now works for a law firm that helps businesses obtain insider privileges in China. Another president of Kissinger Associates, former National Security Advisor Brent Scowcroft, freely mixes public policy advice with private business connections. His consulting firm, the Scowcroft Group, operates out of the same office complex as the nonprofit policy institute he founded: the Forum for International Policy. It was through him that Dean O'Hare, chairman of the Chubb insurance group, secured a meeting with Chinese Premier Li Peng. All the while, Scowcroft has defended China assiduously on issues such as MFN and Chinese sales of nuclear material to Pakistan. In an almost comic twist, Scowcroft blames those sales on U.S. nonproliferation legislation,[36] the idea being that China did it only to save face.

Next to Kissinger himself, the most egregious China Card player is former Secretary of State Alexander Haig, Kissinger's aide during the opening of China. Haig has the distinction of having been the only prominent American to join the October 1989 celebration of the fortieth anniversary of the PRC (i.e., to join Deng Xiaoping in Tiananmen Square just four months after the Tiananmen massacre). As usual he trots behind Kissinger in this matter. Kissinger had openly defended the massacre, saying that "no government in the world would have tolerated having the main square of its capital occupied for eight weeks by tens of thousands of demonstrators."[37]

Haig's continuing role in the defense of MFN and as a critic of anyone who defends Taiwan has earned him a good deal more than praise from the Chinese. Deng saluted his "courage," but what counts are the contracts. One of the major clients of Haig's consulting group, Worldwide Associates, has hauled in billions of dollars in business deals with the Chinese.[38] Haig is not one to be concerned about theoretical contradictions, but more might be expected from his realist mentor, Kissinger.

These putative conservatives join neoliberals in the creation of a foreign policy more suited to the Commerce Department than the State Department. In this corporate agenda, where profits rather than values have the last word, trust becomes a matter of economic calculation. Japan knows that China weighs more heavily on this scale than any other Asian country. China, in turn, was banking on this calculation when it brazenly intensified its domestic oppression and regional intimidation, even as it sought WTO entry and selection as the site of the 2008 Olympics.[39]

In the absence of trust, America's military supremacy will not suffice to maintain even minimal security on the Rim. Nor will good trade relations compensate for bad trust relations. The distrust Asians increasingly feel toward America is not due to any Huntingtonesque clash of civilizations. It is a product of a new corporate virulence in American life, engulfing everything from medical care to foreign policy. Much as Deng Xiaoping brought market socialism to China, recent American presidents have thrown their weight behind a new market liberalism. No country on the Rim trusts either system very far.

Fortunately there is still an Other America, just as there is an Other Korea and an Other Asia, where values are not measured in profits. This is the motive force behind America's communitarian movement, whose concept of the good society reaches beyond statism and economism.[40] Insofar as the oppositional Others of East and West recognize their common adversary in corporate globalism, their grassroots values may yet serve as building blocks for bridges rather than walls—solidarity rather than culture clash. Effective resistance to globalization must begin with this pragmatic "concert of Others."

NOTES

1. Jorge Larrain, *Theories of Development: Capitalism, Colonialism and Dependency* (Cambridge, UK: Polity Press, 1989), 156.

2. Benedict Anderson, "From Miracle to Crash," *London Review of Books* 20, no. 8 (April 16, 1998), <www.lrb/v20/n08/ande2008.htm>.

3. Quoted in Larrain, *Theories of Development*, 116.

4. Anthony Reid, "Merdeka: The Concept of Freedom in Indonesia," in David Kelly and Anthony Reid, eds., *Asian Freedoms: The Idea of Freedom in East and Southeast Asia* (Cambridge, UK: Cambridge University Press, 1998), 141–160, 141, 155, 156.

5. François Godement, *The Downsizing of Asia* (London: Routledge, 1999), 195.

6. Ralph Pettman, "What Is 'Asian' About Asian Development?" Asian Studies Institute Publications (September 28, 2000), <www.vuw.ac.nz/asianstudies/publications/working/asiandevelopment.html>.

7. Tamara Straus, "Protest in Prague," *Nation* (October 23, 2000), <www.thenation.com/doc.mhml?I = 20001023&s = strauss>. Left anti-globalists like Dirlik (*After the*

Revolution: Waking to Global Capitalism [1994]) and the late Daniel Singer (*Whose Millenium? Theirs or Ours?*) thus end up on common ground with a conservative like Gray (*False Dawn: The Delusions of Global Capitalism* [1998]), while on some issues, such as environmental responsibility, liberals like William Greider (*One World, Ready or Not: The Manic Logic of Global Capitalism* [1997]) and David Korten (*When Corporations Rule the World* [1995]) end up in the company of a communitarian conservative like Amitai Etzioni (*The Spirit of Community: The Reinvention of American Society* [New York: Touchstone, 1993], 10). Even some nominal globalists find a place on this spectrum. The cosmopolitan Bryan Turner, for example, is increasingly at odds with corporate globalization, while George Soros, the transnational financier, argues forcefully for political action against the inroads of market fundamentalism (*Open Society: Reforming Global Capitalism* [New York: Public Affairs, 2000], 119).

8. This shift away from older Left totalities bears comparison with the post-Marxist postmodernism of Laclau and Mouffe, which also embraces multiple sites of struggle; but, as Carl Boggs discerns, that flight from Marxist reductionism ends up privileging discursive and micropolitical concerns at the expense of structural and public ones (*The End of Politics: Corporate Power and the Decline of the Public Sphere* [New York: Guilford Press, 2000], 217). By contrast, broad-spectrum resistance to corporate globalization is by its very nature a public and "macro" affair. This convergence of multiple oppositions, prompted by a common globalist adversary, breaks the inertia of postmodernism's retreat from metanarratives of resistance. So too it resolves some of the tension associated with Huntington's "clash of civilizations." A global counteraccord is beginning to take shape at the intersection of the most pressing "macro" issues: world hunger, peace and security, human rights, and environmental sustainability.

9. Daniel Singer, "Seattle from the Seine," *Nation.* (January 3, 2000), <http://past.thenation.com/issue/000103/0103singer.shtml>.

10. Jim Delahunty, "APEC and Auckland," *Monthly Review* 51, no. 7 (December 1999), <www.monthlyreview.org/1299dela.htm>.

11. Naomi Klein, "Cries in the Streets in L.A." *Nation* (September 4–11, 2000), <www.thenation.com/issue/000904/0904klein.shtml>.

12. Arif Dirlik, *The Postcolonial Aura: Third World Criticism in the Age of Global Capitalism* (Boulder, Colo.: Westview Press, 1997), 142.

13. "IMF Chief Rolls Out Reform Plans," *New York Times* AP Online (September 20, 2000), <www.nytimes.com/aponline/sports/AP-IMF-Summit.html>.

14. "After Genoa," *Nation* (August 6, 2001), <www.thenation.com/doc.mhtml?I=20010806&s=editors>.

15. Jane Perlez, "U.S. Report Harshly Criticizes China for Deteriorization of Human Rights; Russia Also Faulted," *New York Times* International (February 26, 2000), <www.nytimes.com/library/world/Asia/022600china-rights.html>.

16. David E. Sanger, "New Realism Wins the Day as Senate Passes Trade Bill," *New York Times* International (September 20, 2000), <www.nytimes.com/2000/09/20/world/20ASSE.html>.

17. "Senate Votes on China Trade Bill," *New York Times* AP International (September 19, 2000), <www.nytimes.com/aponline/world/AP-US-China-Trade.html>.

18. Peter Beinart, "The Return of the Bank," *New Republic* (August 3, 1998), <www.tnr.com/archive/0898/080398/beinart080398.html>.

19. Barbara Slavin, "U.S., China go from Confrontation to Cooperation," *USA Today* (July 30, 2001): 6A.
20. Robyn Lim, "Asia's Nuclear Arms Race," *Asian Wall Street Journal* (November 8, 1999): 10.
21. Lim, "Asia's Nuclear Arms Race," 10.
22. Frank Ching, "Japan and India Forge New Links," *Far Eastern Economic Review* (September 7, 2000), <www.feer.com/0009_07/p32eoa.html>.
23. "Asia's Shifting Balance," *Economist* 356, no. 8186 (September 2, 2000): 15.
24. Frank Ching, "Korea Fallout. U.S.–China Tensions," *Far Eastern Economic Review* (September 14, 2000), <www.feer.com/_0009_14/p34eoa.html>.
25. Brad Roberts, Robert A. Manning, and Ronald N. Montaperto, "China: The Forgotten Nuclear Power," *Foreign Affairs* 79, no. 4 (July–August 2000): 53–63, 53.
26. Pedro B. Bernaldez, "China: Next Superpower?" *Korea Times* (September 7, 2000): 6.
27. Elizabeth Feizkhah, "Making Friends," *Asiaweek* (June 15, 2001), <www.asiaweek.com/asi . . . magazine/business0,8782,129537,00.htm>.
28. "U.S. Rejects China's $1 Million Plane-Parking Bill," *New York Times* AP report (July 8, 2001), <www.nytimes.com/2001/07/08/world/08CHIN.html>.
29. Satu P. Limaye, "Tokyo's Dynamic Diplomacy: Japan and the Subcontinent's Nuclear Tests," *Contemporary Southeast Asia* 22, no. 2 (August 2000): 322–339, 322–323.
30. Ted Galen Carpenter, "Japan, Reluctantly, Re-Awakens," *China Post* (September 7, 2000): 4.
31. Chester Dawson, "Friends Indeed," *Far Eastern Economic Review* (October 19, 2000), <www.feer.com/0010_19/p20region.html>.
32. Gearóid Tuathail and Simon Dalby, "Introduction: Rethinking Geopolitics— Towards a Critical Geopolitics," in Gearóid Ó Tuathail and Simon Dalby, eds., *Rethinking Geopolitics* (London: Routledge, 1998), 1–15, 4, 5.
33. Yosef Lapid and Friedrich Kratochwil, eds., *The Return of Culture and Identity in IR Theory* (Boulder, Colo.: Lynne Rienner, 1996).
34. Bryan S. Turner, *Classical Sociology* (London: Sage Publications, 1999), 138.
35. Charles Hutzler, "China Is Reading Between the Lines Again," *Wall Street Journal* (August 1, 2001): A10.
36. John B. Judis, "China Town," *New Republic* (March 10, 1997), <www.thenewrepublic.com/textonly/031097/txtjudis031097.html>.
37. Quoted in Doug Ireland, "Take Him Away," review of *The Trial of Henry Kissinger* by Christopher Hitchens, *In These Times* (August 20, 2001), <www.Inthesetimes.com/web2519/ireland2519.html>.
38. Judis, "China Town."
39. William H. Thornton, "Selling Democratic Teleology: The Case of the Chinese Fortune-Tellers," *International Politics* 37, no. 3 (September 2000): 285–300, 291–292.
40. Amitai Etzioni, "Introduction: A Matter of Balance, Rights and Responsibilities," in Amitai Etzioni, ed., *The Essential Communitarian Reader* (Lanham, Md.: Rowman & Littlefield, 1998), ix–xxiv, xii.

Index

About the Author

William H. Thornton is professor of literary and cultural theory at National Cheng Kung University, Taiwan.